STRATEGIC LABOR RELATIONS

Kenneth A. Kovach

University Press of America, Inc.
Lanham • New York • London

University Press of America, ® Inc.
4720 Boston Way
Lanham, Maryland 20706

3 Henrietta Street
London, WC2E 8LU England

British Cataloging in Publication Information Available

Library of Congress Cataloging-in-Publication Data

Kovach, Kenneth A.
Strategic labor relations / Kenneth A. Kovach.
p. cm.
Includes bibliographical references.
1. Industrial relations--United States. 2. Labor laws and legislation--United States. I. Title.
HD8072.5.K683 1996 331'0973--dc20 96-44800 CIP

ISBN 0-7618-0581-8 pbk

ISBN 978-0-7618-0581-6

Table of Contents

Readings

Readings

Legal Considerations **Page**

Public Employees

Cases

Cases

Page

Do We Still Need Labor Organizations?

In light of recent history, the answer may surprise you.

It is common knowledge today that organized labor is losing strength in numerical and political terms as well as in the influence it exerts over the rest of the labor force. Numerically, labor unions have gone from 42% of the labor force in the 1950s to less than 16% today with every indication that this downward trend will continue. Were it not for the large number of newly organized public employees, the numbers would be even more ominous for labor unions. Further, the author contends that because of the restrictions on unions in the public sector (many cannot discuss wages and are prohibited from striking), the value to labor as a whole of a certain number of *public* employees organizing is not nearly as great as a like number of *privately* employed workers organizing. Thus, even the decreasing numbers may not tell the whole story of labor's deteriorating position.

Losing Clout

Politically, it should be clear to even the most casual observer that unions are losing their clout. The day when the powerful labor boss could "deliver" the labor vote, and hence was admitted to the inner circles of politics and politicians, is gone. It is hard to image a modern day John L. Lewis working closely with the President to draft key pieces of legislation or inviting members of Congress to his office to "discuss" their votes on upcoming issues - practices that were once a source of pride and status for powerful labor leaders. Labor's present political influence can best be gauged by its track record on such major issues as the Common Situs Picketing Bill, the Striker Replacement Bill, and Labor Law Reform - all defeats.

While organized labor has long been felt to be the trend-setter for wages and terms of employment with the rest of the labor force following with a certain time lag, even here we are witnessing the declining strength of unions. Except in a few big industries (steel, automobile, etc.) where unions enjoy a virtual monopoly, the increasing number of non-unionized firms has reintroduced the cost of labor as a comprehensive factor in market strategies. More and more frequently unions have had to consider the impact of their economic demands on the employer's ability to attract enough business to maintain employment levels. The construction industry is the most dramatic and widely known example of this phenomenon, but it is happening in an increasing number of less publicized instances. The "Southern Strategy" of the automobile employers, the move to the South of the big steel companies, and the inability of the mining unions to organize new mines are all indicators that even in industries long considered union strongholds, this factor will become increasingly important in the future.

A Look Backward

The question growing out of the above discussion is obvious: Do we still need labor organizations? Is it now possible that they have outlived their usefulness?

To answer questions such as these, it is important to take a brief look at labor history. Such a look back reaffirms one of the more important lessons to be learned from history in general: if people are pushed hard enough, are subjected to adverse enough conditions, they will take actions they would never have dreamed of had things been more equitable. It is only within the context of the time that today's labor student can understand why otherwise normal individuals would sit in unheated Michigan and Ohio automobile plants in the middle of winter for 44 days or why they would barricade themselves in steel mills and vow to fight to the death unless working conditions were improved. Read about what workers did to organize the first textile unions, the first mining unions, the first railroad unions, and then ask yourself if you would be willing or able to endure what they did. The author contends that you would probably be willing to if you were subjected to the treatment that those individuals were and if you realized that your children were destined to spend their lives in the same conditions.

The purpose here is not to discuss the historical plight of the American worker, yet it is crucial to understand what this plight was. For the first 150 years of this country's independence, the American worker was free politically but a virtual slave industrially. A look backward at management practices such as company-owned housing, water supplies, stores, etc., with their inflated prices, the payment of workers in company scrip, the unsafe and unhealthy working conditions, the unbelievably long workweek, the ridiculously low wages making it impossible for most families to live on the earnings of a single breadwinner, the completely arbitrary employment and personnel practices, and the company police forces, to mention only a few (in fact, the complete lack of consideration of the worker as a human being) puts the remarkable growth of labor unions in the early 1900s in a different light. Certainly at this point in U.S. history, workers were ready to support any type of organization that promised them relief from their miserable industrial existence. Thus, labor unions filled a real need: they brought humanitarianism to the workplace and a degree of dignity to the American worker.

Yet, ironically enough, because of their success unions have eradicated most of the conditions that led to their foundation. Thus, an often heard argument today is that while unions were necessary once, they are no longer necessary now. Proponents of this argument contend that the American worker today enjoys a higher standard of living than ever before and that we now have laws such as the Fair Labor Standards Act, the National Labor Relations Act, the Occupational Safety and Health Act, etc., which set a floor for wages, working conditions and general treatment of employees below which no employer is allowed to go. Thus, unions are not needed to address conditions of exploitation; the law has stepped in.

The Deterrent Effect

While there is much support for this point of view, there are exceptions to it. While laws and subsequent conditions of employment may have changed, basic human nature has not. While it may be a pessimistic assessment of humanity and one with which the reader will likely disagree, a certain percentage of your fellow human beings will take advantage of you if the price is right. Through the ages, history has repeatedly proven this to be a truism, and anyone who does not realize it is either uninformed, extremely idealistic, or naive. While the laws provide deterrents in the form of minimum acceptable standards, it would certainly be unacceptable to the majority of our working population to exist at these minimum standards. For many, even a small retreat backward, be it in terms of compensation, working conditions or safety standards, would be completely unacceptable. Yet if the law were the only minimum, the only deterrent, there would be plenty of room for retreat in the standards enjoyed in the workplace by the majority of the U.S. labor force.

The biggest single deterrent, besides the law, to the reduction of standards in the workplace is the combined action of the workers - call it a "union" or any other name you wish. This action does not even have to come to pass to serve its purpose, for in many instances the mere possibility of such action is sufficient. There can be no doubt that the level of benefits received by many nonunion workers today is in part buttressed by their employers' desire to reward them at such a level that they remain unorganized.

Thus, while unions may have outlived their usefulness in terms of their original objectives, they are still needed because of what the author would refer to as their "deterrent" effect. Although the traditional browbeaten working conditions in which unions were formed has been replaced by today's more humanistic, less extreme conditions, unions continue to be the instrument inhibiting exploitation of the worker. The irony is that even those individuals in the blue-collar sector who would suffer first and most if unions were to disappear tomorrow do not realize the vital role labor organizations play in today's economy. It is not necessary for unions to be as strong as they once were, for the problems they are trying to correct are not as severe. The government has taken over part of their original purpose through various pieces of legislation. Yet it is still vital that labor organizations continue to exist, not only for those who benefit directly from them, but also for those who believe in the need to maintain the dignity of the worker. Unions find themselves in the same peculiar position as the military in that what they cause to happen may not be nearly as important as what they cause *not* to happen. This fact alone, in the author's opinion, continues to make unions what they have always been - an absolute necessity to the well-being of the work force.

Organized Labor's Deteriorating Condition

Any serious student of organized labor is aware that the American labor movement has experienced, and will continue to experience, hard times. Its membership is declining, the industries upon which its strength was built are in serious trouble, and unfavorable demographic, economic and political trends have seriously weakened its once unparalleled influence. Many who work in the field view this as a favorable trend, destined to mitigate problems from high inflation and unemployment to an unfavorable balance of payments, while others see it as a threat to the "checks and balances" necessary for reasonable labor management relations. Regardless of one's perspective, there can be no doubt that the deteriorating position of organized labor and its resultant effects in other sectors of the economy is one of the major socio-economic trends in the U.S. over the past twenty-five years.

The author proposes to examine this phenomenon by dissecting the problem itself and discussing its various components: exploring the major factors contributing to the problem; looking at the response to the problem by management, the government and independent consultants; and finally by assessing labor's potential for rectifying the situation.

The Problem

There are three equally important components of labor's present unenviable condition, one being numerical, one political and one jurisdictional. Numerically, the picture could not be worse for labor organizations. Despite the growth in the labor force over the last twenty-five years, unions now have fewer dues-paying members than they did in 1980. In the last seven years alone, total membership has dropped from twenty million to barely over sixteen million, and there is every indication that this trend will continue. Obviously, with the increasing number of jobs and the decreasing number of union members, the percentages present an even more ominous picture than the absolute numbers.

Organized labor's percentage share of the labor market has dropped from 42% in 1954, to 28% in 1965, to 18.8% today.[1] This numerical decrease (which translates into dues, which translates into economic clout) is the independent variable that drives all the other dependent variables discussed in this article. Organized labor has long dismissed this trend as attributable to demographic factors, but the validity of this claim is undermined when one considers the magnitude of the numbers. Any institution that loses ten percent of its membership while the universe from which it can draw increases twenty-five percent, is in serious trouble. The numbers,as they say, speak forthemselves.

Politically, the loss of influence by organized labor is obvious. Every American who follows the news is aware that labor poured more than ten million dollars and deployed thousands upon thousands of volunteers to support the Democratic candidate in the latest presidential election. Their politically stated goal was to deliver sixty-five percent of the union households for Democrats while holding Republicans to thirty-five percent. Exit polls showed that nearly one-half the labor households voted Republican.[2] Yet one must look beyond this well-publicized failure to understand the severity of the political component of labor's deteriorating condition. The failure to wrestle a new Labor Law Reform Bill out of Congressional committee, the revision of the Davis-Bacon Act, the lifting of import quotas on Japanese automobiles despite labor opposition, the fact that two more states have Right-To-Work Laws than was the case five years ago, and the high probability that the Administration's sub-minimum wage for teenagers will weather the AFL-CIO's attack, all speak loudly and clearly to labor's political condition. Regardless of what advances it achieves at the bargaining table (an area to be discussed later), unless labor reverses its political direction, it may well "win a few battles but lose the war."

Jurisdictionally, the overwhelming percentage of organizing successes have appeared in the public sector. Over twenty percent of total union membership is now in this area. In the federal sector, sixty-one percent of the work force is now represented, while in the non-federal public sector, thirty percent are represented. Even in these sectors, however, the growth is slowing markedly since the big increase of ten years ago. More important is the fact that these new public members are being recruited to replace (not in addition to) private-sector members. With many in the public sector being prohibited from negotiating over wages and technology, from striking, and from covering their union with a security clause, one must question whether public sector employees give labor organizations as much clout as an equal number of their private sector counterparts. Thus, the numbers tell only part of the story regarding labor's deteriorating position. The jurisdictions covered by the numbers provide additional insight.

The Factors

There are five major factors contributing to the present condition of organized labor:

- the outcome of certification and decertification elections,
- the shift from blue to white-collar jobs in the economy,
- the increasing number and percentage of women in the work force,
- the generational and philosophical gap between union leaders and members, and
- the National Labor Relations Board.

Regarding union elections, even among the decreasing number of workers receptive enough to listen to labor's message, the numbers bode ill. Over six hundred bargaining units decertified their unions in each of the last three years. Unions have won less than one-half of the certification elections in each of the last ten years and have lost three-quarters of the increasing number of decertification elections during the same time period. When studied longitudinally, one sees that these trends are, in fact, accelerating and will probably continue into the foreseeable future.

Another contributing factor is the shift we have seen in this country away from blue-collar manufacturing jobs to white-collar, service-oriented jobs. While the blue-collar manufacturing worker has traditionally been the cornerstone of the movement, there was only a 0.4 percent growth in such jobs over the past five years. The blue-collar base of organized labor has been dependent upon industries that are shrinking, automating, closing, moving, or going international. The millions of new jobs created have been almost exclusively in the white-collar, service-oriented sector where union organizing success has been mediocre at best. While efforts to organize this sector have increased drastically in the last decade, the successes have not been of such a magnitude to offset the losses in the blue-collar sector. Thus, labor, while it is making progress in the white-collar area, is not advancing rapidly enough to keep pace with the industrial shift from blue to white-collar work.

Additionally, the increasing number and percentage of females in the work force is a factor that should not be underestimated when diagnosing labor's present condition. Over the last ten years, the percentage of women unionized has fluctuated between 11% and 13% compared with 25% for men. As women, who are organized at approximately one-half of the rate of men, constitute an increasing percentage of the labor force, unions have increased their efforts to organize this "pink-collar" sector. Effort should not be confused with results, however, since as stated above, the percentage of women organized has not increased noticeably over the last few years.

One big problem in this area has been unimaginative union leadership. Fortunately for organized labor, groups such as the Coalition of Labor Union Women, The National Education Association and the Service Employees International Union, with their female leadership and large female membership, are working hard from *within* the system to educate the traditional white male hierarchy to the importance of organizing drives aimed at women and to the issues essential to such drives (pay equity, health and safety issues, equitable job classifications, child care, etc.). Despite the best efforts of such groups, however, it does not appear that women will become full-fledged members of the labor community in the near future. They continue to be concentrated in the job fields where unions are not well entrenched: administrative, service, part-time, and high- technology industries with many small and union-resistant companies. For these reasons, the increasing number and percentage of females in the work force is a contributing factor to organized labor's deteriorating position.

The generational and philosophical gap between union leaders and members must also be recognized as a factor. The union work force, in addition to becoming smaller, is becoming younger and better educated. Many old-line union leaders have failed to recognize the fact that this change makes it impossible to conduct business as they did twenty years ago. The new generation of union members have become disenchanted with their ossified and lethargic leaders, and they see the traditional union structure as incapable of responding to their needs and desires because of the type of individuals who hold key hierarchical positions. Additionally, young workers (unlike their parents) take a living wage as a given, not a benefit to be earned. They see work as more than just a financial necessity, and the relative generosity of state and supplemental unemployment benefits exacerbates this feeling. The post-war baby boomers are - and will continue to be - labor's dominant age group until the second decade of the 21st century. The fact that they are confounding labor's establishment with values and needs different from their parents is even more threatening than the normal young-versus-old split. Their increasingly middle-class outlook, made possible by the struggles of the two preceding generations of union members, makes them less likely to devote themselves to the labor cause. Their present is no longer measured by fears of the past but by hopes for the future.[3] The changes within this generation gap are critical, because it is in the industries with the most union growth potential that the problem is most acute. Better educated workers in the high-technology industries may well come to regard the unions as bureaucratic entities and as much a damper on their aspirations as any unenlightened corporation. One of the most serious threats to future union growth may come from this generational schism.

The final contributing factor to labor's condition is the National Labor Relations Board. Labor leaders have been unable to protect their members from what they perceive to be (and what under previous administrations would have been) violations of the National Labor Relations Act, the Railway Labor Act, the Labor Management Relations Act, and the Labor Management Reporting and Disclosure Act.

The reasons for this are twofold. First, the number of enforcement personnel, as well as the budgets of the agencies administering these acts, has been cut drastically. This creates a backlog that discourages the filing of charges and it means that, among those filed, a smaller percentage can actually be heard and, if need be, prosecuted. Second, present appointees to political positions within the regulatory agencies have shown no reluctance to reverse previous and, in many cases, long-standing decisions.[4]

The Responses

Responses to the situation discussed in the first section of this article have come from three main sources: management, local governments, and independent consultants. Management's most direct response has been to relocate to the Southeast and Southwest. In the last twenty years, the number of manufacturing jobs grew by forty-five percent in the Southeast and sixty-seven percent in the Southwest. It is crucial for the reader to realize that the *jobs* moved first, then the well-documented population shift was pulled along. It is somewhat of a "chicken and egg" phenomenon, but large numbers of individuals cannot relocate unless there are jobs available at the new location. Certainly, their very presence will create some new jobs, particularly in the service sector, but with the sophisticated logistics system in this country today, it is not as imperative as it used to be that most jobs be performed within the immediate, geographic market they serve. Hence, in the classic economic push-pull situation, the jobs *pushed* first and the population was then *pulled*. As a result, for the first time since Reconstruction, the Northeast and Midwest (once our industrial heartlands and solid union strongholds) no longer hold the majority of the American population.

A response favored by other companies has been to transfer jobs overseas or to subcontract work to countries with lower wage scales. The average consumer would be hard-pressed to notice the difference in quality between the work of a unionized American seamstress and a Taiwanese seamstress, yet a company will surely notice the ten-to-one wage differential. The result is that management shifts union jobs not only to the American South but to foreign countries as well.

A final management response has been to seek "give-backs" at the bargaining table. Many times unions are faced with the alternatives of either granting these concessions or losing some or all of their jobs. Major contracts settled during the last year produced wage increases of 2.8 percent over the life of the contract versus 6.6 percent increases five years ago. In fact, non-union wage increases have been exceeding those of union workers during recent times.[5]

Local government has been another contributor to unions' deteriorating condition. While management's response is to relocate, many local governments have begun to compete to be the beneficiaries of this relocation. In an attempt to retain or attract private capital, state and local governments have begun to give present or prospective industrial citizens tax and labor law relief. The creation of a "pro-business climate" is one of the major marketing points local jurisdictions are using to attract industry. Conversely, jurisdictions presently housing these industries have been forced to grant similar relief in an attempt to hold onto what they have. One need only look at the tax base and resultant city services and physical plants in industrial centers across different geographic regions to realize the magnitude and implications of this phenomena.

Finally, a new breed of independent consultant has surfaced as a response to labor's plight. Use of these **union-avoidance** consultants has become fashionable, widespread and effective. Such consultants as Stephen Cabot, Anthony McKeown, Alfred DeMaria, and Scott Myers are making fortunes teaching management how to keep a company union-free. Their success is based on their ability to convince employers that treating employees properly makes good economic sense. Stephen Cabot states that employers should blame themselves if their workers unionize, because it may well be an indication that they have not been fair, even-handed, or open-minded.[6] Success rates approaching 90 percent in keeping unions out are an indication of the effectiveness of such consultants. In addition to the success rate, the high fees paid to such people are easily justified when one stops to consider the economic advantage to a large company of remaining union-free. Rational economic thought connects the economic benefits to the company, to the high fees they are willing to pay for this service, and to the high number of individuals attracted to this line of work. Hence, the final response is simply the end result of economic evolution.

Conclusion

The logical question to be addressed in light of all the above is: "What can labor do now?" Given the magnitude and diversity of the factors contributing to the problem, there are no simple answers. Addressing one or two particular aspects of the problem at a time will not be enough.

First, there must be a philosophical rapprochement between organized labor's leadership and the work force of the present day. These leaders must recognize that the nature of American business has changed and that things will never be as they were when they were young workers. The reality of a better educated, high-technology or white-collar, service-oriented work force must be dealt with. Extensive use of simple attitude surveys among present and potential union members would go a long way toward making decision-makers within the unions aware that the use of self-reference criteria is no longer appropriate. Unlike thirty years ago, when today's decision-makers were elected to their positions, today's workers and potential union members have a middle-class outlook that gives rise to different objectives, images, and behavior than their parents.

Until today's union leader realizes this and reacts accordingly, little will be done to improve the unions' position. Attitude surveys are a quick, inexpensive way to find out about respondents' desires, attitudes, etc., so that the labor organization can bring itself and its actions in line with those of the individuals it is trying to attract. The author believes that such surveys will show that today's worker expects more than wages from the job, regards demands for wage increases beyond a certain point as job-threatening, and sees incessant union bickering over trivial work rules as needless and unproductive. Health and safety, job enlargement and enrichment, quality of work life, and pay equity may well emerge as issues labor should be addressing more vigorously at the bargaining table. Progress in these areas may well be the key to enrolling the new, better educated and female members the unions need so desperately to attract.

Additionally, more emphasis must be placed on retraining programs for workers displaced by automation and less on the lock-step protectionist policies of the past. For example, labor spends money to lobby for import quotas on automobiles. If one-half the money were spent on retraining existing workers for the new jobs in that industry, not only the union, but the industry and the entire economy would be that much better off.

Another tactic labor should try is to play economic hardball through the use of the billions of dollars in union pension funds. Shifting, or threatening to shift, these monies to "encourage" companies or local governments to modify their thinking and actions in the area of labor relations holds tremendous potential. The dollar value of corporate stock and local government securities held by union pension funds makes this, like the use of attitude surveys, a direct and immediate response by labor to its present situation.

While attitude surveys, retraining programs and pension funds all offer hope for the unions, the author must close on a pessimistic note. These and many other policies that could be recommended must still be implemented through those at the top of the hierarchy. In a survey of seventy-nine top labor officials, several agreed that arrogance, inability to prepare successors, dogmatism, adherence to outdated ideas, and shortsightedness are problems with the leadership of organized labor today.[7] The movement has lost its role as a cause for many leaders and is now simply a job. Many are more interested in holding union office for money and power than they are in affecting significant change.

If this is truly the attitude of many union leaders, and the author feels it is, then to expect them to distribute attitude surveys and respond accordingly (shift bargaining emphasis toward retraining and enrichment and use the pension funds as suggested above) is to expect too much. The author has proposed what he feels are the best and most immediate solutions, but one must be realistic enough to realize that human beings must be willing and able to implement them. Given the current composition of labor leaders and their attitudes toward their jobs, one should not attach a high degree of probability to their trying these ideas on a large scale. Given the magnitude of the problem, piecemeal implementation by individual leaders will not suffice.

Thus, the "human" factor becomes the overriding one in this situation and causes the author to be pessimistic about any reversal in the condition of organized labor in the foreseeable future. Those species and institutions that do not adapt over time become *at worst* extinct or *at best* lose their position of dominance. Organized labor has not adequately adapted to economic, environmental or sociological changes. As a result, it has lost much of the strength it enjoyed thirty or forty years ago. The real problem for labor today is not that this has occurred (for these things go in cycles), but that there is no effective, coordinated attempt being made by the leadership to reverse the situation. The most ominous question for a labor leader today should be: "Given present trends and your inability to combat them, what in the world will you look like in ten or fifteen years?"

Endnotes

[1] Broder, David S., "A 'New Day' For Unions," *The Washington Post*, March 10, 1985.

[2] Erlick, Mark, "Hammer Out A Warning," *The Progressive*, October 1989, p. 18.

[3] Tyler, Gus, *The Political Imperative: The Corporate Character of Unions*, (MacMillan Publishing Company, 1968), p. 290.

[4] Silbergeld, Arthur F., "How Recent NLRB Decisions Have Tilted Toward Management on Critical Issues," *Management Review*, July 1989, pp. 14-15.

[5] English, Carey W., "Why Unions Are Running Scared," *U.S. News and World Report*, September 10, 1989, p. 62.

[6] English, Carey W., "Business is Booming for 'Union Busters'," *U.S. News and World Report*, May 16, 1988, pp. 61-64.

[7] Graham, Harry and Heshizer, Brian, "Are Unions Facing a Crisis? Labor Officials Are Divided," *Monthly Labor Review*, August 1989, pp. 24-25.

Employee Motivation: Addressing a Crucial Factor in Your Organization's Performance

ABSTRACT

One thousand employees were asked to rank order ten rewards in terms of motivational value. Immediately thereafter, the subjects' supervisors were asked to do the same, ranking the rewards as they thought the employees had. Results were compared between the two groups as well as between subgroups of employees differentiated by sex, age, income level, organization level, and job type. Cases where statistically significant differences were and were not found are discussed, possible explanations are offered, and implications for manipulation of reward systems are proposed.

Introduction

This study asked 1,000 employees to rank order ten possible rewards and found that "interesting work" was preferred in the majority of the cases. If this is the answer, then all that is necessary is to make all of the work in industry interesting and we will have happy, productive employees who come to work on time and do not leave. Unfortunately, not all jobs can be made interesting and more importantly, what is interesting to one person might not be interesting to another person.

The direct supervisors of the employees might not be able to recognize the differences between their employees and make sure that all employees were in jobs that were interesting to them. However, when these supervisors were asked their opinions on what their employees wanted from their jobs, the supervisors claimed their workers' highest preference was not for interesting work but for good wages. If the immediate supervisors are to be believed, all a company has to do is make sure it pays good wages to all of its employees.

The second solution, i.e., good wages, is probably easier to implement than interesting work, but the employees say this is not extremely high on their list of preferences. Thus, there appear to be some differences in managers' and employees' perceptions.

This article compares results of three surveys concerning employee and supervisory rankings of ten motivational items, discusses individual differences between groups of employees and supervisors, and looks at the manipulation of reward systems. It is hoped the information presented will shed some light on the question of why workers work and what an employer or supervisor can do to attain full productivity.

Survey Results

In 1946, employees were asked to rank ten "job reward" factors in terms of personal preference. The results were:[1]

1. Full appreciation of work done
2. Feeling of being in on things
3. Sympathetic help with personal problems
4. Job security
5. Good wages
6. Interesting work
7. Promotion and growth in the organization
8. Personal loyalty to employees
9. Good working conditions
10. Tactful discipline

A similar questionnaire was given to industrial employees in 1981 and again in 1994. By 1981, there were changes in what workers wanted compared to 1946. Interesting work was positioned in the number one slot and sympathetic help with personal problems was moved to the number nine slot. By 1994, the list looked like this:

1. Interesting work
2. Full appreciation of work done
3. Feeling of being in on things
4. Job security
5. Good wages
6. Promotion and growth in the organization
7. Good working conditions

8. Personal loyalty to employees
9. Tactful discipline
10. Sympathetic help with personal problems

The workers surveyed in 1946 came from a different environment than the workers of 1994. America had just come out of a depression and gone through a war. In 1994, after almost fifty years of relative prosperity and a rise in the standard of living beyond the imagination of the workers in 1946, it is not surprising that the list of what workers want from their work has changed.

If we consider the list of employee ratings as relating to Maslow's hierarchy of needs[2] or to Herzberg's hygiene theory,[3] it becomes fairly obvious that in the United States organizations have done a better job of satisfying the basic or "deficit" needs of the worker than they have in satisfying the ego or self-fulfillment needs.[4]

In each of the 1946, 1981, and 1994 studies, supervisors were asked to rank the list of job rewards as they believed the employees had ranked it. Their rankings remained almost the same for each year:

1. Good wages
2. Job security
3. Promotion and growth in the organization
4. Good working conditions
5. Interesting work
6. Personal loyalty to employees
7. Tactful discipline
8. Full appreciation of work done
9. Sympathetic help with personal problems
10. Feeling of being in on things

The above rankings by the supervisors show that not only had their collective perception of factors that motivate employees not changed over the last fifty years, but also that they have little realization of the importance of Maslow's hierarchy of needs or Herzberg's extrinsic and intrinsic factors in motivation. Most importantly, a comparison of employee and supervisor rankings shows that the latter group has a very inaccurate perception of what motivates the former.

Why have managers, assuming they are aware of the almost five decades of research, chosen to ignore the theories of motivation?

Specifically, why do managers continually place wages at the top of their hierarchy and put the other motivators that both Maslow and Herzberg consider essential for job satisfaction at the bottom of their list? Several reasons are possible for the supervisors' apparent neglect of the conclusions drawn from behavioral scientists' research.

One reason could be that supervisors feel employees do not believe it is socially desirable to be interested in money and other basic needs and thus pay lip service to more socially acceptable factors such as interesting work, even though these are not in fact the factors that most motivate them. Or, on the other hand, it might just be possible that employees are better witnesses to their own feelings than their supervisors. Another reason for this disparity might be that managers chose the rewards they have less responsibility for, such as pay raises, which are usually determined by formalized organizational policies, as opposed to values that stem from the personal relationships between supervisors and employees, thus "passing the buck" when it comes time to fix the blame for poor levels of employee motivation.

These explanations are largely intuitive and untested. However, one theory the author believes may explain this phenomenon is what he calls "self-reference;" i.e., managers offer workers rewards that would motivate managers (that is, themselves), but this may not necessarily be what will motivate their employees. David McClelland, in his studies, found that supervisors are usually high achievers who are interested in concrete measures that reflect how well they have done - namely, money.[5] For them, it is a quantifiable way to keep score. As stated above, there is a significant difference between the supervisors' rankings of employee rewards in 1946 and employee rankings in 1946, and a significant difference between the two in 1981 and 1994. Thus, managers appear to remain out of tune with the wants of their employees. Despite a tremendous volume of behavioral research into what motivates employees, supervisors' self-reference is still as much of a problem today as it was after the Second World War. This is a sad commentary on the implementation of motivation research results in the workplace.

Differences Between Subgroups

The survey taken in 1994 also divided employees into various categories, something the earlier surveys did not do. Just as there are differences between what employees want over time, there may also be differences between categories of employees based on sex, age, income level, job type, and organization level. (See Table 1 for the subgroups studied in the 1994 survey).

Table 1 Survey Statistics

1,000 Employees	100 Supervisors* (1st and 2nd level)
Sex	Sex
(S1) M = 622	(S1) M = 76
(S2) F = 378	(S2) F = 24
Age	Age
(A1) Under 30 = 202	(A1) Under 30 = 16
(A2) 31-40 = 348	(A2) 31-40 = 29
(A3) 41-50 = 325	(A3) 41-50 = 40
(A4) Over 50 = 125	(A4) Over 50 = 15
Income Level, Annual	Income Level, Annual
(I1) Under 20,000 = 135	(I1) Under 25,000 = 6
(I2) 20,001-30,000 = 360	(I2) 25,001-40,000 = 34
(I3) 30,001-40,000 = 334	(I3) 40,001-50,000 = 39
(I4) Over 40,000 = 171	(I4) Over 50,000 = 21
Job Type	Job Type Supervised
(J1) Blue-collar unskilled = 350	(J1) Blue-collar unskilled = 31
(J2) Blue-collar skilled = 291	(J2) Blue-collar skilled = 27
(J3) White-collar unskilled = 206	(J3) White-collar unskilled = 23
(J4) White-collar skilled = 113	(J4) White-collar skilled = 19
Organization Level	Organization Level Supervised
(O1) Lower Non-supervisory = 418	(O1) Lower Non-supervisory = 34
(O2) Middle Non-supervisory = 359	(O2) Middle Non-supervisory = 37
(O3) Higher Non-supervisory = 139	(O3) Higher Non-supervisory = 29

* Supervisors surveyed are directly connected with employees surveyed.

When the subset data is analyzed against the total employee response, only two groups do not meet the null hypothesis, which specifies that the distribution of the total response is equal to the distribution of each subset. One of these groups is the under-thirty age group, and the other is the group with income under $20,000. (See Table 2 for comparison of total employee response to each employee subset response.)

Table 2 Response Distribution

	S	E	S1	S2	A1	A2	A3	A4	I1	I2	I3	I4	J1	J2	J3	J4	O1	O2	O3
Interesting Work	5	1	1	2	4	2	3	1	5	2	1	1	2	1	1	2	3	1	1
Full Appreciation of Work Done	8	2	2	1	5	3	2	2	4	3	3	2	1	6	3	1	4	2	2
Feeling of Being in on Things	10	3	3	3	6	4	1	3	6	1	2	4	5	2	5	4	5	3	3
Job Security	2	4	5	4	2	1	4	7	2	4	4	3	4	3	7	5	2	4	6
Good Wages	1	5	4	5	1	5	5	8	1	5	6	8	3	4	6	6	1	6	8
Promotion and Growth in the Organization	3	6	6	6	3	6	8	9	3	6	5	7	6	5	4	3	6	5	5
Good Working Conditions	4	7	7	10	7	7	7	4	8	7	7	6	9	7	2	7	7	7	4
Personal Loyalty to Employees	7	8	8	8	9	9	6	5	7	8	8	5	8	9	9	8	8	8	7
Tactful Discipline	9	9	9	9	8	10	9	10	10	9	9	10	7	10	10	9	9	9	10
Sympathetic Help with Personal Problems	6	10	10	7	10	8	10	6	9	10	10	9	10	8	8	10	10	10	9

NOTE: S = Total Supervisor Response, 1994; E = Total Employee Response, 1994.

When the subset data is analyzed against the supervisor rankings, all but three groups do not meet the null hypothesis, which specifies that the distribution of the supervisors is equal to the distribution of each subset. These groups are the under-thirty age group, the under-$20,000 income group and the lower organizational level. (See Table 3 for a Chi Square analysis of total supervisor response to each employee subset response and for total employee response to each employee subset response. See Table 4 for supervisor/subgroup agreement by factor.)

Table 3 Employee vs. Supervisory Responses

E 1994 vs.			S 1994 vs.		
Subgroup	Chi-Square	Sig. Level	Subgroup	Chi-Square	Sig. Level
S1	1.28	N.S.	S1	34.28	.01
S2	3.71	N.S.	S2	41.61	.01
A1	22.44	.05	A1	8.52	N.S.
A2	4.72	N.S.	A1	31.62	.01
A3	6.50	N.S.	A3	44.79	.01
A4	9.67	N.S.	A4	86.78	.01
I1	27.18	.05	I1	9.21	N.S.
I2	2.83	N.S.	I2	39.08	.01
I3	1.20	N.S.	I3	46.12	.01
I4	4.03	N.S.	I4	69.32	.01
J1	4.65	N.S.	J1	28.92	.05
J2	9.59	N.S.	J2	24.53	.05
J3	9.13	N.S.	J3	49.01	.01
J4	3.78	N.S.	J4	46.08	.01
O1	11.53	N.S.	O1	13.36	N.S.
O2	.36	N.S.	O2	45.99	.01
O3	4.49	N.S.	O3	72.54	.01

Note: E = Total Employee Response; S = Total Supervisor Response.

Table 4 Supervisor/Subgroup Agreement by Factor -- 1994

Supv Rank	Tactic-Reward	Subgroups Agreeing		Pop.	Percent of Total
1	Good Wages	A-1	Age under 30	202	20.2
		I-1	Income under $20,000	135	13.5
		O-1	Lower Non-Supervisory	418	41.8
2	Job Security	A-1	Age under 30	202	20.2
		I-1	Income under $20,000	135	13.5
		O-1	Lower Non-Supervisory	418	41.8
3	Promotion and Growth in the Organization	A-1	Age under 30	202	20.2
		I-1	Income under $20,000	135	13.5
		J-4	White-Collar, Skilled	113	11.3
4	Good Working Conditions	A-4	Age over 50	125	12.5
		O-3	Higher Non-Supervisory	193	19.3
5	Interesting Work	I-1	Income under $20,000	202	20.2
6	Sympathetic Help with Personal Problems	A-4	Age over 50	125	12.5
7	Personal Loyalty to Employees	I-1	Income under $20,000	135	13.5
		O-3	Higher Non-Supervisory	193	19.3
8	Full Appreciation of Work Done		None		
9	Tactful Discipline	I	Aggregate	1000	100.0
		S-1	Males	622	62.2
		S-2	Females	378	37.8
		A-3	Ages 41-50	325	32.5
		I-2	Incomes $20,001-30,000	360	36.0
		I-3	Incomes $30,001-40,000	334	33.4
		J-4	White-Collar, Skilled	113	11.3
		O-1	Lower Non-Supervisory	418	41.8
10	Feeling of Being in on Things		None		

Subgroups Finding No Common Ranking with Supervisors

A-2 Ages 31-40
A-4 Age over 50
I-4 Incomes over $40,000
J-1 Blue-Collar, Unskilled
J-2 Blue-Collar, Skilled
J-3 White-Collar, Unskilled

Males Versus Females

When one analyzes male versus female responses by the Chi Square technique, no significant statistical difference in the distribution of rewards is found between the two. However, when one looks at the ranking of values in Table 2, it is found that females rank "full appreciation of work" in first place while males rank it in second place. "Sympathetic help with personal problems" is ranked seventh by females as opposed to tenth by the males. This indicates that perhaps female employees place greater importance on interpersonal relationships and communication than male employees - a difference that should be noted by managers. Women in the workplace today do have different problems than men because many are still trying to cope with their traditional role of homemaker along with that of employee. This could cause them to seek more appreciation of work and more help with personal problems.

Age Groups

The age groups analyzed consisted of under-thirty, thirty-one to forty, forty-one to fifty, and over fifty. As mentioned above, the under-thirty group showed the greatest disparity in its distribution from the total responses of all groups, but showed the greatest similarity to the supervisors' estimate of how employees would respond. The difference between how the under-thirty group responded when compared with each of the other age groups is statistically significant. The under-thirty group chose good wages, job security, and promotion and growth as its first three choices. This could indicate that because they are new workers, they have not yet fulfilled their basic needs according to Maslow. When comparing the under-thirty group to the thirty-one to forty age group, it is noteworthy that the thirty-one to forty group still places job security high on its ranking but as one moves up through the age groups, the basic needs become less important to the respondents. Thus, industry seems to do well in taking care of the basic needs of the employees, at least for those who stay past their fortieth birthday.

The over-fifty workers have some anomalies in their ranking of rewards. They place "sympathetic help with personal problems," "good working conditions," and "personal loyalty to employees" as moderately high on their list of preferences. Again, as one ages, personal problems become more of a factor. (See Table 5 for the Chi Square analysis of the age groups.)

Table 5 Age Distribution

Subgroups	Chi-Square	Sig. Level
A1 vs A2	22.86	.05
A1 vs A3	33.67	.01
A1 vs A4	84.21	.01
A2 vs A3	14.65	N.S.
A2 vs A4	43.95	.01
A3 vs A4	12.67	N.S.

Income Group

The low income group (under $20,000) also showed a response pattern that was quite different from the total employee responses and similar to the supervisors' expectations. The responses were also statistically different from the other income groups. As with the low-age group, the low-income group placed "good wages," "job security," and "promotion and growth in the organization" in the primary positions. The next two income levels (through $40,000) showed little difference in their responses and differed from the low-income group only in that they placed "good wages," "job security," and "promotion and growth in the organization" in a moderate position in their list of preferences. Interestingly, the over-$40,000 group placed "job security" as third in importance. Perhaps the increased income causes a desire to retain it, thereby increasing the importance of job security. (See Table 6 for Chi Square analyses of income levels.)

Table 6 Income Level Distribution

Subgroups	Chi-Square	Sig. Level
I1 vs I2	27.69	.05
I1 vs I3	34.92	.01
I1 vs I4	60.77	.01
I2 vs I3	1.87	N.S.
I2 vs I4	13.53	N.S.
I3 vs I4	5.53	N.S.

Job Types

The comparison of the blue-collar, unskilled responses with those of the white-collar, unskilled workers showed significant differences. The unskilled blue-collar group gave top ranking to "interesting work," "full appreciation of work done," and "good wages," whereas the unskilled, white-collar worker showed a greater interest in "good working conditions," and a lesser interest in "good wages." The unskilled, blue-collar worker was more interested in "job security" than the unskilled, white-collar worker, whereas the unskilled, white-collar worker placed more value on "promotion and growth in the organization."

When one compares the skilled, blue-collar with the skilled, white-collar worker, fewer differences are found. The most significant difference is that the blue-collar skilled do not seem to place much value on full appreciation of work done. One could assume they are intrinsically content with their work, since in the majority of cases their tasks are well-defined and self-contained, while the tasks of white-collar workers tend to be more open-ended and the worker is more dependent on supervisory feedback for the definition and assessment of the job. "Job security" was more important for the blue-collar skilled, whereas "promotion and growth in the organization" was of more importance to the white-collar skilled.

Comparing the blue-collar unskilled to the blue-collar skilled, one finds the most significant difference between the two to be the placement of "full appreciation of work done." The blue-collar skilled rated this factor sixth out of ten, whereas the blue-collar unskilled placed it as number one in importance. When one compares the white-collar unskilled to the white-collar skilled, a significant difference is found between how the two groups rated "good working conditions." The unskilled, white-collar worker placed working conditions as number two in importance, whereas the skilled worker placed it as number seven. (See Table 7 for a Chi Square analysis of the job levels.)

Table 7 Job Type Distribution

Subgroups	Chi-Square	Sig. Level
J1 vs J2	30.31	.01
J1 vs J3	17.67	.05
J2 vs J4	11.01	N.S.
J3 vs J4	16.56	N.S.

Organization Level

The organization levels were divided into lower, middle, and higher non-supervisory categories. The comparison of the lower with both the middle and the higher levels produced statistically significant differences. The largest difference between the lower organization level and both higher groups was that the lower organization level employees rated "good wages" as number one and "job security" as number two, whereas both the middle and higher levels rated "interesting work" and "full appreciation of work done" as numbers one and two. Again, one must return to the satisfaction of the basic needs before the higher needs are expressed as an important and relevant concept when evaluating employee satisfaction. (See Table 8 for the Chi Square analysis by organization level.)

Table 8 Organization Level Distribution

Subgroups	Chi-Square	Sig. Level
O1 vs O2	30.30	.01
O1 vs O3	61.92	.01
O2 vs O3	7.29	N.S.

Reward System Manipulation

All three surveys showed supervisors feel that money, i.e., high wages, is the major motivator of their employees, whereas only three of the employee subgroups rated money as the most important reward. These subgroups were the under-thirty group, the under-$20,000 income level, and the lower organization level employee.

Why do managers choose to ignore the reward responses given by the majority of the workers under their supervision? This question was addressed earlier in this article, and it was suggested that managers operate under a self-reference system. That is, they rank rewards as they would want them for themselves and assume their employees would subscribe to the same ranking. If this is true, and the author would point to the survey results to show that it is, then how can management be encouraged to base its employee policies on more objective interpretations of employee motivations?

One way to encourage more objectivity in structuring reward systems is to do attitude surveys such as the survey described herein. This survey revealed that supervisors do not know what their employees want and also revealed differences between employee subgroups that management should take into consideration when structuring reward systems. Managers need to be aware that reward practices should be designed to fit the needs of particular persons working under particular conditions. Using the present survey as an example, reward systems could be manipulated as follows for the various groupings:

Males Versus Females

Males were more inclined to prefer interesting work, whereas females seemed to need more appreciation of work well done. Efforts should be made to design the job format to provide more interest to both groups, since both marked interesting work as one of the two primary rewards. Managers should take into account the fact that female workers have more need of appreciation and should, therefore, engage in more verbal communication intended to foster such a feeling. Also, managers should be more aware of the needs of women for sympathetic help with their personal problems and thus be willing to spend more time with them on such problems than they do with male subordinates.

Age Groups

Flexible pay incentives might be used effectively with the under-thirty workers since they seem to be concerned about their basic needs, while the higher age groups could be expected to respond more positively to job enrichment and job enlargement programs. One group, the forty-one to fifty group, placed as number one "the feeling of being in on things." Systems of "top-down" vertical communication within the organization would appear to be particularly effective with this group. Perhaps supervisors dealing with the forty-one to fifty-year-old group could make an effort to include this group in discussions of policy, even if their input and ideas are not always implemented. The over-fifty group places as moderately important "good working conditions," "personal loyalty to employees," and "sympathetic help with personal problems." An awareness of these needs by the manager could make these employees more productive.

Income Groups

The lower income group is primarily concerned with "good wages" and would respond to incentive pay programs. They are moderately concerned with "interesting work," "full appreciation of work done," and "the feeling of being in on things." All of the other income groups are primarily concerned with "interesting work" and "full appreciation of work done." A job enrichment/job enlargement program would probably work for all income groups except the lowest one, while an incentive pay program (piece-rate, Scanlon plan, etc.) might be a good investment in regard to motivating lower income employees.

Job Types

The most striking difference between the unskilled, blue-collar worker and the unskilled, white-collar worker is the difference in emphasis placed on "good working conditions." The unskilled, white- collar workers judged this to be second in importance on their list of preferences and were the only group that rated this factor so high. The supervisors of this group should be able to address the physical working conditions for the unskilled, white-collar worker by simple environmental analysis and reap some motivational return.

The difference between the blue-collar, skilled and the white-collar, skilled is significant in the positioning of "full appreciation of work done." The blue-collar, skilled worker evidently has a high self-awareness of his/her job and how well s/he does it, whereas the white-collar worker has little sense of self-awareness concerning his/her job and needs outside confirmation of its worth. The blue-collar, skilled worker should be included in more decision-making activities, as s/he seems to have a need for being in on things. The skilled, white-collar worker would respond to the same stimuli as the skilled, blue-collar worker but for a different reason. For the skilled, white-collar worker, greater participation in decision-making activities gives him/her the feedback needed to define the job and better opportunities to receive the exposure needed for advancement.

Organization Level

Employees at the lower organizational level would respond to pay incentives and greater job security, and in the middle and higher levels to job enrichment/job enlargement programs. Respondents in the middle organizational level ranked job security in the number four position, the same position as the total respondent ranking. Thus, the insecurity experienced by workers in the industrial sector is a factor that should be considered seriously by management. Evidently job security matters when you do not have it, as evidenced by the under-thirty group ranking it in the number two position, and the over fifty group (a group with the most seniority) ranking it as seventh. The higher organization level group, probably those with the most security, ranked job security in the number six position. Again, one finds evidence to support Maslow's contention that fulfilled needs no longer motivate.

Attitude Surveys

With the exception of two groups, the under-thirty group and the under-$20,000/year group, all of the respondents ranked "interesting work" in one of the three top positions. Jurgensen, in a study that drew on a thirty-year practice in a large utility company of asking job applicants to rank-order job characteristics in terms of importance to the applicants, came up with a similar result.[6] Over this period of time, job security declined in importance and "type of work" increased in importance. Furthermore, Jurgensen sorted the respondents out by groups according to educational attainment and found that higher educated persons attached more importance to type of work, while those with only high school diplomas attached more importance to job security. The author would argue that since our labor force contains a higher percentage of persons with post-secondary education each year, the increasing importance of interesting work is to be expected and will continue in the future. Making work interesting is not an easy task, however; it is much easier to pay more, to make work cleaner and safer, even to insure reasonable job security, than it is to make some kinds of work interesting. As stated previously, perhaps job enlargement and enrichment are ideas worth trying in the future on a far larger scale than has been done in the past. Organizations without considerable numbers of younger, lower-paid workers may well take a long look at these behavioral concepts.

The author would never argue that attitude surveys are the only answer needed to all motivation problems, for it goes without saying that job satisfaction is a difficult thing to measure. It is tied to the expectations of the worker who answers the questions and is difficult to evaluate against a fixed scale of intensity. At what point, for example, do the cumulative negative feelings of an individual add up to an overall assessment that s/he is dissatisfied with the job? Only the individual can make such an overall judgment. However, this doesn't mean that we can't generalize from these surveys. For example, we can say that based on these surveys, it appears that in most cases the basic needs of the worker are met by today's U.S. organizations. That is, wages are not a burning issue except with the under-thirty-year-old age group, the under-$20,000-a-year pay group and the lower organizational level employees. What is important to the majority of employees surveyed is "interesting work," "appreciation of work," and the "feeling of being in on things." Obviously, then, supervisors should make every effort to be aware of the importance of these particular values and encourage upper-level management to become involved in job restructuring programs and constructing better formal communication systems within the organization. They should be aware that the employees want to be appreciated and should make an effort to give credit where credit is due, and whenever possible, include all levels of employees in some form of decision making so that the employee has a feeling of belonging and participation.

The more often surveys are taken, the more likely managers will heed them and take a personal interest in the progress of programs that they have initiated. It would also enable them to spot potential dissatisfaction factors that could arise because of changes in the make-up of the work force and in the background of the employees. But above all, frequent surveys would help to impress managers with the importance of taking the needs of employees into account. To know what the specific needs are, attitude surveys are necessary, and because of today's rapid changes in our society and organizations, these surveys need to be administered often. Self-reference, a major problem in employee motivation for at least fifty years, will not and cannot be eliminated or even minimized any other way!

The results of attitude surveys should also be disseminated to the supervisors directly in charge of the employees and not held in the hands of upper-level management. This may help to dispel the false notion held by supervisors that their employees are motivated by high wages above everything else. Gellerman, in 1963, stated that "myths die hard. It is quite clear that money's reputation as the ultimate motivator is going to be a long time a-dying."[7] As the present survey shows, this myth is still alive and flourishing with most supervisors in the business sector.

Maslow would contend that under current business conditions most American employees have lower-level or deficit needs substantially satisfied. Therefore, such management strategies as increasing employee incomes or strengthening job security will not accomplish as much as is often expected. The results of these surveys both bear out Maslow's contention and yet point out that there exists a degree to which various respondents' job circumstances are or are not providing sufficient rewards in each job area. The author believes this survey serves an important function in pointing out both the problem of self-reference in motivation and the differences between subgroups of employees in terms of motivational factors and their relative importance.

It must be remembered, however, that each organization's labor force may well score differently when given the present survey. The results discussed herein may be vastly different than those obtained from a particular employer. The resulting conclusions drawn would, of course, be different in such a case.

What the author has found after twenty years of research and consulting in the area of employee motivation is that it is crucial for the organization to address this area. Employee motivation is a key factor in determining long-term employer success levels. Yet, ironically enough, it is an area overlooked by many organizations. Surveys such as the one discussed in this article must be properly structured before they are administered, and must be properly analyzed after the fact. This is not an easy job, but given its importance, it is one that should be undertaken with all deliberate speed. In most organizations (yours?), the time to address this issue was yesterday!

Endnotes

[1] Kovach, K.A., "Why Motivational Theories Don't Work," *S.A.M. Advanced Management Journal*, Spring 1980, p. 56.

[2] Maslow, A.H., "A Theory of Human Motivation," *Psychological Review*, July 1943, pp. 370-396.

[3] Herzberg, F., et al., *The Motivation to Work*, (New York: John Wiley & Sons, 1959).

[4] Filley, A.C., and House, R.J., "Some Empirical Evidence About Needs Theory, Managerial Motivation and Compensation," *Michigan Business Studies*, University of Michigan, Ann Arbor, 1972, p. 239.

[5] McClelland, D.C., "The Role of Money in Managing Motivation," *Managerial Motivation and Compensation*, 1972, p. 527.

[6] Jurgensen, C.E., "Job Preferences: What Makes a Job Good or Bad?" *Journal of Applied Psychology*, 1978, p. 63.

[7] Gellerman, S.W., "Motivation and Productivity," *AMA*, New York, 1963, p. 64.

Management By Whom?

Trends in Participative Management

A subject of increasing controversy in the field of management is the application of participative techniques to non-managerial personnel. Such techniques have been widely used - and even more widely debated. The debate involves the philosophical question of whether it is proper for workers to be included in such traditional management areas as planning, operational decision making and performance evaluation. It also involves questions of capability and motivation which challenge the potential effectiveness of whatever participative strategies are utilized. While the philosophical question broadly embraces virtually all such strategies, the question of effectiveness more pragmatically addresses the results to be obtained by using worker participation in structuring jobs, defining management-labor relationships and managing the firm itself.

Of the two issues, pragmatic effectiveness is of more importance. A negative finding for effectiveness would surely render the philosophical question moot.

A wide variety of participative techniques have been used in many different job environments, but the range of such techniques is basically limited to those that are relatively traditional in concept, representing a "bottom-up" approach and a group of more recently developed techniques that involve "top-down" participation.

The bottom-up approaches embody the goal of providing the worker with managerial values through participation in operational decisions, communications or benefits. These programs include such well understood and popular techniques as job enlargement, job enrichment, management by objectives, team building, and profit sharing.

The top-down approach envisages the worker or groups of workers in an executive role, participating directly in decision making, e.g., long-range planning. This participation includes the worker in actions and responsibilities traditionally reserved for the Board of Directors or the Chief Executive Officer. The European experience in this area involves participation mandated by law, with detailed and explicit procedures developed over a long period of time. The American experience, on the other hand, is based on localized programs, usually initiated by management.

By examining the current status of bottom-up and top-down approaches to worker participation in the management of an organization, it is possible to draw some conclusions concerning the future application of these approaches in the United States.

Bottom-Up Approaches

Job enlargement, one bottom-up approach, is the process of providing more variety in the number of tasks contained in a given job. Moving from the specific, individual job description to an enlarged responsibility for a wider scope of activities is the primary objective of the job enlargement process. For example, a machine operator's job may be narrowly defined to machine a specific material. Alternatively, the job may be enlarged or broadened by also requiring the person to obtain materials, maintain the tools and equipment and inspect the work. This method of involving workers in a greater variety of activities is viewed by many theorists as the most basic participative strategy.

Over the years, researchers have found that worker participation in a wider range of physical activities reduces fatigue and boredom, thereby increasing expected productivity. Job enlargement, however, does not represent an attempt to increase significantly the worker's sense of personal achievement or share of responsibility for results.

Strategies for enhancing the employee's personal identification with a job are called job enrichment. This approach, successfully adopted by the Texas Instrument Corporation and other firms, attempts to build employee motivation by loading a person's job with components of responsibility and autonomy, so that the individual then identifies with important managerial goals. There is considerable evidence that job enrichment can exert a positive influence on workers' attitudes and productivity. Nevertheless, the potential for generalizing this approach is controversial since some critics claim that reported results are unrepresentative. In summarizing prevalent reservations about the validity of the many enthusiastic reports of job enrichment successes, the author would point to the following shortcomings of research in this area:

- Selective reporting of results, distorting any evaluation of the effectiveness of the programs;

- Too few empirical studies, representing a limited range of working environments; and
- Biased results, reflecting the views of managers who initiated the programs of job enrichment, not the views of workers or unions.

The last point suggests that part of the difficulty in implementing job enrichment is that it is management imposed rather than a product of workers' or unions' initiative.

Management By Objectives (MBO) is a strategy for involving lower-level managers and rank-and-file workers in the planning and evaluation process that directs employee efforts toward organizational objectives. The technique was first proposed by Peter Drucker in the 1950s. Since then, it has been elaborated and systematized for use in virtually every organization and has enjoyed widespread popularity.

MBO has been used extensively in industry during the last three decades, but observers have noted mixed results. While some firms have embraced MBO enthusiastically, others have found it more difficult to apply than anticipated. In particular, the benefits of joint manager-subordinate goal-setting and review have been questioned. While MBO has become a popular managerial tool in government as well as business, there have been questions about its efficacy in motivating public-sector employees.

Team building is a concept that assumes that group participation in work activities will develop positive job attitudes and motivate individual members of work groups. Much attention in training managers has been devoted to this method. Like MBO, team building approaches are oriented to managerial recognition of the value of contributions by subordinates. Despite a great deal of managerial enthusiasm for this method, it remains to be seen whether subordinates will prove to be as enthusiastic as their superiors, i.e., those individuals who initiate group decision making and problem solving and normally retain final authority.

Profit sharing approaches to employee participation vary considerably, but they do share a common assumption - a belief that workers will be motivated to excel in their jobs when their compensation depends on the organization's profits. There have been some notable successes in this area, such as the Lincoln Electric Plan. Many other attempts at profit sharing have been disappointing or, at best, have yielded mixed results.

In the author's opinion, this grab bag of approaches makes it difficult to praise or blame any of the participative strategies outlined above - even in those situations where there are clear-cut results shown to be beneficial or harmful to employee morale or productivity. This is not to say, however, that other individuals have found it similarly difficult to pass judgment on the value of these participative techniques. Labor leaders in particular, as we shall now see, have consistently been very outspoken in their criticism of them.

The Union Perspective

Generally, organized labor has looked with skepticism on the traditional approaches to participative management discussed above. Most of these techniques are viewed as the theoretical constructs of academics who lack practical experience in day-to-day contact with non-supervisory employees. One objection is the implicit assumption made in participative plans (e.g., job enlargement, job enrichment, MBO, etc.) that the job can become a major part of the individual's life - that it can be made challenging enough to produce an attitude change toward the job. In certain situations this is true. It is in those instances that the traditional participative programs work best.

When the skills and intellect of the individuals performing the job are at a level high enough to allow them to incorporate significant enlargement or enrichment features into their present job description, such programs are successful. If the job is at a high enough level in the organization to include meaningful and challenging objectives or if the responsibility increases from job enrichment are not simply a facade, then the program has a chance of leading to a desirable employee attitude change. But in some lower-level jobs, where employees' possession of intellectual abilities and skills is demonstrably poor, participative programs have had little success. Among urban blue-collar workers, for example, the track record of participative management programs has been nothing short of disastrous. So, in the area where changes envisioned by the introduction of such programs are most urgently needed - at the lowest levels where major motivation and identification problems arise and the potential for increased productivity is greatest - participative management programs have realized the least success.

The sector of the labor force where these programs are least successful is precisely that sector where unions have their strongest representation. It is not surprising, therefore, that unions generally look with disfavor on such programs. Labor organizations question the practicality of these programs. It is not simply because they see them blurring the traditional "us and them" labor-management relationship (as many have charged);

rather, it is because the very people who belong to these labor organizations are the ones holding the lower-level jobs where the programs have realized the least success.

Is there a cause and effect relationship between the variables involved? Is it union opposition that causes these programs to fail at lower organizational levels, or do the programs fail for other reasons? To answer that question, it is necessary to examine employee attitudes.

Since the days of Frederick Taylor and Scientific Management, it has been an article of faith among the management of manufacturing concerns that, for production efficiency, jobs need to be broken down into small increments with a specific task assigned to each worker. This in turn has created hundreds of thousands of repetitive, unchallenging jobs. Naturally these are the jobs where the identification, motivation and increased productivity expected to be gained through participative management are most needed, but they are also the types of jobs that (if held by an individual for a number of years) can cause an employee to adopt a very negative mental attitude toward the work.

This mental attitude is manifested in attempts, usually through a union, to get more time away from the job. More holidays, vacations, sick leave, etc., are demanded, since the worker now seeks satisfaction not *at* the job, but *away* from it. This same attitude can also result in demands for more monetary compensation to tolerate the same job. If a worker likes the job, a given rate of pay may be enough to keep him or her in it. If the person hates the job, he or she will invariably insist on more reward for the same level of performance. After years of conditioning in this approach to their employment, is it any wonder that many of these employees who belong to unions by virtue of their position are not wholeheartedly embracing participative management?

The situation is made even worse by the changing educational, financial and social levels of the typical union member. The blue-collar sector of the union movement is becoming better educated and better paid, while a larger percentage of overall union membership is white-collar and professional. The better educated and more financially secure employees become, the more they resist superficial attempts at participation. Even profit-sharing plans will suffer in terms of the attitude changes they seek to foster. As employees become better educated, they begin to expect more than a paycheck from the job.

These forces indicate the need to introduce employer practices reflecting genuine participation by employees in the operation of the enterprise. Instead of techniques that emphasize employee input at the lowest organizational levels, "top-down" plans would give employees a collective voice in operating decisions traditionally made by upper-level management. The introduction of such plans is crucial to improve not only the mental health and attitude of the individual employee but also the performance of the firm and, if implemented on a wide enough scale, the economy as a whole. While not seen as a cure-all in and of itself, the emergence of a top-down approach to management is a beacon of hope on an economically bleak horizon.

Top-Down Participative Management

"Top-down management" is usually defined as management that makes decisions, sets the rules, enforces standards, and generally exercises all the traditional powers of the owner/entrepreneur. "Top-down participation," on the other hand, implies sharing by the employee/worker in this process. Major decisions concerning the direction of the firm, products and markets, plans and policies, and conditions of work and employment are set by, or with major input from, the worker/employee. The philosophy of a property right in the job underlies the concept of top-down participation and may explain in part the resistance of management to worker participation in the direction of the firm.

Such top-down participation has taken many forms in the industrialized nations, many of which have carried the concept much further than we have in the United States.

In Germany, *Mitbestimmung* (codetermination, an equal say in management) is required by law. In this mandated system, one-third of the supervisory board (comparable to a Board of Directors in U.S. corporations) is drawn from the workers. The board is responsible for the overall operation of the firm, including the development of plans and policies, the allocation of funds, and decisions on issues such as products, marketing areas, etc. It also appoints a management board to conduct the day-to-day business of the firm.

Work Councils, comparable in a very broad sense to union locals in the United States, must be formed in any German firm employing more than five workers. Blue-collar and white-collar workers are represented proportional to their numbers in the company. The Work Council does not bargain for wages, and working conditions are normally negotiated on a regional or national basis. The Council, however, has a right to codetermination in deciding such issues as job evaluation, piece rates and wage structures, working hours, overtime arrangements, breaks and holiday schedules, staffing policies - including guidelines for recruiting, assigning and dismissing workers, measures to mitigate the effects of layoffs on workers facing dismissal, training, occupational safety and welfare schemes, allocation of company housing, and workers' conduct on the shop floor.

Hiring, discharge, work allocation, promotion, and demotion decisions require the consent of the Council. Unilateral action by the employer in these areas is not allowed.

In the actual conduct of the business of the firm, the powers of the Work Council are more limited. In firms with more than 100 employees, the Work Council appoints an economic committee. The committee has the right to obtain information on such major issues as manufacturing methods, automation, production programs, and the financial condition of the firm. Analysis of this information is the responsibility of the economic committee. The consent of the Work Council is required for major actions such as plant closings and staff cuts.

The author has done extensive research in this area over the last ten years and has concluded that there is little possibility of such a system gaining a significant foothold in the United States. Countries such as ours, where a traditionally adversarial role has existed between labor and management, will take at least a generation to embrace such a system. While economic factors are indeed moving us in this direction faster than many would like, it will still take a considerable amount of time to develop a model that fits within our capitalist frame of reference.

A review of our country's labor history reinforces the idea of the voluntary basis of our labor/management relations and reduces the likelihood of adoption of the European method of codetermination. Systems like codetermination are the result of national law (unlike the normal give-and-take between American management and labor), confirming that European industrial democracy was fought for and gained within the political arena. Codetermination's political origins in Germany have resulted in hundreds of pages of manifold, complex legislation, bearing little relation to laws in this country. In the author's opinion, American workers and their representatives have both the expectation and the desire for two things that codetermination restricts: the freedom to create/operate systems independent of governmental influence and the freedom to contest any ensuing labor/management system.

In contrast to the mandated system of workers contractual presence on joint committees, there are situations where the American worker actually can own all or part of the firm and have management rights by virtue of such ownership. The Employee Stock Option Plan (ESOP) and its management arm, the Employee Stock Option Trust (ESOT), are employment benefit plans in which a company (usually a small, closely-held corporation) sells its stock to its employees. These plans work in conjunction with, or as replacements for, the normal retirement plans. The author would hypothesize that an employee owned firm (either completely employee-owned or partially owned through an ESOP) should have (a) increased profitability, (b) a better growth record, (c) increased productivity, (d) more employment stability, and (e) fewer work stoppages.

Summary

What is happening in the United States is not the codetermination system mandated in Germany. Yet neither is it the level of employee ownership some envisioned after the successes of employee takeovers at Youngstown Sheet and Tube or Kaiser Steel. Instead, we see management reluctantly granting both bottom-up and top-down participation to workers in return for economic concessions. Boundaries, systems, and rules are being formulated every day in the American workplace in individualistic *ad hoc* ways. Both labor and management have resisted the intrusion of the legislative process into this area, and for this the author applauds them. In the long run, a more equitable and less burdensome system will evolve based on the uniquely American combination of cooperation and confrontation between labor and management.

Health Care Cost Containment: An Impossible Dream?

The escalating cost of employee health care has become a major threat to the balance sheet of most major U.S. employers. No human resource issue has consumed as much time and energy or generated as much anxiety since the Employee Retirement Income Security Act of 1974 forced employers to come to grips with the solvency of their pension plans.

The magnitude of the problem can be summed up in one startling statistic: health care costs are rising at the rate of 20% per year - four times faster than the consumer price index![1] At present, the United States spends 11% of its gross national product on health care with projections indicating that this figure will reach 15% by the year 2000. This is a far greater percentage than any other industrialized country and, in absolute dollars, represents over $1.5 trillion.[2] Without some control, health care costs will seriously threaten the financial stability of major employers across all industries and thereby threaten our entire economy. Something must be done, and it must be done soon.

Realizing the need for action, the federal government, employers (individually and collectively), and employees have begun to address the problem. Thus far we have accomplished the easiest part of the task - identifying the causes of the problem.

Problem Causes

There are numerous factors contributing to the escalating costs. One is the increasing instance of malpractice claims, forcing overly cautious doctors to require more tests. Another is the unique system in the medical profession whereby those generating the demand for test and laboratory work (doctors) are also the suppliers (often through their own laboratories). Both of these factors have generated considerable publicity. Likewise, the percentage of total cost consumed by overhead or administrative expenses has been frequently mentioned as an explanation for the staggering growth in costs.

All three of the above-mentioned factors are minor, however, when compared to the costs associated with the new medical technology and the changing demographics of the United States population.[3] It is the latter two that are the biggest single contributory factors, not only in terms of absolute dollars, but also in terms of employer perceptions.

Addressing these points, the Midwest Business Group on Health surveyed its 150-company membership to assess employers' perceptions on causes of health care cost increases. The results are presented in Table 1.[4]

Table 1

Cause	% Respondents Indicating Major Cause
Medical technology	53%
Aging population	39%
Physicians using unnecessary tests	36%
Excessive employee protection by insurance	34%
Outpatient prices increasing	32%
Employers inattentive for too long	14%
Hospital inefficiency	12%
Insurers doing too little	10%
Excessive mandates on coverage	7%
Administrative costs added to total expenses	7%
Physicians earning too much	2%

Medical technology is the most frequently perceived problem today. It borders on the miraculous, but it is not without a price. Heart bypass surgery averages $20,000 per artery, a heart transplant averages $115,000, and a liver transplant today costs $175,000. To the patient and family in need, the cost may be irrelevant at the time of demand; but sooner or later, someone is going to have to pay the supplier. The increasing use of nuclear magnetic resonance imaging testing may eliminate the need for many surgical procedures, but the equipment costs over $1.5 million and each test costs several thousand dollars. Sooner or later we, as a nation and as individuals, must be willing to perform a medical costs/benefit analysis. The moral dilemma raised at that point is an obvious one: what monetary value do we put on the cost of a human life? The escalating cost of medical technology will soon force us to confront the benefit side relative to the cost side, rather than simply marveling at the benefits as we have done in the past.

The other major factor driving up medical costs is the aging U.S. population. The U.S. Census Bureau projects that 13% of our population will be 65 years of age or older in the year 2000 - compared with 10.7% in 1980. Also, by 2020, the over-65 age group will have increased by two-thirds from 1980 to 17.3% of the total population. Moreover, 5% of the population will be 85 years of age or older in 2020 compared with 1% in 1980.[5]

The latest amendment to the 1967 Age Discrimination in Employment Act removed the upper age limit for the protected class. As a result, this aging of the population will naturally result in an aging of the U.S. work force. Since older employees, as a group, incur greater health care costs than younger workers, this aging of the work force will cause employer health care costs to increase dramatically.

Thus, it can be seen that while many factors are contributing to increasing health care costs, technological advances and the aging of the work force are perceived to be the two biggest culprits.

Solutions

Having identified the causes of the problem, employers are now searching for solutions. In the mid-1980s, a number of employer groups and trade associations began to extol the virtue of exploring various purchasing strategies as a necessary first step in controlling health care costs. Presently, five major purchasing strategies are being utilized by employers. These strategies are presented in Table 2.[6]

Table 2

Purchasing Strategy	Cost Savings*	Quality Activities
Employee sponsored specific procedure purchasing initiative	$100,000 annual savings	Review mortality data procedures; examine reputation
Employer group purchasing initiative for comprehensive services	10% to 40% discounts off billed charges; 1% to 6% annual increase in total health expenditures for some companies	Utilization data used to identify problem areas. Some starting to implement quality improvement principles
Utilizing insurer-sponsored nationwide Provider networds	As little as 10% total expenditure increase in first three years	Rely on insurer efforts
Encouraging competition among Health Plans	One community experienced annual increases of 1.3% to 13.7% over the last five years for all plans; HMO and PPO rate increases of 4.8% to 8.1% in the last five years	Patient satisfaction surveys, including quality issues. Professional review organizations examine health plan quality assurance activities
Community-wide health care resource planning	8.2% annual increase between 1984-96	Mortality rates declined during 1992-96. Applying case-mix severity adjustment tools to payment system

* Nationwide annual health expenditure increase = 20%.

A majority of employers have begun to shift a greater percentage of premium costs to employees as a second tactic addressing cost containment. There is no doubt that this shift has only just begun and will continue through the 1990s. During 1989, employees paid nearly 30% of their collective $500 million health care premium out-of-pocket. This figure is up almost 10% from 1985[7] and by the end of this decade may reach 50%.[8] The depth of employer feeling on the issue of cost shifting is delineated in Table 3, where labor and management were asked which health care concessions they would seek in the next decade to control costs.[9]

Table 3

Health Care Concessions

	Labor	Management
Denying coverage for dependents of members who hold jobs elsewhere	34%	4%
Increasing union members' out-of-pocket payments or cost sharing	18%	70%
Reducing coverage in the most expensive areas, e.g. mental health and substance abuse	18%	16%
Reducing retirees' benefits	2%	8%

While the previously mentioned trends are the most universally adopted tactics to address the problem, there are numerous others being implemented by smaller segments of employers. Health Maintenance Organizations (used by 18% of employers), Preferred Provider Organizations (11%), and health education and fitness programs (4%) are the ones that have received the most publicity.[10] The first two have not resulted in the savings predicted a few years ago, since they are both subject to the double whammy of technology and an aging work force that has affected the more traditional plans. Health education and fitness programs may well have long-term benefits but will not impact in a time period that is short enough to help with the present problem.

Because these and many other lesser-used programs have failed to stem the escalating cost of health care, some employers are now starting to support the most drastic solution of all - national health insurance. Twenty-five percent of all employers feel that it is likely that the government will institute a national health plan by the year 2000.[11] It is also believed that the government will regulate medical fees. Among employers, the question is not whether there will be national insurance but *when* there will be a national health plan. Marriott, AT&T, Dupont, Chrysler, and American Airlines are just a few of the companies that support a national health care plan.

In this type of program, government would decide how much society would spend on health care. Doctors would, in fact, collect less per patient; however, claims would be settled at a higher rate and faster.[12] Under such a system, health care would be rationed according to need as opposed to the current method of price rationing. All members of society would receive equal health care. This is an extremely socialistic concept for the distribution of any commodity. The author doubts that the system would be operated as efficiently and as fairly as its supporters claim. However, health care is not a commodity that can be sold in a price market. It cannot morally be sold to the highest bidder. Rationing on the basis of need may be the only way to avoid continuous rapid growth of health care costs.[13]

Conclusion

As Table 4 [14] indicates, health care cost containment is one of the major problems facing U.S. industry today.

Table 4

Top Six Labor-Related Issues for the Business Community in the Next Decade

	Labor's View			Management's View	
1.	Health care benefits	34%	1.	Rising health care costs / cost containment	22%
2.	Job security	30%	2.	Labor-management cooperation /non-adversarial relationships	22%
3.	Retirement / pension funds benefits	22%	3.	Health care benefits	14%
4.	Wage / pay increases	20%	4.	Global competition / protection of U.S. jobs	14%
5.	Rising health care costs / cost containment	18%	5.	Retraining / education of work force; preparation for new technology	18%
6.	Global competition / protection of U.S. jobs	16%	6.	Productivity improvement	14%

Strategies already implemented have thus far failed to control the problem, yet everyone acknowledges something must be done soon. The push for a system of national health insurance by huge private-sector employers, who historically have viewed lesser instances of government intrusion as a step toward socialism, indicates how desperate the situation has become.

The answer may not lie in piecemeal solutions such as those discussed in this paper (HMOs, PPOs, fitness programs, cost shifting, purchasing strategies, etc.), but in some total program coordinated by an umbrella, private-sector group formed solely to address this problem. It is the author's opinion that if a number of large employers voluntarily formed such a group and coordinated across employer members all of the cost control tactics discussed herein, the results would be pleasantly surprising. No one should be naive enough to believe that this will solve the entire problem, but the degree of success would be such that other employers would follow the lead. This option is worth exploring first, as it is far preferable to government intervention in the form of national health insurance - both in terms of efficiency and total cost to individual taxpayers.

This may strike some as a drastic, unrealistic approach to the problem, but at this point in time we must be willing to try something different. If previously conceived and/or presently implemented solutions had worked, we would not have a need for articles such as this. The time to address this problem was yesterday. The solution to this problem had better come before too many tomorrows!

Endnotes

[1] *National Institute of Business Management, Inc.*, Bulletin (1989), Vol. 40 , Number 33, Section 1.

[2] Special Bulletin: *Rising Costs, Diversified Group Administrators, Inc.*, National Association of Employee Benefit Administrators (1991).

[3] Relman, A., "Confronting the Health Care Crisis," *Technology Review* (1989), Vol.92, No.7.

[4] Midwest Business Group on Health (1990), "Health Program Management: Experience and Expectation," *MBGH Member Survey*, p. 5.

[5] "Medical Miracles," Special Supplement, *Wall Street Journal,* 4/1/91, p. 4.

[6] Cited at note 4 above, p. 7.

[7] Cited at note 5 above, p. 4.

[8] Martin, S., "What Americans Spend on Health Care," *U.S. News and World Report*, 6/8/90.

[9] *Ibid.*

[10] Schachner, K., "Group Health Options for the Future," *Newsweek*, 4/21/90.

[11] "Employees to Pay More for Benefits," *Futurist*, Vol. 23, 11/12/89.

[12] Cited at note 3 above.

[13] "Health Care Rationing," *Science Magazine*, Vol. 248, 5/11/89.

[14] Special Report, "How Today's Organizations Control the Cost of Health Care," *Bureau of Labor Research*, (1991).

Manager, Political Activist, Labor Leader, Statesman:

The Remarkable Life of ASA PHILIP RANDOLPH

ABSTRACT

Asa Philip Randolph was many things to many people. He was a tireless crusader for African-American rights, a strategic manager and planner, a political activist, and a labor leader. Many of the changes he brought about and many of the conditions he created continue to shape American culture today. This article traces the career of this remarkable individual and highlights the contributions he made to U.S. society.

Introduction

Asa Philip Randolph was born into a poor family on April 15, 1889 in Crescent City, Florida. His father, a country preacher, hoped his second son would follow in his footsteps and take up the religious life. While Asa never became interested in this vocation, he did learn many principles of public speaking from observing his father. He performed well in his segregated elementary school and graduated as valedictorian from Jacksonville's Cookman Institute, a college-preparatory school.

Having no money for college, Randolph moved to Harlem in 1911 to find work. There he married Lucille Campbell Green in 1914. During his early years in New York, Randolph attempted to organize his fellow employees to seek better working conditions and higher wages. He tried to organize a group of porters and a group of waiters but the employees were afraid to stand up to management for fear of being fired. Randolph was later successful in coordinating an effort among elevator and switchboard operators and established his first union in 1923, The Elevator and Switchboard Operators Union. His intelligence and public speaking abilities quickly moved him from organizing small, local labor unions to speaking at large union meetings. Thus, his career as a labor leader began.

It was during those early days in Harlem that Randolph first confronted the problem of managing and leading others over whom he had no institutional authority. During these days Randolph relied on his charismatic style of leadership. He developed this style out of necessity, and it was to serve him well throughout his life.

Randolph enjoyed reading about African-American labor leaders and other leaders such as Bill Haywood, Ghandi, Karl Marx, Elizabeth Gurley Flynn, and Eugene Debs. His philosophies were shaped by these individuals and he became an avid supporter of the socialist system, sometimes entertaining thoughts of communism. Socialism, he thought, was the way to salvation for African-Americans, and in his early years in unions he argued for this system. With time, however, he drifted away from socialism and advocated working within the democratic system, peacefully trying to strengthen the power of organized labor.[1]

In 1917, Randolph and his longtime friend, Chandler Owen, began the *Messenger*, a labor newspaper that claimed to be the only radical African-American paper in America. The *Messenger* was successful even though at first it only reached the middle class socialists. Since Randolph was a pacifist, he used the *Messenger* to urge African-American men not to join the war effort in the late 1910s. He could not understand why African-Americans would want to enlist and fight for democracy abroad when there was no democracy for them in the U.S..[2]

At the *Messenger* Randolph became proficient at delegating responsibility to staff while he concentrated on strategic planning in areas of editorial policy and financing. Even at this early stage of his career, and lacking formal management training, it was obvious that Randolph had an understanding of basic management principles.

The Brotherhood Movement

With all the publicity that Randolph received from the *Messenger*, he was in great demand to assist African-American groups. One of the groups that approached him was the Pullman porters. Ashley L. Totten, a Pullman Railroad sleeping car porter, asked Randolph to come and speak to other porters about forming a union. He accepted Totten's offer to lead the new union and in 1925, in an Elks Lodge in Harlem, the Brotherhood of Sleeping Car Porters (BSCP) was born. "Fight or be Slaves" was the motto the Brotherhood adopted.[3] This union became the single largest representative of African-American workers in America.

The porters saw Randolph as a dynamic speaker capable of leading their union. Since Randolph was not a porter, he was not threatened with being fired by the Pullman Company. One of the early problems with the formation of a union was that the porters were scattered all over the country and were constantly moving about. The new union had to devise a way to reach all of them even though there was no money to hire men to organize the workers. Randolph saw the porters as the ideal group to strengthen African-American unionism because they worked on railroads all over the country. He raised $10,000 and toured the entire country to form a solid union to fight the Pullman Company.

In 1925, while touring the country, Randolph met Milton Webster in Chicago. Webster was fired from his job as a Pullman porter after 20 years of service for "insubordination." His insubordination consisted of trying to organize a union of porters. The porters had a great deal of respect for Webster and would follow any man he endorsed to lead them. Webster heard Randolph speak of uniting the porters to force the Pullman Company to bargain with them and immediately let it be known that he would back Randolph. Randolph, in turn, appointed Webster assistant general organizer of the Chicago division of the BSCP.

Randolph moved from city to city gathering followers everywhere he went. By the end of 1926, groups of the Brotherhood had been set up in cities all over the country, from New York City on the East Coast to Portland, Oregon and Los Angeles, California on the West Coast.[4]

Randolph kept in touch with the porters through the *Messenger*. Every issue listed the porters' demands:

1. Recognition of the BSCP as the legitimate porter's union and abolition of the Plan of Employee Representation (the company union)
2. An end to tipping and a raise in salary to $150/month
3. A basic 240-hour work month
4. Fair pay for overtime and deadheading (spending time on railway cars without pay)
5. Stop double heading (using two engines to pull more railway cars)
6. Conductor's pay for conductor's work
7. Establishment of a pension plan
8. 4 hours' sleep on the first night out and 6 hours on the following nights.[5]

The *Messenger* was the key to the success of the Brotherhood of Sleeping Car Porters, as it was a channel to reach the porters and their sympathizers throughout the country. Randolph wrote a series of articles describing the poor working conditions of the porters. Porters were overworked and the lowest paid members of the working class. Yet as poor as a porter's job was, it was considered good by the African-American community because African-American men could only find manual labor jobs. African-American males that had any education sought jobs as porters. The Pullman Company was well respected in the African-American community because it was the single largest employer of African-Americans in the U.S.

To prevent the porters from forming their own union, the Pullman Company formed a company union called the Plan of Employee Representation (PER). The company handpicked its leaders and told them how to vote. The BSCP knew that they, rather than the PER, represented the majority of the porters but they still needed to be recognized by the Pullman Company. The BSCP realized that would never happen if there was a company union, yet the members of the BSCP could not publicly denounce the PER or they would be fired (porters were fired even if they were suspected of associating with the BSCP). The Brotherhood, therefore, kept its membership list secret. Because of this secrecy, Randolph had to change his management style from an emphasis on charismatic leadership to an appeal to followers to work for the long range benefit of their organization and their race.

In May 1926, the Railway Labor Act was passed which allowed the railroad workers to organize. Randolph now believed that the Pullman Company had to meet with the Brotherhood. But this law did not apply to the railroad porters. They tried to peacefully and legally get recognition, to no avail. Their only option was to strike. Randolph realized that a strike might be deadly to the union, because the Pullman Company would hire strikebreakers of all races. William Green, President of the AFL, also warned Randolph against striking.

Randolph decided to hedge his bet by mobilizing for a strike but not actually striking. He hoped the threat of a strike would be enough to coerce the Pullman Company into an agreement. When the Pullman Company heard of the strike, it approached Randolph with a deal. If Randolph resigned from the union, the Pullman Company would meet with the Brotherhood. Randolph demanded that the Pullman Company recognize the union before he resigned. The Pullman Company would not agree to do this. Randolph then went ahead and ordered a strike vote. Six thousand Brotherhood members voted in favor of the strike and 17 against.[6]

The Pullman Company called their bluff and, in effect, told the Brotherhood to proceed with the strike. The company was confident that the strike would have little effect on its operation of railway cars. Thinking that the strike would break the union, Randolph called it off. This was a humiliating defeat for the Brotherhood and for Randolph. The Pullman Company fired everyone that it believed had voted for the strike and hired replacements. Membership in the union dwindled from thousands to a few hundred, and union offices were closed all over the country.

Randolph realized that the Brotherhood needed help and turned to the AFL for assistance. The Brotherhood applied for AFL admission in the early months of 1929. The Brotherhood lacked the funds and the membership to obtain an international charter so William Green (AFL President) permitted each district to join independently (which was less expensive). With the support of the AFL, Randolph believed that the Brotherhood's position was now secure.

Throughout his career, Randolph sought such coalitions with groups within the existing power structure. As the manager of an "outside" group, he realized this gave him ties to what many recognized as "legitimate" power. Using this, he could work for change from both within and outside the system.

The Stock Market Crash of 1929 worsened the conditions faced by the Brotherhood. Many businesses closed and people lost their jobs. This was especially difficult for African-American workers because white workers were now desperate enough to take their lowly positions. Many porters lost their jobs and looked to the union for help. Most Brotherhood offices closed, and the leaders started to live from day to day. Even though the Brotherhood membership was at an all time low, the Pullman Company sent Randolph a $10,000 check to stop working for the Brotherhood. Randolph immediately returned the check and declared that he was not for sale. This incident gave the Brotherhood and Randolph a much needed boost. After this, everyone knew that Randolph was loyal and would not stop fighting until the Brotherhood was accepted by the Pullman Company.

The passage of the National Industrial Recovery Act (NIRA) and the Emergency Transportation Act (ETA) in 1933 helped almost every potential union or union member in the country except the porters. These two Acts did not cover porters. The ETA, designed for railway workers, did not include the porters because Pullman technically was not a railroad company. The porters were also excluded from the NIRA, designed for everyone but railway workers, because under the terms of this legislation, porters were defined as railway workers. Therefore, the porters were not covered under either piece of legislation.

Randolph went before Congress and insisted that the porters be included in future railroad legislation. At Randolph's insistence, President Roosevelt amended the Railway Labor Act in 1935 to include porters. This law required corporations to negotiate with unions that represented a majority of their employees. The Pullman Company also found a way around this law. The Company secretly founded the Pullman Porters Protection Association (PPPA) with a few porters loyal to the company. The Pullman Company said that they would not recognize the BSCP because the real union was the PPPA.

In 1935, using all the money in their treasury, the Brotherhood conducted an ambitious membership drive. This paid off as membership and dues increased significantly. William Green announced that the Brotherhood would be admitted into the AFL as a full member. In 1935, the Brotherhood proudly took its place among the 105 official AFL international unions and made history by being the first African-American union to become affiliated with the federation. Even though the AFL accepted the Brotherhood, the Pullman Company still asserted that the PPPA was the porters' true representative.

Randolph again went to Congress to protest the Pullman Company tactics. The federal government intervened and supervised a vote of the porters to determine which union they preferred. The overwhelming winner was the Brotherhood.

On July 29, 1935, the Pullman Company agreed to a meeting with the leaders of the Brotherhood. The union met with the Pullman Company's President, A. J. Curry. Pullman executives kept stalling on an agreement hoping that the amended Railway Labor Act of 1935, which included the porters, would be declared unconstitutional in court.

In the spring of 1936, the Supreme Court ruled that the amended Railway Labor Act was constitutional. On August 25, 1937, twelve years to the day since the first Brotherhood meeting in Harlem, the Pullman Company finally agreed to a contract. They signed the first labor contract between a large American corporation and a union of African-American workers. The porters gained higher salaries, shorter working hours, and job security.[7] Asa Philip Randolph was the chief union negotiator.

Other Labor Organizations

The Brotherhood continued to advance the civil rights cause by helping other African-American laborers. African-American women were unionized under the BSCP and were called the Ladies Auxiliary. In 1938, the Brotherhood also helped form the Joint Council of Dining Car Employees and the International Brotherhood of Red Caps on airlines. The Red Caps, known today as Sky Caps, worked in the same poor conditions as the porters on the railroads. The Brotherhood's reputation even spread to Canada, and in 1946 the Brotherhood organized the porters of the Canadian Pacific and the Northern Alberta Railways.

With the law on its side (Executive Order 8802), Randolph helped form the Provisional Committee for the Organization of Colored Locomotive Fireman in 1941. There was a shortage of firemen on the railroads, but railway companies were still not hiring trained African-American men. The Brotherhood sued the all-white Brotherhood of Locomotive Firemen and Engineers for colluding with the railway companies in preventing the hiring of such men. In 1944, the Supreme Court outlawed the collusion between the railway companies and the all-white union and forced them both to pay damages.[8]

In 1936, a group of young African-American intellectuals approached Randolph about forming an organization to unite the African-American community. Randolph helped form the National Negro Congress (NNC) to further African-American rights organizations and to help African-Americans cope with the depression. Unfortunately, the NNC was not successful in bringing African-American groups together because the NAACP never endorsed the NNC. These two organizations should have been allies, but the NAACP saw the NNC as a potential threat to its influence in the African-American community and as a competitor for funds. The main reason for the demise of the NNC was the infiltration of the organization by Communists. Randolph left the NNC when it overwhelmingly voted against U.S. participation in World War II. He realized that its views were vastly different from his own and were detrimental to the success of African-American organizations. The NNC did, however, give Randolph practical civil rights experience.

Early Civil Rights

In 1939 when World War II broke out in Europe, the U.S. needed to increase its defensive capabilities. The military build-up helped the domestic economy and created many new jobs. By 1940, the U.S. economy had taken a healthy upturn, and defense-related firms had numerous job openings. African-Americans flocked from southern states to northern urban areas for these jobs, but most companies refused to hire them.

Randolph voiced his opposition to the companies' policies at a convention of the BSCP in September, 1940. He urged the President, Congress, and especially the African-American community to fight for equal opportunity in defense-related and government jobs. He also called for desegregation in the armed forces and the elimination of Jim Crow laws. Eleanor Roosevelt attended the convention and influenced the President to investigate.

President Roosevelt met with Randolph but only agreed to minor concessions concerning African-Americans in the Air Force. Randolph responded by beginning strategic planning for a march on Washington on July 1, 1941, to bring together over 10,000 marchers supporting his cause. He also established the March on Washington Committee which for decades after would remain a powerful force in coordinating civil rights activities. The response was overwhelming and two months before the planned march, over 100,000 people were scheduled to attend.

Roosevelt, desperate to avoid the bad publicity and possible violence, issued Executive Order 8802 which made it a crime for government funded companies to refuse to hire applicants based on race. It also established the Fair Employment Practices Committee to enforce the Order.[9] Randolph called off the march feeling that he had been victorious. Compliance with the Executive Order, however, was slow until the bombing of Pearl Harbor on December 7, 1941. When the U.S. entered the war, Randolph refrained from coordinating any marches or protests for fear of being labeled an anti-war activist.

After the war, Truman requested legislation for a draft which required African-American men to join a segregated army and navy. Randolph capitalized on this to launch an effort to fully desegregate every branch of the armed forces. After a fruitless meeting with President Truman, Randolph and his colleague, Grant Reynolds, met with the Senate Armed Services Committee and delivered their civil disobedience ultimatum. They declared that if the draft was implemented with the armed forces still segregated they would recommend to men of all races that they not sign up, but instead march peacefully against it. This received the attention of the Senate and the President but produced no concrete action. A poll conducted by the NAACP after Randolph's "ultimatum" revealed that 70% of African-American draft-age men would refuse to sign up for a draft if segregation continued.

In 1947, Randolph established the Committee Against Jim Crow in Military Service and Training to fight against military segregation. This Committee was later named the League for Non-Violent Civil Disobedience Against Military Segregation. This organization coordinated pickets in front of the White House and Congress threatening widespread civil disobedience if Truman's draft became law. In June, 1948, the draft was signed into law without a desegregation clause.

Randolph immediately went into action organizing marches, pickets, and boycotts throughout the U.S.. Realizing that he might be imprisoned for coordinating such acts, Randolph said, "I am prepared to oppose a Jim Crow army until I rot in jail." Randolph's management expertise was now on display as he deliberately made himself the focal point of the struggle. This political pressure eventually forced Truman to sign Executive Order 9981 on July 26, 1948 which stated that African-Americans were to be treated exactly the same as whites in the army and the navy.

The Civil Rights Movement Matures

The beginning of the civil rights movement is marked by the refusal of an African-American woman, Rosa Parks, to give up her bus seat for a white person in Montgomery, Alabama in 1955. After Parks' arrest, E. D. Nixon, a disciple of Randolph's, began coordinating a boycott of Montgomery buses. Another of Randolph's colleagues, Bayard Rustin, was sent to help coordinate the bus boycott, which lasted until passage of the Civil Rights Act of 1957.

While still leader of the BSCP, Randolph took an active role in desegregating schools in the South. Even though the Supreme Court ruled in 1954 that segregating in public schools was unconstitutional (*Brown v. Board of Education of Topeka*), some southern states blatantly ignored the ruling, which sometimes led to violence.

On April 24, 1956, Randolph organized "The State of the Race" conference in Washington in which leaders of diverse African-American organizations representing over twelve million people concluded that the pace of the civil rights movement was too slow. Leaders at the conference issued a statement which called for the abolition of school segregation and new civil rights legislation to mandate fair employment practices.[10] This conference, however, failed to speed progress on civil rights and never convened again.

Disappointed in his effort to unify African-American leaders, Randolph joined forces with Martin Luther King, Jr. and the NAACP in coordinating and supporting a number of marches on Washington called Prayer Pilgrimage marches. The NAACP provided much of the financial support for the marches and, in turn, Randolph pledged "uncompromising support" for the association, warning white supremacists "to keep their evil hands off" the organization. The largest of these marches took place on May 17, 1957 and involved over 20,000 people at the steps of the Lincoln Memorial. Dr. King attended many of the marches, but President Eisenhower conveniently was out of town for the events.

President Eisenhower finally focused his attention on school desegregation after sending troops to Little Rock, Arkansas to prevent mob violence at a local high school. He called for a meeting of African-American leaders to discuss racial problems and invited Randolph "because he was a respected citizen in whom most Americans had complete faith."[11] Randolph presented Eisenhower with a nine-point program which would help fully integrate public schools in the U.S.

After Eisenhower showed little response, Randolph invited 100 African-American and white leaders to a New York conference where Dr. King recommended a march on Washington which would include thousands of school-age African-Americans. The NAACP volunteered financial support for the event. Randolph organized the march and on October 25, 1958, 9,500 African-American and white students converged on the Lincoln Memorial to show their discontent with segregated schools. Even though the President refused to meet with the leaders, Randolph called the march a success because of the pageantry and drama it supplied. After the Youth March of 1958, Randolph established a committee that would coordinate many other similar marches for the same cause. Over the next two years, these marches brought thousands of children to the steps of the Capitol. Though no major legislative victory was achieved, the marches enabled Randolph to forge alliances between African-Americans' rights organizations, churches, white liberals, and organized labor which would prove instrumental in carrying out the historic march on Washington in 1963.

Randolph with the AFL-CIO

After the AFL accepted the Brotherhood as a full member in 1935, Randolph began fighting against racial discrimination from within. When the CIO was formally expelled from the AFL in 1937, Randolph kept the Brotherhood in the AFL to fight discrimination "where it's at." Randolph succeeded in persuading many AFL members to oppose discrimination, but the Federation's leadership would not cooperate.

Randolph financed most of the civil rights activities discussed thus far using funds from the BSCP. When membership in the Brotherhood waned in the 1950s due to a decline in railway transportation, Randolph turned to the AFL-CIO for financial support. Randolph had many friends there and persuaded the organization to support the civil rights movement.

After being elected vice president of the AFL-CIO in 1957, Randolph concentrated his efforts on purging the organization of member unions which practiced discrimination. The Federation's policy stated that unions could be expelled for corruption and communism but not for civil rights violations. In 1955, at an AFL-CIO convention, Randolph called for the ouster of unions that prohibited African-Americans from joining. This was the first time civil rights issues within the Federation were brought up at a convention.

These comments from the podium enraged George Meany (President of the AFL-CIO) because Randolph had not consulted him first. Tension between Randolph and labor leaders in the AFL-CIO ran high after this speech because many southern labor leaders opposed union integration. This is one of the few times Randolph violated one of his management practices of building an alliance with an established power base within an organization before pushing for internal change. Like any good leader, he did not make this same mistake twice.

Frustrated with the lack of support from the AFL-CIO, Randolph established the Negro American Labor Council (NALC) in 1960 to fight for first class citizenship for African-Americans and full equality of opportunity for all minority groups in every facet of employment. Randolph stated that the NALC was not a union but merely an organization to strive for equality. Randolph, however, kept his position in the AFL-CIO so he could make changes from within. In March 1961, he announced his "code of fair racial trade union practices" to the AFL-CIO leadership. This code denounced AFL-CIO policies and called for an end to racial segregation in the federation's unions within six months. It also called for establishment of a mechanism to enforce the new policy. The AFL-CIO leadership, especially Meany, strongly opposed this code and condemned Randolph for his slanderous accusations of the Federation. After the NALC and many white leaders pressured the Federation on Randolph's behalf, the AFL-CIO, in effect, apologized to Randolph and adopted a policy to "work harder to make sure all men in unions were treated equally."[12] By late 1961, the NALC was waning in membership but Randolph still used it as a base to launch his next big accomplishment: the 1963 march on Washington.

The March on Washington

In 1961, Randolph conceived a plan to coordinate a massive march on Washington to show his displeasure with the pace of the civil rights movement. He was appalled by statistics showing that more African-Americans attended segregated schools in 1961 than in 1952; that more African-Americans were unemployed in 1961 than in 1954; and that the median income of African-Americans had slipped from 57 to 54 percent of that of whites in the same time period.[13] He obtained immediate support from large African-American organizations like the NAACP, National Urban League, Congress On Racial Equality, and the Southern Christian Leadership Conference. Randolph's major objective was to obtain more jobs and better pay for African-Americans.

At the same time, Martin Luther King, Jr. was planning a march on Washington for the passage of a strong civil rights bill. Since Randolph felt two marches would diminish the strength of each, he joined forces with Dr. King and called the unified march, "The March on Washington for Jobs and Freedom." The leadership made two demands of the federal government: 1) promptly pass a civil rights bill enforcing school desegregation and ending police brutality; and 2) establish a federal Public Works program which would ensure an expanding economy, a $2 minimum wage, and the end of discriminatory practices in government offices, private businesses, and trade unions.

On August 28, 1963, Washington saw the largest protest in the nation's history attended by people of all races. Randolph gave the opening speech to the 250,000 attendees and later introduced Dr. King who delivered his famous, "I Have A Dream," speech. The march was entirely peaceful and a great success in Randolph's eyes. This event marked the first time that such a large number of white moderates showed their support for the cause. Partially as a result of Randolph's efforts, the 1964 Civil Rights Bill was passed by Congress and signed by President Lyndon Johnson. A. Philip Randolph took part in the signing ceremony.

Trophies in His Cabinet

Randolph had been widely recognized in many arenas for his contributions to the African-American labor movement and civil rights.

Universities presented Randolph with honorary degrees, the NAACP awarded him the Springard Medal, New York honored him with an A. P. Randolph Day, and President Johnson presented him with the highest civilian medal, The Medal of Freedom. Today streets are named after him and his old high school bears his name. There is no doubt that he deserves these honors, for perhaps no man contributed more to the cause of African-American labor and civil rights.

Asa Philip Randolph died on May 16, 1979 at the age of 90. During his lifetime Randolph helped many African-American unions achieve not only better pay and better working conditions but also equality in major labor organizations. His efforts drove discrimination from not only the AFL-CIO but also from the U.S. Armed Forces, companies receiving government funding, and some schools in the South. Randolph united people with his vision and determination, creating solidarity and strength in the labor movement. His non-violent methods proved to be effective in furthering the African-American cause. Asa Philip Randolph was the first to give vision, organization, and dignity to the African-American labor force. For this, he deserves a special place in labor history. It is unfortunate that his contributions are largely unknown and unnoticed by students of labor and management history today. This article is written in tribute to Asa Philip Randolph.

Endnotes

[1] Wright, Sarah, *A. Philip Randolph: Integration in the Workplace*, New York, Silver Burdett Press, 1990, p. 32.

[2] *Ibid.*, p. 51.

[3] Santino, Jack, *Miles of Smiles, Years of Struggle: Stories of Black Pullman Porters*, Urbana, Ill., University of Illinois Press, 1989, p. 37.

[4] *Ibid.*, p. 71.

[5] McKissack, Patricia and Frederick A., *A Long Hard Journey: The Story of the Pullman Porters*, New York, Walker and Company, 1989, pp. 60-61.

[6] *Ibid.*, p. 93.

[7] Wright, *op. cit.*, pp. 86-89.

[8] Pfeffer, Paula F., *A. Philip Randolph, Pioneer of the Civil Rights Movement*, Baton Rouge, La., Louisiana State University Press, 1990, p. 92.

[9] Wright, *op. cit.*, p. 97.

[10] Pfeiffer, *op. cit.*, p. 175.
[11] *Ibid.*, p. 179.
[12] Wright, *op. cit.*, p. 111.
[13] Pfeiffer, *op. cit.*, p. 240.

Subconscious Stereotyping in Business Decisions

By educating individuals about the legal aspects of employment discrimination, university courses, employer-sponsored training programs, various human relations seminars, and other sources are serving a valuable purpose - but they are addressing only half the problem. An individual may be extremely knowledgeable regarding the legal side of discrimination and yet, without consciously being aware of it, still discriminate in decisions involving such matters as selection, placement, promotion, training, and compensation. Based on evidence collected during numerous consulting experiences, the author is convinced that this continues today even among the most "enlightened" individuals, and that this implicit discrimination is most likely to be based on race or sex. In the following study, sex is the key variable:

The "Who" and The "How"

To test this contention, a sample of 512 graduating college seniors, 271 males and 241 females, were surveyed. All subjects were taking a Human Resource Management course that devoted considerable time to equal employment and fair employment practices. Thus they had all been recently schooled in the legal aspects of employment discrimination and were more sensitized to this issue than might otherwise have been the case. Any implicit discrimination found in decisions made by this group might, therefore, underestimate the extent of the problem in the general business community.

Before being given the survey, the subjects were told that they would be evaluated on the quality of their responses to the various situations presented and that the evaluation would be a factor in the grade awarded in the course. In this way, it was hoped that commitment to the exercise would be increased with fewer subjects simply 'going through the motions.' Subjects were told to respond to the situations as if they were the Human Resource Manager of a large business organization.

They were then given eight incidents, each necessitating a typical human resource decision (e.g., hiring, firing), with forced-choice responses.[1] Each incident was presented in two forms - one with a female as the individual primarily involved in the incident (female version) and one with a male primarily involved (male version).

Of the 271 males in the subject group, 135 were given the male version of each incident and 136 were given the female version. Of the 241 female subjects, 120 were given the male version of each incident and 121 the female.[2] No subject was given both versions of any one incident since this (a) would not be realistic - having two identical applicants differing only by sex, and (b) would make fairly obvious the intent of the study, thus distorting the findings, since few people would respond in an overtly discriminating manner. It was, after all, subconscious discrimination that the author was interested in.

Responses to Eight Incidents

The first three incidents involved a conflict between responsibilities on the job and at home. It is the author's belief that when these conflicts arise most individuals expect the male to place job responsibilities first and the female to give first priority to the home.

Incident 1

Jack and Judy Garrison have been married three years. Jack is an aspiring business executive and Judy is a successful free-lance writer. This is part of a conversation they had after coming home from a cocktail party at the home of an executive in Jack's division.

Judy: Oh, boy, what a bunch of creeps. Do we have to go to these parties, honey?

Jack: Judy, you know we have to. These things mean a lot to me. Tonight I had a chance to talk to Mr. Wilson. On the job, it would take a week to get an appointment with him. I was able to get across two good ideas I had about our new sales campaign, and I think he was listening.

Judy: Is Wilson that fat slob who works in marketing, the one with the dull wife? I spent ten minutes with her and I nearly died! She's too much. Jack, the people there tonight were so dull I could have cried. I prefer to talk to people who know what is going on in the world, not a bunch of half-wits whose main interests are their new cars and spoiled kids. I tried to talk to one guy about Virginia Woolf and he didn't even know who she was. These people are incredible. Do we have to go to another cocktail party again next week? I'd like to see a play instead. What an uncouth bunch in the business world.

Jack: One of my main ambitions is to get ahead in the business world. You know that these parties are required for bright junior executives coming up in the organization. And I'm a bright junior executive. If we don't go, who knows which of the other junior executives will get to Wilson with their good ideas?

Judy: Can't you relax and work a 40-hour week? That's what they pay you for.

Jack: I guess I'm too ambitious to relax.

Judy: I'd still like to go to the play. At least we could think about real problems.

Jack: And I'd be a mediocre, lower-management nobody for the rest of my career.

Judy: I want you to be a success, Jack. But the idea of spending more evenings talking to idiots is too much!

The "female version" had Judy as the aspiring executive and Jack as the reluctant spouse with all other details being identical. Subjects were then asked to choose one of three responses.[3]

Incident 1

	Female Version	Male Version
a. The spouse should go to the parties and stop making such an issue of it.	30%	72%
b. The junior executive should attend the parties alone.	42%	18%
c. The junior executive should stop attending the parties.	28%	11%

It is obvious from these results that the subjects expected the female to suppress her personal desires and support the male in his work role to a much greater extent than they expect the male to support the female in a similar situation. Such expectations make it easier for a male to succeed in balancing career and home demands than a female. Obviously, the male will have more assistance and less resistance in doing so.

The second incident looked at these competing demands from another angle.

Incident 2

> Ruth Brown, an accountant in the main office, has requested one month's leave beginning next week. She has already taken her vacation this year. She wants the leave to take care of her three young children. The day care arrangements the Browns had made for the period covered by her request suddenly fell through, and they have been unable to make other arrangements satisfying their high standards. Ruth's husband is principal of a junior high school, and he cannot possibly get off during the next month.
>
> The problem is that Ruth is the only person experienced in handling the cost section in the accounting department. We would either have to transfer an accountant with the same experience from another section or train a replacement for only one month's work. I have urged Ruth to reconsider this request, but she insists on going ahead with it.

I have also checked with the legal department, and we do not have to hold the position open for Ruth if she insists on taking the whole month off.

I would appreciate it if you could give me your decision on this as soon as possible.

The male version was identical except it involved Ralph Brown whose wife was a principal. Subjects were then asked if this was an appropriate leave request and whether they would grant leave with pay or without pay.

Incident 2	**Yes - Female Version**	**Yes - Male Version**
a. Is this an appropriate leave request?	51%	31%
b. Would you grant leave with pay?	72%	56%
c. Would you grant leave without pay?	11%	3%

In this case, the results indicated that sex stereotyping benefits females. A leave request for child care was considered acceptable by more than one-half of the subjects when it was made by a female but by less than one-third of the subjects when it was made by a male. As in the first incident, the evidence suggests that when a job/home conflict arises, the male is expected to accommodate his work schedule, while it is more acceptable for the female to miss work and devote her energies to the home.

Such stereotyping creates increasing problems for both husbands and wives as more and more wives pursue careers. Women will find it hard to advance as long as most employers believe that their first allegiance is, or should be, to the home and not the job. At the same time, males are going to find themselves more often in situations where their absence from work is necessary because of a working spouse, yet where their employers view the reason for such absence as unacceptable.

Incident 3

Situation three presented a direct career conflict between husband and wife:

> As you know, Ronald Cooper is a computer operator in my section. He has played a key role in computerizing our inventory system. Recently Ronald's wife was offered a very attractive managerial position with a large retail organization on the West Coast. They are seriously considering the move. I told Ronald that he has a very bright future with our organization, and it would be a shame for him to pull out just as we are expanding our operations. I sure would hate to lose him now.
>
> What do you think we should do about the situation?

The alternate form had Rhonda as the computer operator and her husband offered the job on the West Coast. Subjects were asked to choose from among four alternative responses.

Incident 3

	Female Version	Male Version
a. Try to convince the operator that too much has been invested in his (or her) career to leave now.	41%	88%
b. Don't try to influence the operator.	60%	11%
c. Offer the operator a sizable raise as an incentive to stay.	22%	28%
d. Try to find an attractive position for the employee's spouse in the organization.	8%	8%

It is obvious from the response pattern that the subjects viewed male employees as more worthy of retaining than female employees even when the qualifications of each were the same.

When looking at responses to the first three situations, one gains some insight into why absenteeism and turnover rates are higher for females than males even when they are at the same organization and compensation level. If employers do not make as much effort to retain females as they do males and if, as seen in Incident 2, females are more readily granted unscheduled absences, is it any wonder that the government reports slightly higher absenteeism and turnover rates for females than for males? [4]

The fourth and fifth situations dealt with an employee's unacceptable conduct - the question being what disciplinary action, if any, should be taken.

Incident 4

> I have a problem and I don't see how to solve it. It concerns one of the design engineers, Jill Diller, who has worked for me for the past 15 months. Jill persists in arriving late every morning. She is always 10 minutes late, more usually 15 minutes to one-half hour. I am at my wit's end. I have tried everything I can think of - private discussions, written reprimands, threats, sarcasm, and more. She is still late every morning.
>
> When Jill walks into the office, the work stops and everyone watches. Some of the designers are even joking that Jill's coming in late has something to do with her recent engagement. I don't like to get too tough with a creative employee like Jill, but her behavior is bound to hurt morale in the department.

The male version involved Jack Diller. Subjects were asked to select from among three courses of action.

Incident 4

	Female Version	Male Version
a. Suspend for one week for continued tardiness.	72%	64%
b. Threaten to fire and follow through if necessary.	51%	42%
c. Don't make an issue of tardiness.	8%	11%

In the case of both the female and male employee, the subjects considered the situation serious enough to warrant the more severe actions. Yet they were slightly more inclined to take such action when the employee involved was a female. This may be connected to the value the subjects attached to employees of different sexes, as exhibited by the responses to Incident 3. Both the willingness to risk losing an employee through more severe disciplinary actions and the lesser effort made to retain female employees seem to provide insight into the value the subjects placed on employees of different sexes. The response patterns indicated that, when all else is equal, males were viewed as more valued employees. More effort was put into retaining them and severe discipline was less likely to be used for fear of losing them.

Incident 5

Situation five involved unacceptable personal, rather than work, conduct:

> I would like to get your advice on a matter of great sensitivity involving one of the junior executives in our organization. It has been brought to my attention by an unimpeachable source that Bill Holman, assistant comptroller in my division, is having an affair with a prominent young socialite. I understand it has reached the point where any day now Bill's wife will publicly denounce the socialite as a homewrecker. I have been reluctant to bring this up, but I know Bill's marital problems will hurt his work. I would appreciate any advice you could give me on this.

The female version involved Renee Holman having an affair with a young playboy. Subjects were asked to select from among three responses:

Incident 5

	Female Version	Male Version
a. Do nothing unless the junior executive raises the issue.	50%	52%
b. Advise junior executive to see a marriage counselor.	40%	56%
c. Confront employee and threaten termination unless affair stops.	3%	4%

The only real difference between male and female respondents in this situation seemed to be in response (b). Subjects were more likely to advise a male employee to see a marriage counselor than a female employee. The author would speculate that the almost identical results to response (a) may have to do with the equal number of male and female subjects given each version. It may be that members of one sex (regardless of which one) are less likely to approach members of the opposite sex on issues such as this. For response (a) then, it is not a question of the sex of the participant but of the sex of the subject relative to the participant.

Response (b) indicates that the subjects were more willing to correct the unacceptable behavior of male than female employees even when this behavior was of a personal rather than a work nature. When the unacceptable behavior was personal (Incident 5) rather than work-related (Incident 4), the subjects were willing to expend more effort on male than on female employees.

Incident 6

This situation is becoming all too common today. By playing a numbers game, the organization has hired enough females to comply with the law but through subtle forms of unintentional sex discrimination does not allow them to develop as managers to the same extent that equally qualified males do. The females' comparative lack of advancement in the organization is then used as evidence that they are not as well suited for the work. This failure to advance can also lead to higher rates of absenteeism and turnover and thus perpetuate the cycle.

The difficulty here is that the decisions as to who advances may be made on the grounds of legitimate individual qualifications and may not be discriminatory at all. The discrimination occurred earlier, however, when females (because of employers' subconscious discrimination) were not given the same opportunities to develop as males. Incident 6 addresses this type of situation.

> I am pleased that we have the opportunity to send a representative to the Dunbar conference on production supervision. I know from personal experience that it is a high quality conference, and it has developed such a favorable reputation in this area that it is considered an important form of recognition for those who are selected to attend.
>
> I have reviewed our supervisory staff quite carefully and have narrowed the choice down to two people, both of whom I feel are qualified to attend. Unfortunately, we can send only one person, and I will leave the final selection up to you, depending on what you feel we want to emphasize. The two candidates are Susan Adams and John Elms.
>
> Susan Adams is supervisor of knitting unit A. She is 25, married, and has no children. She has been employed by our company for three years. She is a college graduate with a general business degree, and we consider her to have good potential for higher level positions.
>
> John Elms is supervisor of knitting unit B. He is 43, married, and has two teenage children. He has been employed by our company for 20 years. He is a high school graduate. He has been a steady, conscientious employee, advancing gradually from a helper's job to his present position. This may be as high as he will

be able to go judging from our assessment of the information in his file. Selection for this conference would mean a great deal to John.

In the alternate form, the two names were reversed. Subjects were asked to select one of the two to attend the conference. When all responses were considered collectively, without differentiation by sex of the individual involved, the following results emerged.

Incident 6

Send 25-year-old: 31%
Send 43-year-old: 69%

Hence, regardless of sex, the majority of subjects felt that the older employee should be sent. When the results were sorted by the sex of the individual, however, the following occurred:

Send 25-year-old female: 23%
Send 25-year-old male: 39%

These results indicated that the subjects, when selecting younger workers with career potential to participate in a developmental conference, were more likely to expend company resources if the employee were a male - even when all other qualifications were equal.

Incident 7

This situation dealt with a selection/promotion decision for a position requiring extensive traveling:

> Pursuant to our recent discussion about the need to recruit a Purchasing Manager for the new operation, I have developed a set of brief job specifications and have located a candidate who may be suitable for the opening. Will you please review the attached resume and give me your evaluation?
>
> Job requirements for Purchasing Manager:

The major responsibilities of the new Purchasing Manager will be to purchase fabrics, materials and clothing accessories (buttons, belts, buckles, zippers, etc.) for the production of finished goods.

For the most part, the Purchasing Manager will have to travel around the country visiting wholesalers and attending conventions and showings. The person hired for this position should have a knowledge of the quality of raw materials and have the ability to establish a fair price for goods purchased in large quantities. The person selected for this position will have to travel at least 20 days each month.

RESUME

Name:	Mr. Carl Wood
Position Applied For:	Purchasing Manager
Place of Birth:	Cleveland, Ohio
Marital Status:	Married; four children, ages 11, 8, 7, and 4
Education:	B.S. Business Administration, Ohio State University
Relevant Work Experience:	One year as purchasing trainee, Campbell Textiles, Inc. Ten years' experience in various retail clothing stores in sales, buying and general management.
Interviewer's Remarks:	Good personal appearance, seems earnest and convincing. Good recommendations from previous employers.

The female version had Mrs. Karen Wood as the candidate. Subjects were asked to answer three questions.

Incident 7

	Yes-Female Version	Yes-Male Version
a. Would you select this candidate?	23%	33%
b. Is the candidate favorably suited for the job?	33%	38%
c. Does the candidate have the potential to remain on the job?	30%	35%

Subjects apparently felt that employees with this set of characteristics, regardless of sex, were not suited for the position in question. The author believes that the presence of four young children was the deciding variable for the subjects.

Yet in all three areas of inquiry, males were selected more often or rated more favorably than females. This response pattern seems to indicate that the subjects were exhibiting the same values evidenced in the responses to Incident 2. That is, the first allegiance of males belongs to the job and of females, to the home and/or family. This type of subconscious sex stereotyping makes it more acceptable for a male to be selected for a job involving extensive travel than a female - even when both have the same employment qualifications and the same situation at home.

Incident 8

The final incident addressed the family vs. work dilemma even more directly:

> We are at the point where we must make a decision on the promotion of Cathy Adams of our Human Resources staff. Cathy is one of the most competent employees in the corporate Human Resources office, and I am convinced that she is capable of handling even more responsibility as Bennett Division Human Resources Director. However, I am not altogether certain that she is willing to subordinate time with her family to time on the job to the extent that may be required with Bennett.

> I have had the opportunity to explore with her the general problem of family versus job, and she strongly believes that she would rarely stay late at the office or participate in weekend meetings. She believes that her first duty is to her family and that she should manage her time accordingly. This viewpoint has not affected her performance in the past, but it could be a problem in the more demanding position as head of Human Resources with the Bennett Division.

The male version involved Gerald Adams. Subjects were given three possible courses of action.

Incident 8

	Female Version	Male Version
a. Do not promote.	34%	10%
b. Persuade the candidate to make a stronger job commitment prior to promotion.	29%	32%
c. Base the promotion on past experience.	40%	58%

The responses to (a) and (c) indicated that identical family demands and/or commitments did not disqualify males to the same extent they disqualified females. Not only were females expected to yield to family demands in the work vs. home dilemma (as shown in the previous situations) but even if they set priorities identical to those of their male counterparts, the males were still given more consideration for the job. The effects of this type of sex stereotyping will be difficult, at best, to overcome.

Conclusion

The conclusions to be drawn from this study are obvious. If the subjects used here are any indication, there is a good deal of unintentional, subconscious sex stereotyping taking place in the business sector of our society. The author feels quite strongly that, if anything, these responses underestimate the extent of the problem. The subjects were younger than most people in business, were college educated, and were undergoing a learning experience (the Human Resource Management course) that sensitized them to the area of employment discrimination. It is reasonable to expect that responses from such a group would be different from those of a more general sample.

While we as a society can legislate against overt discrimination, equally important and necessary are efforts to eliminate the type of subconscious stereotyping evidenced in the present study. Even if all members of the business community fully comply with the written laws regarding equal/fair employment, the barriers erected by the underlying, unfair attitudes found in this study will still be imposing. This study has tapped some deep-seated, gender-based values - and found them to be resistant to change, despite education. Only after this more difficult type of prejudice is eliminated will real equal employment opportunity be attained. Making people aware of the pervasiveness of the problem is the first step.

Endnotes

[1] These incidents were taken from an earlier survey conducted by Benson Rosen and Thomas Jerdee published in 1974: "Sex Stereotyping in the Executive Suite," *Harvard Business Review*, March-April 1974.

[2] In the present study, responses were tabulated by the sex of the fictitious individual involved in the incident, not by the sex of the respondent - although the number of respondents by sex was the same for both the male and female version of each incident. In a follow-up study, the author intends to tabulate responses by the sex of the respondent.

[3] In this and certain subsequent situations, the responses do not total 100 percent since more than one response was possible.

[4] Bureau of National Affairs, Inc., *Bulletin to Management*, 1995. Information on absenteeism and turnover is published quarterly in the bulletin.

National Right-To-Work Law: An Affirmative Position

The historic right of the states to outlaw the firing of employees who refuse to pay dues to labor unions is reaffirmed by Section 14(b) of the Taft-Hartley Act which states that: "Nothing in this Act shall be construed as authorizing the execution or application of agreements requiring membership in a labor organization as a condition of employment in any State or Territory in which such execution or application is prohibited by State or Territorial Law."[1] State laws forbidding this firing for refusal to pay dues are popularly known as Right-to-Work laws, because they safeguard the individual's right to work as either a voluntary union member or as a nonunion employee.

Because of the existence of Section 14(b), all 50 states are empowered to adopt Right-to-Work laws. Such statutes or constitutional provisions are now in effect in the following 21 states:

Alabama	Kansas	South Carolina
Arizona	Louisiana	South Dakota
Arkansas	Mississippi	Tennessee
Florida	Nebraska	Texas
Georgia	Nevada	Utah
Indiana	North Carolina	Virginia
Iowa	North Dakota	Wyoming

In the remaining 29 states, workers can legally be compelled - and millions are being compelled - to join labor organizations in order to earn their livelihood. Union/company agreements requiring all employees to pay union dues are explicitly sanctioned by Sections 7 and 8(a)(3) of the National Labor Relations Act.

The battle over Right-to-Work laws has been raging since the enactment of Section 14(b) and arguments pro and con have been expressed and debated over the years. This article will shed some light on this very complex issue by doing the following:

- Presenting the problem (issue); that is, should Americans be compelled to join labor unions?
- Discussing Right-to-Work support, including the National Right-to-Work Committee and its purposes and goals;
- Presenting arguments on both sides of the issue with the view towards providing support for National Right-to-Work legislation; and
- Presenting conclusions/justification for a National Right-to-Work law.

The Problem

Today, under the sanction of federal laws, unions and management can make agreements whereby employees can be forced into a union. Under compulsory "union shop" and "agency shop" agreements, the employee must either join or pay dues and fees to the union or be fired from their job.

This situation exists in 29 states. Only in the 21 states which have enacted state Right-to-Work laws, authorized by the federal law, can employees exercise freedom of choice to join or not join a union.

The right of workers to organize has been perverted to include the right to compel employees to join or pay fees to labor organizations against their will and the right to compel employers to herd their employees into unions. Right-to-Work laws seek to remedy these flagrant abuses of power.

Supporters of Right-to-Work laws believe that union democracy tends to be stifled under conditions of compulsory unionism, because there is little need for union leaders to be responsive to a captive membership. Right-to-Work simply means that an individual has the right to join or financially support a union and a corollary right to refrain from joining or supporting a union, without losing a job.

The following practices are examples of what can, and often does, happen under compulsory unionism:

- Workers are subject to unlimited amounts of monthly dues and assessments.

- A portion of workers' dues is used, without their knowledge, to support political parties to which they may be opposed.
- Union officials can call all employees out on strike without a secret ballot vote of the employees.
- Seniority of older workers means nothing when company-union agreements give super-seniority to union officials.
- A worker can be discharged from a job if late in paying monthly dues, regardless of the reason.
- The salaries of union officials can be raised to any amount without approval of the rank-and-file members, even though the members are compelled to contribute the money which pays the salaries.
- Local unions are dominated by the national and international unions through such gimmicks as trusteeships and the merging of several locals. The worker has no voice in such manipulations.[2]

Support For Right-to-Work Laws

The supporters of Right-to-Work laws are many and varied, including the National Right-to-Work Committee, legislators, educators, authors, workers, and even some union officials.

The National Right-to-Work Committee, organized in 1955, is a public interest organization incorporated as a nonprofit organization for only one purpose: to protect the right of citizens to obtain and hold jobs whether they belong or pay fees to unions or not. The Committee's more than one-half million supporters and members include employees (both union and nonunion), business firms, homemakers, clergymen, educators, and people from all walks of life.

Over the years, the Committee has won steadily increasing recognition for its work in exposing and combating the evils of compulsory unionism. Today the Committee is widely regarded as the most effective organization in labor matters when the issue of compulsory unionism is involved.

The Committee demonstrated its effectiveness by blocking an all-out drive by union officials in 1956 to repeal Section 14(b) of the Taft-Hartley Act, which affirms the right of states to enact Right-to-Work laws. In 1970 the Committee scored another very significant victory when the Congress voted to include Right-to-Work protection in the Postal Reform Bill. It has successfully fought off attempts since then to repeal that provision of the Law.

The Committee has helped defeat repeated attempts to repeal or emasculate state Right-to-Work laws, and has backed successful efforts to strengthen those laws in several states. It has blocked efforts to extend compulsory unionism to public employees in state after state and at the federal level. It has been instrumental in the introduction of, and mobilization of, grass roots support for legislation providing for a national Right-to-Work law, guaranteeing freedom of choice for federal employees, and prohibiting the use of compulsory union dues for political purposes.

Details of the National Right-to-Work Committee's program are:

1. Conduct a national education program designed to alert the American people to the wrongfulness of compulsory unionism and to bring about understanding of the Right-to- Work principle.
2. Safeguard Section 14(b) of the Taft-Hartley Act (that section of the national labor law which reaffirms the right of states to have Right-to-Work laws).
3. Preserve all existing Right-to-Work guarantees for public employees.
4. Provide assistance in organizing statewide citizen movements to promote, enact, and protect state Right-to-Work laws.
5. Work to preserve legislation which curbs the use of compulsory union dues for political activity, protect public employees at all levels of government against compulsory unionism, prevent compulsory unionization of farm workers, and ultimately provide national Right-to-Work protection covering all employees.[3]

There are a large number of other supporters of Right-to-Work - too numerous to discuss here. There follows, however, a small sampling of some of these supporters and selected statements they have made.

Jameson G. Campaigne, author of *American Might and Soviet Myth*, stated:

> The freedom of the checked-off man will not come from action by unions. It can only come through both Federal and State legislation. The most vital provision of any such law is the abolition of the compulsory check-off and the prohibition of compulsory union membership ... only when the individual working man is free to decide for himself whether to support union policies, support union political candidates, support a strike or oppose it, and

> work to change his union leadership if he wishes - only when his human rights to these actions are protected by law will he be a free man again. The end of the check-off and the abolition of compulsory union membership are the key to the liberation of the American worker so that he can use his powers for himself and for the commonwealth.[4]

John McClellan, the former U.S. Senator from Arkansas, stated:

> If I were a wage earner, I might well be inclined to join a union. I would not want to be compelled to join.

Everett M. Dirksen, former Minority Leader, U.S. Senate from Illinois stated:

> Is there a greater right? Is there a more important right? Is there a more fundamental right than the right to make a living for one's self and for one's family without being compelled to join a labor organization?

David Lawrence, editor and columnist, stated:

> No organization should have the privilege of keeping from their jobs any workers who wish to perform their services. The big question is whether individual liberty really prevails in America and whether every citizen is to be permitted to enjoy the freedom that is so often extolled.[5]

Samuel Gompers, courageous founder of the modern American labor movement, stated:

> There may be here and there a worker who for certain reasons unexplainable to us does not join a union of labor. This is his right no matter how morally wrong he may be. It is his legal right and no one can dare question his exercise of that legal right.[6]

Major Arguments Against Right-to-Work Laws

The issues involved in the Right-to-Work controversy are highly sensitive ones. Well intentioned people on both sides are caught up in the wave of emotionalism. Proponents of Right-to-Work laws feel they are defending a basic individual liberty. On the other hand, opponents of Right-to-Work legislation feel they are fighting for the very lifeblood of the labor union movement. Add to this combination the traditional chasm between certain members of both unions and management who have not accepted the idea of accommodation and resolution of differences through negotiation, and the setting is perfect for a highly charged campaign.

The major arguments on behalf of compulsory unionism, made by Right-to-Work opponents, are as follows:

1. "Union security," that is, the strength of the union, depends upon universal acceptance of membership as a condition of employment.
2. Majority rule is a democratic principle, and a minority of workers who will not voluntarily support the union should be compelled to do so to solidify the power of the majority.
3. The union negotiates contracts for the benefit of all employees of a craft or class, and those who do not voluntarily contribute support to an organization which benefits them should be compelled to do so or they will be 'free riders'.
4. The power of discipline over all workers should be available to the union so that it may insure the fulfillment of contracts and other assumed obligations.

Not one of the foregoing arguments can be maintained against the facts, nor can they justify the oppression and denial of individual liberty which is the inherent wrong of compulsory unionism. Let us now examine each of the above arguments in turn.

Union Security

Labor union leaders and other opponents of Right-to-Work laws argue that the inability of unions to arrive at union shop agreements with employers strikes at the core of union security and strength. Yet it is a simple historical fact that the unions have existed as voluntary organizations in Right-to-Work states for fifty years. Since their existence is not in jeopardy in these states, they have no need to compel unwilling workers to join and pay dues.

Those in favor of Right-to-Work laws argue that unions do not need further strengthening, because they are adequately protected under present law. In his book, *The Case for Right-to-Work Laws*, the Reverend Edward

A. Keller, C.S.C., states that union security clauses are an effective way to exercise the right of unionism but they are not a necessary means. No one has proven that compulsory unionism is the only reasonable and normal means of security for labor unions today. The protective labor laws of both the federal and state governments can, should, and do give adequate and reasonable security to unions in the United States.[7]

It is also hardly debatable that a voluntary organization of workers united for self-help is inherently a much stronger organization than a union composed to a considerable extent of unwilling members. Many of the strongest friends of organized labor have pointed out that the strength of unions as voluntary organizations would be greatly weakened by converting them into compulsory monopolistic organizations. If legally permitted, these would inevitably require detailed regulation by government which would otherwise be unnecessary.

Two members of the National Defense Mediation Board, Judge Charles E. Wyzanski (former Solicitor in the Department of Labor) and former Senator Frank P. Graham, both made this point in opposition to compulsory unionism. President Franklin D. Roosevelt made a similar public pronouncement. Justice Frankfurter in the state "right-to-work" cases (335 U.S. 538) quoted extensively from the late Justice Brandeis who held that:

> The ideal condition for a union is to be strong and stable, and yet to have in the trade outside its own ranks an appreciable number of [men] who are non-unionists...Such a nucleus of unorganized labor will check oppression by the unions as the unions check oppression by the employer.[8]

Majority Rule

Critics of Right-to-Work laws contend that democratic principles require the minority to support the majority.[9] This is an unnecessary argument, especially when applied to Right-to-Work, because our laws and customs already require the minority of employees who are not members of a labor union to accept the terms and work under the contract(s) of the majority. This is similar to the requirement that any minority or dissenting group in a community must accept the laws enacted by the majority representatives. But even in the case of public laws, a dissenting minority or a political party in opposition is not required to stop its opposition nor is it required to contribute to the political support of the majority party.

Even members of the majority are at liberty to withdraw from such an association.

Those who espouse compulsory unionism are essentially adopting the communist theory that there should be only one party to which everyone should give allegiance and support. Inside the party there may be disagreements, but no one is permitted to go outside and support an opposition movement.

The claim of democratic majority rule by compulsory unionism is a pure fraud. Our democratic theory of majority rule is based on the preservation of minority opposition and the possibility of shifting the majority power. When workers are required to join and support a union regardless of their desire to oppose it, the whole democratic basis of majority rule disappears. It is supplanted by a type of majority rule that has no place in a democratic society.

Free Riders

Much emphasis is placed on the argument that, since the union negotiates for the benefit of all workers of a unit or class, all such workers should be compelled to contribute to the cost of maintaining the union activities. This argument has a superficial appeal, but it is both fundamentally unsound and highly deceptive in fact.

The argument is fundamentally unsound because, throughout our society, voluntary organizations carry on activities which benefit a great many who do not contribute any financial or other support. Fraternal organizations, churches, and civic and political organizations exist and work for the benefit of a large number of persons who contribute no support. It would be absurd to suggest that whenever a voluntary organization benefits any group of people it should be empowered to compel them by law or by economic pressure to contribute support. The argument is also highly deceptive for three reasons:

First, only a part of the dues and assessments of the unions is devoted to negotiating contracts. The unions have a great many activities such as political campaigns, social and economic propaganda, insurance, etc., to which no one should be compelled to contribute, particularly when a member can gain no personal benefit.

Second, the real objective of forcing all workers to join unions is, as the union leaders themselves admit, not so much to compel them to pay their share of an expense as to compel them to accept the discipline of the organization. Workers who become members add to the economic and political power of the union.

Third, the unions sought and obtained by law a special privilege: the right to represent any minority of non-member employees and to make contracts binding on any such minority. The unions took away, by law, the right and freedom of individual employees to contract for themselves - and now the unions demand that non-members be compelled to pay for having their freedom of contract taken away and exercised against their will. The non-member is not a "free rider" but a captive passenger.

Power of Discipline

The argument based on the need for an increased power of discipline, which is being made with increasing vehemence, rests on the theory that nonunion employees, who cannot be disciplined by depriving them of their employment, are a menace both to the union and to the employer because they will not live up to contract obligations. This is a fraudulent argument because the nonunion employee is just as much bound as the union employee to carry out the obligations of the trade agreement.

Also, without being made a member of the union, the independent worker is subject to employer discipline to an even greater degree than a union member. If s/he breaks contract obligations or refuses to obey management orders, s/he can and will be disciplined by the employer and will not have any union backing in a recalcitrant position. On the other hand, if a union member gets in difficulty with management, the union is obligated to provide support.

What the unions really mean is that they want the power of discipline over all employees, particularly so employees will all strike or otherwise support the union officials in whatever position they may take that is antagonistic to management. The fact is that the increased power of discipline given to union officials by compulsory unionism is contrary to the interest of both the employer and the nonunion workers.

There are various other arguments brought forward by unions in an effort to prove that a worker is better off as a compulsory member. For instance, the American Federation of Labor contends that if the employee is not a union member the employee has no voice at all in determining rates of pay, hours, or other conditions of employment. Theoretically, this appears to be plausible. But as a practical matter, a union member in one of the huge unions today has as small a voice in determining union policies and programs as the average citizen who is not active in politics has in making the laws.

The most effective voice anyone can have in an organization, unless part of the ruling hierarchy, is the voice of opposition - the voice of criticism. This may be a small voice, but one which can be made effective if it is coupled with the power to withdraw from the organization, to refuse to give it moral and financial support, and to threaten unwise or vicious leadership with the development of a rival faction or organization to challenge its authority.

The unions claim that Right-to-Work laws are an "anti-labor weapon." How can a law be "anti-labor" which provides only that an employee be free from coercion to join a union? How can a law sustaining the freedom of individuals of the laboring class be honestly called an "anti-labor" law?

In the author's opinion the unions are, in effect, claiming that it is against the interests of the worker to be free from such coercion. They are claiming that if the union approves of such coercion then it is "anti- labor" to insist that the employee be kept free from any tyrannical use of this power. It is the unions that have claimed to be the ancient, time-honored enemy of such coercive power being vested in the employer. Is it any better for similar power to reside on the union side? Is the union's argument against what they feel is excessive power one of principle or one of placement?

The agreement for a union shop is called a "union security" agreement. This very designation is a confession that it is not the worker who is made more secure by union shop agreements. Only the union itself - that is, the union officialdom - is made more "secure" by such agreements. These union shop contracts, these "one party" monopolies, make it practically impossible for dissenters to successfully oppose the dictatorial control of a well-entrenched machine of labor bosses.[10]

Summary

The right of workers to organize has been perverted to include the right to compel them to join or pay fees to labor organizations against their will. Right-to-Work laws seek to remedy these flagrant abuses of power. As of this writing, 29 states still do not have such laws.

The only responsible action that would terminate compulsory unionism and the abuses associated with it while protecting the right of citizens to get and hold jobs (whether they belong or pay fees to unions or not), is the

enactment of a national Right-to-Work law. The sooner this happens the better off all involved parties, including labor organizations, will be.

Endnotes

[1] The National Right-to-Work Committee, "14(b) Is Not An Odd Shoe" (Arlington, VA: *The National Right-to-Work Committee*, January 1975), p. 2.

[2] The National Right-to-Work Committee, "What Happened to Liberty and Justice for All?" (Arlington, VA: *The National Right-to-Work Committee*, August 1976), p. 2.

[3] The National Right-to-Work Committee, "The Right-To-Work Issue: Should Americans Be Compelled to Join Labor Unions?" (Arlington, VA: *The National Right-to-Work Committee*, August 1976), p. 3.

[4] Campaigne, Jameson G., *Check-Off*, (Chicago: Henry Regency Company, 1961), p. 20.

[5] Richberg, Donald R., *Labor Union Monopoly*, (Chicago: Henry Regency Company, 1966), p. 11.

[6] The National Right-to-Work Committee, "The Voluntarism of Samuel Gompers" (Arlington, VA: *The National Right-to-Work Committee*, August 1973), p. 3.

[7] Skibbins, Gerald J., and Weyman, Caroline S., "The Right-to-Work Controversy," *Harvard Business Review*, July-August 1966, p. 9.

[8] Richberg, Donald R., *op. cit.*, p. 5.

[9] Skibbins, Gerald J., and Weyman, Caroline S., *op. cit.*, p. 9.

[10] Richberg, Donald R., *op. cit.*, pp. 8-9.

The Labor Position on Repeal of Section 14(b) of Taft-Hartley

Introduction

The basic federal law governing labor-management relations in the United States today is the National Labor Relations Act (Wagner Act) of 1935, as amended by the 1947 Labor-Management Relations Act (Taft-Hartley Act) and subsequent laws. The depression-bred Wagner Act was highly favorable to labor organizations. The Taft-Hartley Act, which was bitterly opposed by labor, nullified and modified some of the Wagner Act guarantees and, in so doing, gave rise to state Right-to-Work laws through Section 14(b).

A Right-to-Work law is a law which prohibits labor-management agreements requiring union membership as a condition of keeping a job. This article will examine the reasons why Section 14(b) should be repealed.

Background

Since the 1940s, the issue of Right-to-Work laws has been an extremely emotional one. Labor unions bitterly resent the tag name of Right-to-Work, saying it is a misnomer for anti-union laws. Supporters of such laws say workers should be free to join or not to join unions.

The major amendments to the Wagner Act were contained in the Taft-Hartley Act which was passed by a Republican Congress in 1947 over President Truman's veto. Passage of the bill followed the heaviest wave of major strikes in U.S. history - some of which had tied up entire industries like steel, coal and automobiles. The strikes reflected labor's desire to catch up with the rest of the economy after a long period of wartime wage controls under which most unions had complied with a 1941 "no strike" pledge made by labor leaders.

The Taft-Hartley Act was, obviously, opposed by organized labor. The Act forbade, among other things, the closed shop and the closed shop hiring hall - a union-run employment service which referred only union members to employers. In addition, Section 14(b) of the Act essentially empowered the states and territories to pass Right-to-Work laws forbidding employers and unions from signing union shop contracts.

Ordinarily, state labor relations laws do not apply to unions and businesses which are involved in interstate commerce or activities affecting interstate commerce. However, the 1947 Taft-Hartley Act created special rules with regard to state Right-to-Work laws. The Taft-Hartley Act itself forbade the closed shop. It permitted the union shop, however, with the proviso that union shop contracts would be legal only in states which did not forbid them. (A union shop contract requires employees to join a union within a specified time after being hired. Employees who refuse to do so must be dismissed.) The effect of this proviso, Section 14(b), was to validate state Right-to-Work laws.

As a result, existing state Right-to-Work laws are applicable to all unions and businesses (unless exempted by the state laws themselves), with one exception - the exception involves the Railway Labor Act. Railroads, airlines and other firms and their employees which are subject to the Railway Labor Act, rather than the Taft-Hartley Act, are not subject to state Right-to-Work laws.

Legislative History Of 14(b) Of Taft-Hartley

The genesis of Section 14(b) follows. Under the House bill, H.R. 3020, a new Section 13 of the National Labor Relations Act was included to ensure that nothing in the act was to be construed as authorizing any closed shop, union shop, maintenance of membership, or other form of compulsory unionism agreement, in any state where the execution of such agreement would be contrary to state law. Many states had by that time (1947) enacted laws or adopted constitutional provisions to make all forms of compulsory unionism in those states illegal. It was never the intention of the National Labor Relations Act, as is disclosed by the legislative history of that act, to deprive the states of their powers to prevent compulsory unionism. Neither the so-called "closed shop" proviso in Section 8(3) of the existing act, nor the union shop and maintenance of membership proviso in Section 8(a)(3) of the conference agreement, could be said to authorize arrangements of this sort in states where such arrangements were contrary to the state policy. To make certain that there should be no question about this, Section 13 was included in the House bill. The conference agreement in Section 14(b) contains a provision having the same effect and was the result of the conference committee's work.

The Case For Repeal of Section 14(b)

The following are major labor arguments for the repeal of Section 14(b) of the Taft-Hartley Act.

Union Security

The union security provision says a worker shall join the union (or commence paying a fee to it) after a certain period of time on the job.

Under the union shop, it is the employer rather than the union who decides what person shall be hired for a job. An applicant is hired only if they have the qualifications for the job. Then, and only then, is the requirement enforced to join the union holding the contract with the employer. Under the union shop contract, the union cannot say whom the employer will hire. Under a union shop agreement, an employee loses his union membership only for failure to pay normal fees and assessments.

As the bargaining representative of all the workers, the union can be most effective - and it can best represent all the attitudes of the workers - when all the workers are members. The strength of a union depends on what portion of the workers belong. In some situations, it is impossible for a union to maintain itself without some sort of union security; and in all situations, union security gives added strength to a union.

Through an effective union representing all the workers, the individual employee achieves a more effective voice in determining the wages paid for work and the conditions on the job. Labor-management agreements, in addition, provide an orderly procedure for the handling of grievances and lay-offs and for the rehiring of workers.

Further, since under the Wagner Act a union, once certified as bargaining agent, must "represent equally all employees in the bargaining unit" (whether union members or not), it seems only fair that these employees be required to join the union.

Labor supporters of the repeal of 14(b) also argue that such repeal would not result in compulsory participation in union activities, because various court rulings have held that although workers in a union shop must pay union dues, they need not participate in union activities. Furthermore, union shops would not automatically follow the repeal of 14(b), because management must agree to their establishment in the collectively bargained agreement.

Individual Rights

Some who oppose union security are apt to say that union security is undemocratic when, in fact, union security is simply an expression of our democratic concept of majority rule. Majority rule is the very basis of our society and civilization.

To argue against union security is, in effect, to argue that the minority has even more rights than the majority - and that goes counter to all the common sense rules for our democratic society. The union shop operates where a majority of the workers have decided in its favor and where the employer has agreed with the union to a union security contract. Minority rights must always be protected, but minority rights cannot be allowed to take precedence over majority rights.

Certainly, there have been abuses by unions under union shop agreements. But few people are aware of the strict codes of democratic conduct which the government, by law, has imposed on unions. No other voluntary organization must meet such requirements of frequent secret ballot elections, freedom to criticize elected officials without reprisal, and democratic procedures for setting policy and making decisions.

The Free Rider

The union's activities on behalf of the workers require funding. If the union is to represent properly all the workers in the group, it must have their participation and financial support. Union dues are an obligation that workers owe to the union that serves them. People who do not join the union, nor support it financially, are receiving a free ride.

Under the Taft-Hartley Act, unions are required to provide services for everyone in the plant or shop included in the bargaining unit, whether they are members of the union or not. These services - bargaining the basic contract, handling grievances, etc., - cost money to provide. Someone has to pay for the time of the people who manage these things for workers in the plant. There is only one place the money should come from - the people who are receiving the service. Since the law requires this service to be provided for all, it is only logical that all should help pay for the benefits received. Yet Section 14(b) is a license to make those services available to all, yet free to some. No other service organization is in this position. No one may be obliged to join such other organizations, but neither do those organizations have to provide service to those on the outside.

Organized labor argues that if Right-to-Work is a valid concept, then Americans should also be free to refuse payment of federal taxes and free to disregard scores of other obligations where majority rule prevails on every citizen in our society.

Uniform Application Of National Law

Section 14(b) is the only provision of federal labor law that is not uniformly applied to all states.

The labor position is that not applying Taft-Hartley uniformly to all states results in "disruptive competition" among states by encouraging business to locate where there is less union activity, mainly in the South.

The House Education and Labor Committee has said "Section 14(b) was an explicit departure from the principle specifically recognized in the basic provisions of the National Labor Relations Act that a uniform national labor relations policy is necessary and desirable." It further stated:

> The isolation of union security as a separate and severable issue to be considered wholly apart from all other matters, is no longer realistic, if indeed it ever was. The fact is that the special treatment given by the statute to this single matter has been the source of continued confusion and uncertainty with respect to a widening span of related matters...[1]

Other Arguments

Union spokespeople believe that Right-to-Work laws are, to a large extent, responsible for the slow growth of unions in the South. They further argue that in many parts of the South, Right-to-Work laws are only one of a battery of anti-labor devices designed to keep unions weak, keep wages low and keep business taxes (for such items as unemployment insurance) low - thereby creating a favorable business climate to "pirate" industry from other areas of the country.

Finally, unions contend that anti-union business groups often put forward Right-to-Work proposals in state legislatures not only for their own sake, but also to absorb the attentions and resources of unions in a fight against the proposals, thus diverting the unions from pushing favorable welfare and tax legislation through the state legislatures.

Summary

Given the reasons set forth above, it is easy to see that Section 14(b) of Taft-Hartley should be repealed. In the words of Samuel Gompers: "Organized labor's insistence upon and work for, not the 'closed shop' as our opponents term it, but the union shop, in agreement with employers, mutually entered into for the advantage of both and the maintenance of industrial peace with equity and justice for both, is to the economic, social and moral advancement of all our people."[2]

The union shop, entered into agreement with employers, is the application of the principle that those who enjoy the benefits and advantages resulting from an agreement shall also equally bear the moral and financial responsibilities involved. Surely no fair-minded American could argue with such a principle.

Endnotes

[1] Report of the House Education and Labor Committee on H.R. 77, Government Printing Office, Washington, DC, June 22, 1965, p. 3.

[2] "The Truth About 'Right-to-Work' Laws," *AFL-CIO News*, Washington, DC, January 1977, p. 2.

The Agency Shop: Arguments Pro and Con

ABSTRACT

The "agency shop" form of union security, whereby certain employees must pay union dues whether they are union members or not, is one of the most detested contract clauses requested of management. The remarkable increase in the number of employers agreeing to such clauses causes the author to examine the issue from a union and management point of view.

A union security provision of collective bargaining agreements is a clause requiring employees to become members of a union or assume some financial obligation to the union. Among the more common forms of union security agreements are the union shop, agency shop, and maintenance-of-membership clauses. The union shop is a form of union security requiring membership in the labor organization as a condition of employment within a specified number of days after an individual begins work. Maintenance-of-membership is a type of union security arrangement demanding present union members to maintain their membership status for the duration of the contract as a condition of continued employment but does not require other employees to join. The agency shop obligates all employees in the bargaining unit who do not join the union to pay periodic dues and assessments, usually a monthly amount equivalent to the amount paid by union members.

The agency shop provision was first introduced in 1946 at the Ford Motor Company in Ontario, Canada. Justice I. C. Rand stipulated that nonunion members of the bargaining unit should not be forced to join the union as a condition for holding their jobs but should be obliged, instead, to contribute the equivalent of union dues for services rendered as a bargaining agent.[1] Justice Rand gave as his main reason for imposing the agency shop provision the elimination of "free riders" - a name given to those nonunion workers in a bargaining unit who enjoy the benefits of union representation but make no financial contribution to the union. The existence of these free riders was made possible by the legal requirement that unions represent everyone in the bargaining unit but the lack of a legal requirement that they join the union. Thus, the union must represent everyone in the bargaining unit, but no individual in the unit is legally compelled to join the union.

Unions in the United States showed little interest in the Canadian decision, however, since the Wagner Act of 1935 had declared the closed shop legal. (A closed shop is one in which union membership is required before the individual receives the job.) Consequently, U.S. unions could avoid the problem of free riders by negotiating for a closed shop provision. It was not until 1947 when Congress passed the Taft-Hartley Act that U.S. unions started to investigate the provisions of the agency shop. The Taft-Hartley Act outlawed the closed shop provision and partially surrendered federal jurisdiction over union security clauses in labor-management agreements. Section 14(b) of the Taft-Hartley Act permitted the states to legislate in the field of union security, provided their laws were "more restrictive than Federal law."[2] Remember that in a closed shop, union membership is required before the individual can be offered employment while in a union shop the individual has a specified number of days after beginning work to join the union. The distinction is important because in a closed shop the union has the first input into the hiring decision, since management can only accept applicants who have first been accepted by the union. In the union shop, management can hire anyone they wish since union membership is secondary.

Thus, Section 14(b) of Taft-Hartley started the Right-to-Work laws which stated that union membership could not be required by unions or employers as a condition for employment in any state which prohibited such agreements. With union shops illegal in certain states, unions became interested in other ways to maintain union membership and dues, including agency shop clauses. As a result, labor unions in the U.S. turned to this device through the 1950s to dodge state Right-to-Work laws banning the union shop.

One of the first unions in the United States that tried to enforce the agency shop clause was a Florida local of the Retail Clerks International Union. It succeeded in persuading an employer, a supermarket, to incorporate an agency shop clause in its contract. As might be expected, the nonunion workers, who up to this point had enjoyed the freedom of not having to pay union dues, objected to this new arrangement. These workers brought suit against the employer and union in the Florida State Courts, and eventually the case went to the U.S. Supreme Court. The Retail Clerks argued that the Taft-Hartley grant of power to the states over union security clauses did not extend to the agency shop.[3]

The Supreme Court ruled that a state court in Florida had the right to interpret the state's Right-to-Work laws to mean that an agency shop was illegal.[4] In other words, the Court held that the States' Rights provision of

Taft-Hartley could be interpreted to permit banning the agency shop as well as the union shop. This meant that agency shops were legal only in states that did not object to them. The unions' reaction was to combat the Right-to-Work movement more vigorously than ever before.

The National Right-to-Work Committee, a pro-business group chartered to combat compulsory union membership, immediately hailed the new ruling as a boost to its drive to increase the number of Right-to-Work states - a drive the AFL-CIO called a "union-busting" campaign.[5] At present there are 21 states with Right-to-Work laws: Alabama, Arizona, Arkansas, Florida, Georgia, Indiana, Iowa, Kansas, Louisiana, Mississippi, Nebraska, Nevada, North Carolina, North Dakota, South Carolina, South Dakota, Tennessee, Texas, Utah, Virginia and Wyoming. Out of these states, Indiana is the only Right-to-Work state where the agency shop is declared legal.

The second case specifically dealing with the agency shop issue involved the United Auto Workers. In 1955, the UAW finally won a full union shop from General Motors. Later on, a problem arose in applying the national agreement to GM plants in Indiana. Although the Indiana Supreme Court had ruled that the state law did not extend to the agency shop, GM refused a UAW demand for it in Indiana. The corporation argued that, regardless of state law, federal law prohibited the agency shop. Company lawyers could not find in the Taft-Hartley Act's authorization of the union shop any duty on the part of the employer to bargain on the agency shop. The UAW then filed an unfair labor practice charge against GM, accusing it of refusal to bargain.[6]

The Supreme Court eventually ruled that GM did not have to bargain on the agency shop issue, stating that state courts had authority to "enforce" Right-to-Work laws in the states that have such laws.[7] The importance of the court decision lies in the fact that it places the enforcement of state Right-to-Work laws in the state and not in the federal government. As noted earlier, after this decision almost all Right-to-Work states prohibited the agency shop.

While it is important to review the legislative history of the agency shop question, it is equally important to understand why there has been so much controversy over this issue.

Labor's Position

One of the main arguments for the agency shop is that Taft-Hartley requires a union that has been certified as a collective bargaining representative of the workers by the NLRB to represent all workers in the bargaining unit whether they are union members or not. Unions feel that individual workers should not be able to receive benefits secured by their union without having to pay some amount for the expenses involved.

The facts show that unions spend large sums of money in negotiating better wages and working conditions for members of the bargaining unit. They are also compelled by law to process grievances and extend contract terms without discrimination to members or non-members. Under these circumstances, it seems unfair for a worker to refuse to pay dues while taking advantage of the same benefits as union members.

As the reader might imagine, the free rider was very much resented by union workers. The agency shop tends to eliminate some of the hostility between dues-paying, non-union workers and the union workers. The strong feeling of resentment toward the free rider is evident in the following quote from a union official in the oil industry:

> You'll find a lot of hot numbers working in the oil industry. The time has come for them to join up, help pay the freight, quit hitchhiking. Persuasion should be used. If that doesn't work, then we'll have to think of something else. The government doesn't allow free loaders at tax time. The union shouldn't either.[8]

In defending the agency shop provision, George Harrison of the Railway Clerks said: "We have always felt that it is manifestly unfair that individual employees should be permitted to obtain all of the benefits which result from the collective bargaining process and be subject to none of the obligations of that process."[9] At the very least, the agency shop would require non-union members to pay for benefits in the collective bargaining process.

Management's Position

Those that object to the agency shop clause contend that it is a form of bribery. To keep a job, an individual must pay money to the union. There is no good reason why a non-union employee, forced to pay dues under the agency shop clause, would decide not to become a member of that union. Hence the practical effect of an agency shop is the same as a union shop. Right-to-Work advocates have consistently argued that the union shop violates workers' rights of free association by compelling them to join a union against their will. If agency shop clauses lead to union shop effects for the majority of workers, then an individual's right to free association has again been violated. It would seem almost foolish for an employee not to join the union since dues are required, and the arrangement inadvertently forces a worker into making that decision.

Management also contends that, in some cases, an individual's religion might prevent them from joining a union or paying dues to a union. To answer this, some union contracts allow those people to pay union dues to a charity.

Another argument against the agency shop concerns the objection of many employees to having any portion of their dues expended for political purposes. Federal law has long forbidden the union to use dues to contribute directly to political campaigns. But until recently even these provisions did not prevent labor organizations from drawing upon dues to defray the costs of lobbying or to pay for political articles and radio and television advertisements for candidates they support.

Conclusion

Arguments on both sides of this issue are compelling and deserving of consideration. As is usually the case, a compromise seems the most equitable solution. This compromise has taken the form of a "service fee" clause whereby non-union members in the bargaining unit pay only their share of the actual collective bargaining costs. All other union-related expenses, such as general promotion, lobbying, political campaigns, etc., are paid for by fees (dues) assessed on union members only. In this way, the stronger objections of both labor and management are addressed.

Endnotes

[1] Masse, Benjamin L., "Is the Agency Shop Legal?" *America*, Volume 107, December 15, 1962, p. 1244.

[2] *Ibid.*

[3] "Victory for Right-to-Work Law: An Issue in 1964 Campaign?" *U.S. News & World Report*, Volume 55, December 16, 1963, p. 108.

[4] "Trouble with the Agency," *Time*, Volume 81, July 14, 1963, p. 91.

[5] "Labor Loses Agency Shop Case," *Engineering News*, Volume 171, December 12, 1963, p. 74.

[6] Masse, *op. cit.*, p. 1245.

[7] "Labor Loses Agency Shop Case," *loc. cit.*

[8] Barbash, Jack, *The Practice of Unionism*, (New York: Harper & Row Publishers, 1956), p. 159.

[9] *Ibid.*, p. 160.

The *Beck* and *Lehnert* Decisions and Their Impact on Union Security Agreements

Kenneth A. Kovach
Peter E. Millspaugh

Introduction

The relationship between employers and employees - labor/management relations - has evolved substantially in the United States over the course of the past 100 years. The agent of change has varied as the times have changed, but each and every time there has been change of any magnitude - either pro-labor or pro-management - one or more agents of change have been present molding the outcome of events and shaping the evolution of labor history. These agents of change can assume many forms and may not be recognized for what they are until enough time has passed to look back at events with an objective, critical eye. They may be extraordinary individuals or the confluence of unique events. They may be violent or peaceful. In the pages that follow, we will consider how the determination of two individuals unknown to one another, Harry E. Beck, Jr. and James P. Lehnert, caused them to become late 20th-century agents of change in the ongoing evolution of labor/management relations in the United States.

Harry Beck and Jim Lehnert will be remembered - with respect or disdain, depending on one's point of view - for years to come because of their determination to stand up and challenge the legitimacy of clauses in union security agreements that permit unions to collect agency fees from non-union members working at agency shops. The validity of the underlying union security agreement was not an issue, since Section 8(a)(3) of the National Labor Relations Act (NLRA) explicitly authorizes an employer and a union to enter into an agreement requiring all employees in the bargaining unit to pay union dues as a condition of continued employment whether or not the employees become union members.[1] What was at issue in both the *Beck* and the *Lehnert* cases was whether agency fees collected under such union security agreements could legitimately be used by the unions for purposes other than "collective bargaining, contract administration, or grievance adjustment."[2]

Harry Beck, who lived in Maryland, knew labor unions and had at one time served as shop steward for the Communications Workers of America.[3] Jim Lehnert, on the other hand, was an academic on the teaching faculty of Michigan's Ferris State College.[4] What Beck and Lehnert shared in common was a recognition that agency fees they were paying to their unions - the Communications Workers of America in the case of Beck and the Ferris Faculty Association (an affiliate of the Michigan Education Association which is an affiliate of the National Education Association) in the case of Lehnert - were frequently being used to support political causes and other purposes to which they were opposed. Accordingly, each went to court to challenge the practice.

Union Security Agreements: A Definition and Brief Legislative History

The concept of an agency shop - in which everyone within a bargaining unit is required to pay the equivalent of union dues whether a member of the union or not - first developed at the Ford Motor Company plant in Ontario, Canada in 1946.[5] The underlying principles of union security agreements were codified in American labor law in Section 8(a)(3) of the National Labor Relations Act. That provision, which is permissive and not mandatory, allows a union which is the certified exclusive bargaining agent for a group of workers to enter into collective bargaining agreements with the employers of those workers stipulating that all workers represented by the bargaining agent must pay representation or agency fees to the union.

Congress authorized the establishment of agency shops out of a sense of fair play. Such shops were intended to benefit workers by correcting abuses of compulsory union membership that had developed under "closed shop" agreements. Simultaneously, they were intended to provide unions with security against free riders or non-union workers who could reap the benefits of a union's representation services without paying for them.[6] The underlying theory is that, under the principle of exclusive representation, a certified union must represent all the workers in a bargaining unit; therefore, it is only fair that all such workers pay their fair share of the union's costs in doing so.

The legislative history of this provision is very explicit and warrants review. As Senator Taft, one of the authors of the 1947 legislation that bears his name, explained on the floor of the United States Senate:

> ...the argument...against abolishing the closed shop...is that if there is not a closed shop those not in the union will get a free ride, that the union does the work, gets the wages raised, then the man who does not pay dues rides along freely without any expense to himself.[7]

Members of the House echoed that view. For example, Representative Jennings pointed out that because members of the minority:

> ...would get the benefit of the contract made between the majority of their fellow workmen and the management...it is not unreasonable that they should go along and contribute dues like the others.[8]

Similarly, Representative Robinson noted that:

> ...If [union-negotiated] benefits come to the workers all alike, is it not only fair that the beneficiaries, whether the majority or the minority, contribute their equal share in securing these benefits?[9]

However, out of deference to "states' rights" advocates, the federal statute authorizing agency shops and hence union security agreements does not supersede or preempt state laws in this regard. According to Section 14(b) of the National Labor Relations Act, the individual states are free to prohibit agency shops and other union security clauses in collective bargaining agreements. The state legislatures in twenty-one "right-to-work" states have, in fact, enacted state laws prohibiting agency shops and other union security agreements.[10]

Nevertheless, the impact of union security agreements on the American work force and in the American political arena should not be underestimated. In order to appreciate the magnitude of the reach of union security agreements the reader should consider the following:

- an estimated 2 to 3 million non-union workers are subject to union security agreements;
- 15.4 million Americans are employed under compulsory union contracts;
- this system generates $10 million per day ($3.8 billion per year) in union staff payroll expenses; and the value of in-kind services for

political candidates generated by this system has been estimated at between $100 million and $350 million in an election year.[11]

Against this backdrop, we will now turn to consider the specific cases of Harry Beck and Jim Lehnert; how these two cases, while similar in many respects, can nevertheless be distinguished from one another in some important ways; and how the United States Supreme Court disposed of each.

The *Beck* Case

Harry Beck, and others who shared his view, was tired of seeing union payments going to support political candidates and causes to which he was personally opposed. They claimed that the expenditure of union funds on activities such as organizing the employees of other employers, lobbying for labor legislation, and participating in social, charitable and political events violated the Communications Workers' duty of fair representation. Organized labor's support of Democrat Hubert H. Humphrey in his unsuccessful bid for the presidency of the United States in 1968 prompted Harry Beck to take action.[12] In order to bring this practice to an end, Beck and 20 of his co-workers - financed by the National Right-to-Work Committee - brought suit against the Communications Workers of America in 1976 challenging the union's use of agency fees for purposes other than "collective bargaining, contract administration or grievance adjustment." After a twelve-year odyssey through the federal court system, the case was finally argued before the United States Supreme Court on January 11, 1988.

The issue was settled six months later when, on June 29, 1988, a divided Supreme Court, in an opinion authored by Justice William Brennan, held that:

> ...fees beyond those necessary to finance collective bargaining activities violated the judicially created duty of fair representation and non-union members' First Amendment rights...

and

> ...The National Labor Relations Act does not...permit a union, over objections of dues-paying nonmember employees, to expend funds so collected on activities unrelated to collective bargaining activities ...[13]

In essence, the Supreme Court concurred with the lower court's conclusion that the union had failed to show that more than 21% of the funds were used in support of collective-bargaining efforts. It further agreed that the Communications Workers of America should: 1) reimburse all excess fees Beck and his 20 colleagues had paid since January 1976; and 2) institute a record-keeping system to segregate accounts for representational and noncollective-bargaining activities.[14]

The *Lehnert* Case

The *Lehnert* case is distinguishable from the *Beck* case in three very significant ways: 1) while Harry Beck was an employee in the private sector, Jim Lehnert was a state government employee serving as a faculty member at Ferris State College in Big Rapids, Michigan; 2) while Harry Beck was challenging the use of agency fees by a single union (i.e., the Communications Workers of America), Jim Lehnert was challenging the utilization of agency fees by a tiered triumvirate (i.e., the Ferris Faculty Association which is an affiliate of the Michigan Education Association which is an affiliate of the National Education Association); and 3) in the manner in which the *Lehnert* court resolved the issue of the use of agency fees for political purposes, specifically, to influence the outcome of pending legislation.

The total agency fee assessed against Jim Lehnert by the Ferris Faculty Association for the 1981-1982 year was $284.00. Of that amount, only $24.80 (or 9%) stayed with the local bargaining unit. The bulk of the funds - the remaining $259.20 - was divided between the state and national affiliates. Of the $284.00 collected under the union security agreement, $211.10 (74%) went to the Michigan Education Association and $48.00

(17%) was forwarded to the National Education Association in Washington, D.C.[15]

In deciding the *Lehnert* case, the Court held that:

> ...the considerations that justify the union shop in the private context - the desirability of labor peace and eliminating "free riders" - are equally important in the public-sector workplace...[16]

However, the Court rejected Lehnert's contention that he should be charged only for those collective-bargaining activities undertaken directly by the Ferris Faculty Association and not costs associated with the Michigan Education Association or the National Education Association. Specifically, the Court decided that in this case:

> ...membership in the local union constitutes membership in the state and national parent organizations ...Consequently, that part of a local's affiliation fee which contributes to the pool of resources potentially available to the local is assessed for the bargaining unit's protection...We therefore conclude that a local bargaining representative may charge objecting employees for their *pro rata* share of the costs associated with otherwise chargeable activities of its state and national affiliates, even if those activities were not performed for the direct benefit of the objecting employee's bargaining unit ...[17]

Prior to the *Lehnert* case, there was a clear and consistent judicial view that use of agency fees for political purposes - specifically, to lobby lawmakers - should be proscribed. The underlying rationale was that since unions traditionally have aligned themselves with a wide range of social, political and ideological viewpoints, any number of which might bring vigorous disapproval from individual employees, to force employees to contribute - albeit indirectly - to the promotion of such positions implicates core First Amendment concerns. As the Court noted:

> ...The right of freedom of thought protected by the First Amendment against state action includes both the right to speak freely and the right to refrain from speaking at all ...[18]

However, in the *Lehnert* case the Court continued to recognize a small exception to the general prohibition of the use of agency fees for political purposes. The reasoning enunciated by the Court took into consideration the inherently political nature of salary and other workplace decisions affecting government employees since the legislature and the employer are effectively one and the same entity. The *Lehnert* court concurred with a New Jersey case decided in 1985 which concluded that:

> ...To represent their members effectively, public sector unions must necessarily concern themselves not only with negotiations at the bargaining table but also with advancing their members' interests in legislative and other 'political' arenas...[19]

The *Lehnert* court then concluded that:

> ...the State constitutionally may not compel its employees to subsidize legislative lobbying or other political union activities outside the limited context of contract ratification or implementation.[20]

Implementation of the *Beck* and *Lehnert* Decisions

While it took twelve years for the *Beck* case to reach its final resolution before the United States Supreme Court and ten years for the *Lehnert* case to be fully adjudicated, those decisions hardly brought the controversy to a close. In neither *Beck* nor *Lehnert* are the Court's decisions "self-enforcing." For the principles enunciated by the justices in these cases to become integrated into the workplace, a method of segregating covered expenditures from excludable expenditures would have to be established; a manageable framework for monitoring and policing union expenditures would have to be implemented; and a mechanism to expeditiously resolve controversies would have to be created. Since the use of agency fees for political purposes inspired both Harry Beck and Jim Lehnert to take the unions to court initially, it seems oddly appropriate that politics should haunt the process during the implementation stage as well.

In the pages that follow, this article will review the National Labor Relations Board's (NLRB) efforts to implement the *Beck* decision; the line of *Beck* administrative proceedings filed with the NLRB subsequent to the

Supreme Court's *Beck* decision; and actions taken by the executive and legislative branches of government designed to shape labor/management relations in the post-*Beck* era.

NLRB's *Beck* Guidelines

Following the *Beck* decision, the National Labor Relations Board issued guidelines to all its regional directors advising them on a broad range of what came to be known as *Beck* issues. These guidelines specified that the threshold test that must be met before any *Beck* rights may be invoked is that the employee must be a "nonmember" of the union. An employee who had never become a full union member or an employee who had resigned full membership in the union would be able to invoke *Beck* rights, as would an employee who attempted to resign from the union but was unlawfully prevented from doing so.

In addition to being a "nonmember," the worker must object to the expenditure of funds for nonrepresentational purposes. The NLRB guidelines were very clear on this point, quoting from a Supreme Court decision rendered more than a quarter century before *Beck*:

> ...[D]issent is not to be presumed - it must affirmatively be made known to the union by dissenting employees. The union receiving money exacted from an employee under a union shop agreement should not in fairness be subjected to sanctions in favor of an employee who makes no complaint of the use of his money for such activities...[21]

In the absence of some objection on the part of the worker, the union is permitted to collect full dues under the union security clause.

Under the NLRB guidelines, if a union spends any portion of funds collected from nonunion members on activities other than "representational" activities, the union has an affirmative obligation to notify all nonunion workers at least once a year:

- that a stated percentage of funds was spent in the last accounting year for nonrepresentational activities;
- that nonmembers can object to having their union security payments spent on such activities; and
- that those who object will be charged only for representational activities.[22]

According to the NLRB guidelines if a nonmember should object, the union must provide the objector with information setting forth the union's major expenditures during the previous accounting year, distinguishing between representational and nonrepresentational functions. In addition, if the union is a local of an international and a portion of union security money is sent to the international, both the local and the international must provide the relevant information.[23] The guidelines expand on this requirement noting that while "absolute precision" cannot "be expected or required,"[24] the information must reveal the major categories of expenses (e.g., "national convention," "organizing," etc.); whether the union considers the expenses to be representational or nonrepresentational; the total sum of expenditures; and the percentage of expenditures that were representational and nonrepresentational. If the objecting employee disagrees with the union's percentage allocation, the employee may challenge the union's determination either by invoking arbitration or by filing a charge with the NLRB. Unions are required to place disputed amounts in an interest-bearing escrow account until the matter is resolved.

The NLRB guidelines conclude with a list of "chargeable" and "nonchargeable" activities. Among the representational activities that are "chargeable" to nonmembers are:

- Collective bargaining, contract administration, and grievance arbitration
- Expenses of litigation incident to negotiating and administering the contract, settling grievances and disputes arising within the bargaining unit, fulfilling the duty of fair representation to the unit, handling jurisdictional disputes with other unions, and conducting other litigation before administrative agencies or courts concerning bargaining unit employees
- National conventions
- Union business meetings and social activities open to member and nonmember employees
- Union publications to the extent that they report on the union's representational activities
- Costs of union benefits available to members and nonmembers alike.

Nonrepresentational, and therefore nonchargeable, activities include:

- Union organizing activities, either in the represented unit or outside of it
- Expenses of litigation that do not "directly concern" the bargaining unit
- Union publications to the extent that they report on nonrepresentational activities
- Costs of union benefits that are not available to nonmembers
- Costs of a union building fund
- Lobbying
- Promotion or defeat of legislation
- Political campaigns
- Advertising related to nonchargeable matters[25]

While some may find the above lists of "chargeable" and "nonchargeable" activities a handy point of reference, others view them with skepticism either because they see them as a backing away from the black-letter law laid down by the Court in *Beck* or because they realize that the promulgation of guidelines provides no assurance that the guidelines will be followed.

NLRB's Enforcement Mechanism

The National Labor Relations Board processes all employee complaints through its Office of General Counsel, which decides whether or not to pursue the complaint. If the general counsel decides to proceed, the complaint is heard by an administrative law judge (ALJ). Decisions rendered by ALJs may be appealed to the five-member NLRB. As of this year, there are approximately 300 cases pending before the NLRB ALJs,[26] many of them *Beck* cases. In fact,
at the time of this writing there are 21 cases pending before the NLRB that involve *Beck* issues.

The backlog of cases - particularly *Beck* cases - at the NLRB is due in no small measure to politics. This is ironic (although not surprising) since the use of agency fees to further political causes was an underlying issue at the very heart of both the *Beck* and *Lehnert* cases. Two Executive Orders - one issued by President Bush in the heat of his unsuccessful bid for re-election, the other issued by President Clinton less than two weeks after he was sworn into office - had a role to play in the off-again, on-again, off-again approach to enforcement of *Beck* rights by the NLRB and the Department of Labor (DOL).

President Bush's Executive Order

In a White House Rose Garden ceremony held on April 13, 1992, President George Bush, with Harry Beck looking on, signed Executive Order 12800. This Executive Order directed the Secretary of Labor to require all companies performing federal contract work to post notices in their plants and offices during the term of their contract informing workers of their *Beck* rights. President Bush also announced at the Executive Order signing ceremony that Secretary of Labor Lynn Martin would be proposing a rule clarifying and bringing up to date requirements for labor organizations to account for how workers' dues are spent. For *Beck* purposes, the most noteworthy proposed revision to forms LM-2 and LM-3 was the inclusion of a new schedule entitled "Statement C - Expenses." This schedule would be used by unions to allocate all expenses among eight new functional categories: contract negotiation and administration; organizing; safety and health; strike activities; political activities; lobbying; promotional activities; and "other."

The promulgation of Executive Order 12800 was characterized by Democrats as "an election year move that Bush bypassed during his first three years in office." Conservatives applauded Bush's move, describing the executive order as "championing individual freedom for American workers," while labor leaders condemned it as a "political gesture" that would ultimately have little impact upon their operations and activities. The reach of this presidential order was hotly contested, with the White House claiming that as many as 3 million workers could be impacted while union leaders said the number was closer to one million.[27]

Four days after promulgation of Executive Order 12800, the Department of Labor published twenty-eight pages of proposed rules revising the manner in which labor unions report their financial condition to the DOL, NLRB, and their members.[28] Fifty-one written comments, filling twelve binders, were received in reply. The rule was soundly criticized by representatives of both labor and management, with many singling out for criticism a proposed union security clause which the Management Association of Illinois said would require "a 17th-grade-level education" to understand. They went on:

> ...The practical impact will be that no employee or applicant for employment will be able to read this union security language and understand his or her rights - a real denial of workplace due process ...[29]

Also deemed highly controversial was the proposed requirement that each bargaining unit independently account for its expenditures in order to measure its compliance with *Beck* requirements. Internationals in particular, and labor organizations in general, took the approach that unit-by-unit accounting would be extremely costly and burdensome. The AFL-CIO estimated that it would incur annual bookkeeping and accounting costs of $192 million (or about $10 per member) if required to implement the proposed reporting requirements.[30] Organized labor also challenged the appropriateness of such reporting, noting that Courts had, in the past, rejected the unit-by-unit accounting theory. Claiming that it is "normal and reasonable" for a union to use its dues from all represented bargaining units to create a pool of resources, the AFL-CIO argued that:

> ...Many national union activities simultaneously benefit more than one bargaining unit...[31]

The AFL-CIO added that requiring unit-by-unit accounting would impose enormous burdens on any multi-unit union and overwhelming ones on any national or international union.[32]

W. James Young, an attorney for the National Right-to-Work Legal Defense Foundation, labelled the AFL-CIO's position as "the rankest form of hypocrisy."[33] Irving Ross, a certified public accountant, said that labor organizations had created a "mystique" about the difficulty of accounting noting that "it's not as burdensome as some would have you believe."[34]

The circumstances under which President Bush issued his executive order - particularly the timing - certainly called into question his political motivations. Invoking the memory of Thomas Jefferson, on whose 249th birthday the order was released, Bush quoted Jefferson's declaration that:

> ...To compel a man to furnish contributions of money for the propagation of opinions which he disbelieves and abhors is sinful and tyrannical...[35]

In addition, the President's action to inform workers of a right they had won four years earlier - an action the President could have taken at any point since he was sworn in as President - happened to occur on the very same day that the executive committee of the AFL-CIO recommended to its membership that they endorse Arkansas Governor Bill Clinton for the Presidency.

President Clinton's Executive Order

In one of his first official acts after being sworn into office, President Clinton issued Executive Order 12836, rescinding President Bush's Executive Order 12800, and "any orders, rules or regulations implementing...Executive Order No. 12800."[36] Claiming that by revoking Executive Order 12800 he was ending the "government's role in promoting this one-sided version of workplace rights," Clinton characterized the Bush order as:

> ...distinctly anti-union as it did not require contractors to notify workers of any of their other rights protected by the National Labor Relations Act, such as the right to organize and bargain collectively...[37]

As one would expect, organized labor praised Clinton's action, while "right-to-work" advocates condemned it. AFL-CIO President Lane Kirkland welcomed Clinton's action as:

> ... the first symbol of renewed commitment to the national labor policy set out in the federal labor laws and to the fair and vigorous enforcement of those laws...

while Rex H. Reed, executive vice president of the National Right-to-Work Legal Defense Foundation declared:

> ... By ordering his labor department to tear down notices of employees' rights against compulsory unionism, Clinton has turned back the clock and thrown the cloak of secrecy over federal contract workers...And with exit polls showing that 45% of unionized workers didn't vote for Clinton, that means nearly four million private sector workers will continue to walk with blinders on, courtesy of the union bosses and Clinton...[38]

Congressional Efforts To Codify *Beck* Rights

Numerous efforts have been made to codify the *Beck* decision since it was handed down by the Supreme Court. The approach generally advocated by the proponents of *Beck* codification would amend the Federal Election Campaign Act of 1971 to include what has been labelled the Workers' Political Rights Act.

The Workers' Political Rights Act would impose more stringent reporting requirements on labor unions regarding their political expenditures. Specifically, it would require labor unions engaged in political activities to provide written annual notification to their members, advising them:

- that members cannot be compelled to pay for the political activities of the union;
- that no employee can actually be compelled to join a union and that (in the case of a union shop) the employees may elect instead to pay an agency fee;
- that the amount of the agency fee shall be limited to the employee's *pro rata* share of the cost of the union's exclusive representation

services to the employee's collective bargaining unit, including collective bargaining, contract administration, and grievance adjustment;

- that an employee who elects to be a full member of the union is entitled to a reduction in dues by the employee's *pro rata* share of the total spending devoted to political activities;
- that the cost of exclusive representation services and the amount of spending on political activities will be computed based on the immediately preceding fiscal year; and,
- on the union's full dues, reduced dues, and agency fees for the current year.[39]

Principal proponents of the codification of *Beck* rights in the Senate have been Senators Orrin Hatch (R-UT) and Mitch McConnell (R-KY). The opposition to their efforts has been led by Senators Howard Metzenbaum (D-OH) and David Boren (D-OK). When on July 31, 1992, the measure was debated and voted upon in the United States Senate, it was defeated by a vote of 59 to 41.

More recently, on May 27, 1994, Texas Republican Tom DeLay introduced in the U.S. House of Representatives the aforementioned Workers' Political Rights Act (H.R. 2307). Noting his concern that "no one is required to tell workers that they have the right not to contribute" to political causes they do not support, DeLay wrote to his colleagues in the House:

> ...What's worse, President Clinton has decided that workers should not be informed of this right...Clearly this is not right. Every member of the Congress who supports our nation's free and democratic heritage should speak out and oppose this abuse of our political process...[40]

Despite the fact that his bill has attracted 71 co-sponsors since its introduction, Representative Charlie Rose (D-NC), who is a member of the House Oversight Committee to which DeLay's bill has been referred, has yet to schedule so much as a single Congressional hearing to consider the merits of H.R. 2307. An analysis of campaign contributions by political action committees (PACs) associated with labor organizations proves enlightening on this point.

Labor's PAC Contributions

Let us analyze the Federal Election Commission reports filed by the ten largest labor PACs. These ten PACs are those of the: International Brotherhood of Teamsters, American Federation of State, County and Municipal Employees, Service Workers International Union, United Food and Commercial Workers, United Autoworkers, United Steelworkers, International Association of Machinists, International Brotherhood of Electrical Workers, Communications Workers of America, and the National Education Association. Further, let our analysis include six election cycles covering the twelve-year period extending from 1983 to 1994.

The findings confirm what many would surmise - labor PACs are major players in the game of electoral politics, and the volume and amount of labor's campaign contributions have increased substantially over the past decade. By overwhelming margins, organized labor's PAC dollars are used to support Democratic candidates for office. Advocates of organized labor would, or course, be quick to point out that it is misleading to imply that PAC giving to incumbents is synonymous with "labor" giving to incumbents. An analysis of FEC reports filed in conjunction with the 1994 Congressional elections indicate that business PACs - those sponsored by corporations, trade associations and cooperative associations - gave candidates an amount three times as large as the amount given by labor PACs. Labor proponents would also note the bipartisan nature of PAC giving, pointing out that $24.9 million went to Senate Republicans.[41]

While all PAC giving may reflect a bipartisan balance, that is hardly the case with the PACs that represent organized labor. The political action committees for organized labor have a clear and unmistakable bias in support of Democratic candidates for office. For the twelve-year period studied, it can be determined that, with the exception of the Teamsters, in no case did a labor PAC give more than 5% of its dollars to support Republican candidates for office. Furthermore, the one exception to the rule - the Teamsters - saw their contributions to Republican candidates consistently decline over the period studied, from 15% in the 1983-1984 election cycle to merely 3% in the 1993-1994 cycle. Meanwhile, with the exception of the Teamsters, none of the labor PACs studied gave less then 93% of their contributions to Democratic candidates during that same period.

Whether or not it is legitimate to do so, numbers such as these provide great ammunition to opponents of organized labor such as Rex H. Reed, executive director of the National Right-to-Work Legal Defense Fund, who claim that President Clinton's action rescinding President Bush's executive order regarding implementation of the *Beck* decision is not the last action President Clinton will take on behalf of organized labor but rather "the first installation of his debt to Big Labor."[42]

Conclusion

The history of America's labor movement provides abundant examples of abuse of worker's rights by parties on both sides of the bargaining table. Our constitutional form of government, which emphasizes individualism, vision, and the entrepreneurial spirit while simultaneously maintaining a commitment to the equality of all, is admittedly vulnerable to abuse. Yet the system of checks and balances present in our form of government also provides workers and management with an appropriate means of redress.

Harry Beck and Jim Lehnert were, in many ways, trapped or caught in a system that had become top-heavy, if not unbalanced, in favor of organized labor - a system that some claim placed higher value on the organization than on the laborer. Common sense and notions of fundamental justice tell us that individuals should not be compelled to support political agendas which they themselves find repugnant. Both Beck and Lehnert challenged the status quo and, over time, affected broad-reaching reforms which impact all who work in union or agency shops. In the post-*Beck* era, support of the union is still required in areas directly related to issues of collective bargaining - the concept of "free-riders" remains anathema - but workers should not be compelled to support the union in areas going beyond collective bargaining.

The *Beck* and *Lehnert* decisions are good decisions, and good decisions make good law and sound public policy. In both cases, the Court refused to stake out an extreme position but rather sought that compromise which would result in a truly equitable decision for all the parties involved.

Political issues were at the heart of *Beck* and *Lehnert* cases, and it is politics that have muddied the waters since these decisions were rendered. Elected politicians, as well as the political appointees of the executive branch of government charged with enforcing these decisions, have interpreted them so as best to conform with their party's political agenda *vis-à-vis* the business community and organized labor. That is something we can expect to see continue, despite the fact that it brings about some generally undesirable yet nevertheless tolerable results, such as the situation where successive executive orders are promulgated, with the second nullifying the first.

As a result of the *Beck* and *Lehnert* decisions, organized labor will find its clout somewhat restricted. Union leaders will be held more accountable to their members as far as the expenditure of funds is concerned. Full and fair disclosure of expenditures should become the norm rather than the exception. While these results will at least marginally diminish the role of union leaders, the status and dignity of the rank-and-file union member will be enhanced.

Organized labor will continue to do battle with "right-to-work" advocates. Each side will doubtlessly claim that they are upholding fundamental American values, and the fact of the matter is that both are doing just that!

We can be certain that politics (which is oftentimes described as "the art of compromise") will continue to dominate this debate. Accordingly, we should expect the dialectical process to continue, which - like our partisan form of government - avoids extreme positions and by and large results in the establishment of norms which do not satisfy the hard-core, extreme partisans on either side, but are tolerable or acceptable to moderates on both sides. This is exactly what has transpired in the *Beck* and *Lehnert* situations. The beat goes on.

Endnotes

[1] 29 U.S.C. §§ 141-187 (1982 & Supp. V, 1987).

[2] *Communications Workers of America v. Beck*, 108 S.Ct. 2641 (1988).

[3] *Harvard Journal of Law and Public Policy*, Vol. 13, No. 2, Spring 1990.

[4] *Lehnert v. Ferris Faculty Association*, 111 S.Ct. 1950 (1991).

[5] Masse, Benjamin L., "Is the Agency Shop Legal?" *America*, Vol. 107, December 15, 1962, p. 1244.

[6] *Ibid.*

[7] 93 *Congressional Record* (1947), p. 4887.

[8] *Ibid.*, p. 3557.

[9] *Ibid.*, p. 3558.

[10] Bairn, Charles W., *The Permissible Uses of Forced Union Dues: From Hanson to Beck*, the CATO Institute, Washington, D.C., July 24, 1992, p. 10.

[11] Larson, John, "Harry Beck's Earthquake," *Policy Review*, 74 (Summer 1989), pp. 74-75.

[12] Devroy, Ann, "Bush Moves to Enforce Union Curb: New Order Covering Political Use of Dues Pleases Conservatives," *The Washington Post*, April 14, 1992, p A-1.

[13] *Communications Workers of America v. Beck*, 108 S.Ct. 2642 (1988).

[14] *Ibid.*

[15] *Lehnert v. Ferris Faculty Association*, 111 S.Ct. 1956 (1991).

[16] *Lehnert v. Ferris Faculty Association*, 111 S.Ct. 1958 (1991).

[17] *Ibid.*, 1961.

[18] *Wolley v. Maynard*, 430 U.S. 705 at 714; 97 S.Ct. 1428 at 1435; 51 L.Ed. 2d 752 (1977).

[19] *Robinson v. New Jersey*, 741 F.2d 598 at 609 (CA3 1984); cert. denied, 469 U.S. 1228; 105 S.Ct. 1228; 84 L.Ed.2d 366 (1985).

[20] *Lehnert v. Ferris Faculty Association*, 111 S.Ct. 1960-1961 (1991).

[21] *Machinists v. Street*, 367 U.S. 740, at 774 (1960).

[22] Collyer, Rosemary M., (NLRB General Counsel), Memorandum GC 88-14, *Guidelines Concerning CWA v. Beck*, November 15, 1988 p. 3.

[23] *Ibid.*

[24] *Chicago Teachers Union, Local No.1 v. Hudson*, 475 U.S. 292 (1986) p. 307.

[25] Collyer, *op. cit.*, pp. 6-7.

[26] Bureau of National Affairs, Daily Labor Report, 139 (April 20, 1994) p. 469.

[27] Devroy, *op. cit.*

[28] *Federal Register*, Volume 57, Number 75, Friday, April 17, 1992, p. 14244.

[29] Bureau of National Affairs, *Daily Labor Report*, 47 (March 12, 1993), p. A-6.

[30] Bureau of National Affairs, *Daily Labor Report*, 8 (January 13, 1993), p. C-1.

[31] *AFL-CIO News*, March 30, 1992, p. 2.

[32] *Ibid.*

[33] Bureau of National Affairs, *Daily Labor Report*, 47 (March 12, 1993), p. A-7.

[34] Bureau of National Affairs, *Daily Labor Report*, Special Report #60, March 31, 1993, p. CC-2.

[35] Bush, George, *Remarks of the President In Signing Ceremony For Beck Executive Order*, Office of the Press Secretary, The White House, Washington, D.C., April 13, 1992, p. 1.

[36] Clinton, William Jefferson, *Executive Order No. 12836*, The White House, Washington, D.C., February 1, 1993, p.1.

[37] Bureau of National Affairs, *Daily Labor Report*, 21 (February 3, 1993), p. AA-1.

[38] Bureau of National Affairs, *Daily Labor Report*, 21 (February 3, 1993), p. AA-2.

[39] DeLay, Rep. Tom, *Worker's Political Rights Act* (H.R. 2307), 103rd Congress at §2(b).

[40] Bureau of National Affairs, *Daily Labor Report*, 106 (June 4, 1993), p. A-9.

[41] *AFL-CIO News*, December 8, 1994, p. 1.

[42] Bureau of National Affairs, *Daily Labor Report*, 21 (February 3, 1993), p. AA-2.

Is Codetermination a Workable Idea For U.S. Labor-Management Relations?

Kenneth A. Kovach
Ben F. Stands, Jr.
William W. Brooks

Participation by employees in decision making at the upper levels of private industry has been the exception rather than the rule in the United States, but there are indications this situation will change. Such diverse individuals as United Auto Workers' Vice-President Irving Bluestone, Undersecretary of Commerce Sidney Harman, and Federal Mediation and Conciliation Service Commissioner Samuel Sackman have spoken of the increasing need for worker involvement in decision making. In addition, experiments with employee participation in such firms as Harman International Industries and Carborundum Co. and the Chrysler-UAW agreement allowing the union president a seat on the company's Board of Directors, are evidence that rhetoric is being replaced, at least in some instances, by action.

To evaluate the potential for this idea in the United States, it is necessary to define several terms and trace the history of one of the more highly developed, legally mandated systems of labor participation in an industrialized nation.

The degree of integration of all members of an organization into the decision-making process ranges from zero (all decisions made by one person) to 100 percent (anarchy). The types of decisions (working conditions, societal responsibilities, production, financial matters, marketing approach, etc.) form subsets within the overall system of decision making.

Originally, the major decisions affecting workers were made by religious leaders or the nobility. With the coming of industrialization, decisions were made by the owners of capital, who regarded workers as one of the means of production. For various reasons - increasing wealth of the workers, higher levels of education in the labor force, greater complexity of the technological means of production, organization among the workers, etc. - it became necessary and desirable to introduce a degree of industrial democracy involving the labor force in the decisions affecting conditions of work, methods of production, and ultimately, financial and investment decisions.

Research into the evolution of this development reveals many descriptive terms. Among the more popular are participative management, industrial democracy, *autogestion* (French for self-management), and *Mitbestimmung* (German for codetermination). It is interesting to note that one of the major indices used in the United States usually lumps these terms under participative management although they mean entirely different things insofar as management, labor, and society are concerned.[1] While it may be true that they are parts of a spectrum along which worker participation may be measured, the results of each can differ greatly, and the workability of each may be dependent upon exogenous factors such as culture, economic development, and other environmental conditions.

Labor leaders, industrialists, and society should be aware of the distinctions and differences among the various levels of organizational democracy, if for no other reason than that the subject cannot be discussed rationally unless the terms are well defined.

Henry Mintzberg pointed out that many movements (degrees of participation, in our terms) hardly touched the United States. He stated that what has instead received considerable attention here is "participative management." In discussing this concept, he dis-tinguished two of its propositions. One of a factual - that is, testable-nature - is that participation leads to increased productivity: involve employees and they will produce more, management is told (e.g., Likert, 1961). The other - a value proposition not subject to verification - is that participation is a value worthy in and of itself: "In a 'democratic' society, workers have the right to participate in the organizations that employ them."[2] The American debate over participative management has focused almost exclusively on the first factual proposition (although the proponents really seem to be committed to the second, value position).

The latter concept - the right of workers to participate in decision making - forms the ideological base for the actions of many European unions. It is also the concept that causes major concern among U.S. managers and, it may be added parenthetically, many U.S. unions. James Furlong said that "the theme of extending to economic life the principles of political democracy - the right of all citizens to help choose their leaders and to express their opinions freely on the choice and fulfillment of group goals - is the real thread that runs through all defenses of *Mitbestimmung* (codetermination)."[3]

Codetermination in Germany

One German experiment is of particular interest. A combination of historical developments - a perception of common interests among industrialists and labor in dealing with an occupying army, and general cultural and social factors - has resulted in legislation that requires the participation of many German workers in decision making at all levels. Since July 1976, German law has given workers near parity with stockholders in controlling the management of approximately 625 major companies employing about five million workers.[4]

In March 1979, Germany's high court dismissed a suit brought by twenty-nine employers' associations and nine companies asserting that the 1976 law undermined property rights and blurred the line between companies and unions in collective bargaining.[5]

The 1976 law, *Mitbestimmung in der Bundes Republic Deutschland*, (codetermination in the Federal Republic of Germany) is the latest in a long series of legislative acts establishing and defining the rights of workers in German industry.

As early as 1848, political representatives of German labor demanded the establishment of factory committees to include workers. Although no legislation resulted from this first parliamentary discussion, worker committees were established in some companies on a voluntary basis. These were consulted primarily on social matters.[6] In 1905, mining companies with more than 100 employees were required to establish worker committees under the provisions of the Prussian Mining Law.[7] This law, and subsequent regulations in 1916 and 1920, established worker committees with full rights of participation in decisions concerning working conditions and limited rights in financial and personnel matters, although final decisions were made by management alone.

The Nazi regime dissolved all trade unions. Union headquarters were occupied by the military and their funds confiscated. Most of the leading trade unionists were arrested, and workers and employees were placed in the German work front.

Following World War II, German industrialists, in an attempt to prevent the decartelization of the steel industry, made common cause with German trade unions in dealing with the occupation authorities. Works councils were established along the lines of the Works Councils Act of 1920. The 1946 Allied Control Council Law No. 22 provided the basis for these councils. Finally, in 1951, the Act on the Codetermination of Workers in the Supervisory and Management Boards of Undertakings in the Mining Industry and the Iron and Steel Production Industry was passed. This was, according to Furlong, the "high-water point in the *Mitbestimmung* movement."[8]

Current German law requires a Works Council (*Betriebsrat*) in any firm employing more than five workers. The Council must represent both blue-collar and white-collar workers in proportion to their numbers in the company. Nationwide elections to the Councils are held triennially. Ballots are secret, and only workers are allowed to vote. The number of representatives elected ranges from one (five to twenty employees) to thirty-one (7,001 to 9,000 employees). In companies with more than 9,000 employees, two additional Works Council members are required for every additional 3,000 employees or part thereof.

Companies with several plants or divisions must establish a central council for the firm. Normally, each Works Council furnishes two representatives to the central council. In conglomerates, a group Works Council may be established at the option of the separate councils.

Certain Works Council members must be released to devote all their time to council matters. The number released ranges from one (in units with more than 300 employees) to twelve (in units with more than 10,000 employees). All members are entitled to four weeks of paid vacation during the first year to attend training courses and other educational functions related to the activities of the council. The firm must provide facilities, information and assistance to the council.

The Works Council does not bargain for wages and working conditions normally negotiated by the unions on a regional or national basis, but it has a right to codetermination - an equal say with management in deciding such issues as:

- job evaluation, piece rates, and wage structures;
- working hours, overtime arrangements, breaks, and holiday schedules;
- staffing policies, including guidelines for recruiting, assigning and dismissing workers;
- social plans, i.e., measures to mitigate the effect of layoffs on workers in the event of reduction;
- training, occupational safety and welfare schemes;
- allocation of company housing; and
- workers' conduct on the shop floor.[9]

Hiring, discharge, work allocation, promotion, and demotion decisions require the consent of the Council. Unilateral action by the employer in these areas is not allowed.

In companies with more than 100 employees, an Economic Council (*Wirtschaft Ausschuss*) of four to eight members is appointed by the Works Council. The Economic Council has limited powers but has the right to information on important issues, i.e., manufacturing methods, automation, production programs and data concerning the financial condition of the firm. Analysis of this information is the responsibility of the Economic Council while final approval of proposed actions of the firm rests with the Works Council.

Codetermination also functions at the management level. In German joint stock or incorporated public firms, a Supervisory Board (*Aufsichtsrat*) is elected by the shareholders and is generally comparable to the Board of Directors in U. S. firms. A Management Board (*Vorstand*) conducts the day-to-day business of the firm. No member of either board may serve on the other. Private, limited liability firms (the most popular form of organization in Germany) are not required to have a supervisory board unless they have more than 500 employees. Smaller private firms with unlimited liability (partnerships, etc.) are outside the limits of the Codetermination Act.

The power of the Supervisory Board to appoint and supervise the Management Board and to make major decisions concerning the goals and objectives of the firm make membership on the board extremely important to the worker. Current law requires three general levels of worker representation on the Supervisory Boards:

1. parity with shareholders in coal, iron and steel producing industries employing more than 1,000 workers;
2. one-third representation in joint stock companies employing up to 2,000 workers and in other limited liability companies employing between 500 and 2,000 workers; and
3. equal representation (with a bias in favor of the shareholders) in firms with a work force of more than 2,000.[10]

The Management Board constitutes the lower half of the two-tier board system. In the steel industry, the workers choose the Labor Director (*Arbeitsdirektor*), although this power is not inherent in current law. The

Labor Director (Human Resource Director in U. S. terms) has specific responsibilities in staff and social matters.

Experience has shown that to fulfill the purpose and objectives of the Codetermination Act and in the interest of the undertaking, concerned persons appointed as Labor Directors should have the special confidence of the employees.[11] Furlong says that "whether the unions in fact control the post will be left to capital and labor to thrash out."[12]

We are beginning to hear discussion of the desirability and practicality of implementing a codetermination system in the United States. It is important, then, to address the issue from the relative perspectives of U. S. management and labor organizations.

The Union Perspective

Since most codetermination schemes already implemented in the United States include the particular labor organization on the governing board instead of, or in addition to, unspecified employee representatives, it becomes imperative to discuss codetermination from an organized labor perspective.[13]

Before doing so, it is important to reemphasize the differences between U. S. unions and their German counterparts. As noted earlier, the Works Councils in Germany have two main roles. They are responsible for plant bargaining over issues - job evaluation, working hours, training, etc. - not dealt with in collective agreements at regional or national levels. Many of these issues are also of primary interest to national unions in the United States. In addition, the Works Council is considered the first and fundamental forum for codetermination.

The wildcat strikes at the plant level that plague so many European industries are virtually unknown in Germany. Strikes can be called only at the regional or national level. If the Works Council and the employer are unable to agree on an issue, either may apply for arbitration by a committee of an equal number of worker and employer representatives and one neutral member.

Unlike members of shop steward committees in the United States, German Works Council members (with the exception of two or three members, depending on the size of the company) are not required to be union members. Any employee aged 18 or older may vote for council members with the only requirement for election being that the candidate must have been with the firm for at least six months.[14]

Much of the real power in unions in Germany rests in small local units rather than at the national level. Unions thus structured will be more receptive to ideas like codetermination than will national unions like those in the U. S. system.

Many alleged experts, while acknowledging the success of codetermination or similar schemes in Germany, Sweden, Israel, etc., contend that similar systems will not work in this country due to the different role of labor organizations in the United States. The ultimate goal of organized labor in many countries where the industrial democracy experiments are working has been to achieve equal footing with management in the operation of the business. Thus, ideas such as codetermination have fit nicely into their long-range objectives. Government legislation of such schemes (e.g., Germany) is viewed by labor as welcome assistance from an unexpected source. In the United States however, organized labor has sought to fill a different role. Most U. S. unions think of themselves as the protectors of employees, as the intercessor variable between workers and management, serving as a safeguard against exploitive management action. The fact is that after "economic gain," the reason given most frequently by new union members for joining is "protection against arbitrary management action." This is evidence of the popular perception concerning the degree to which unions fulfill this role.[15]

This being the case, many U. S. unions question the desirability of sitting with management on codetermination boards. They certainly must work with management and they may wish their members to see them as interacting with management on an equal footing, but a checks-and-balances relationship still may be the more advantageous position from organized labor's standpoint. As Albert Zack, AFL-CIO Director of Public Relations, has said: "It is preferable for U. S. unions to meet company representatives across the bargaining table, rather than trying to get involved in traditional management functions."[16] The feeling of many union officials - that under the present collective bargaining arrangement labor probably bargains on as many, if not more, issues than the number they might under a formal system of codetermination - adds to the conviction that the present way is the best. In addition, many in the labor movement feel that, unlike most European unions, they finally have won equality at the bargaining table; and they are reluctant to throw it away for the promise of equality in the boardroom.

Nevertheless, some unions in the public sector would welcome the introduction of codetermination. Richard Calistri of the American

Federation of Government Employees has said that his organization would be delighted to have codetermination introduced, provided management genuinely cooperates and does not just look out for its own interests.[17] Part of the reason public-sector unions are more positive about codetermination may be that they have not been afforded the opportunity to bargain collectively on as broad a range of issues as have their private-sector counterparts. Thus, for them, the prospect of sitting on a corporate Board of Directors may hold the promise of affecting an increased number of issues, a promise not as easily envisioned by private-sector unions.

Another union perspective is represented by the International Brotherhood of Teamsters, Warehousemen, and Helpers of America, who regard the question of codetermination in U. S. industry as moot. While agreeing that it might benefit organized labor, the Teamsters contend that implementation in this country would be both impractical (the membership is not seen as favoring it) and counter to the free enterprise system.[18]

The only major private-sector union to endorse the idea wholeheartedly appears to be the United Auto Workers (UAW). As mentioned earlier, UAW Vice-President Irving Bluestone and Undersecretary of Commerce Sidney Harman have worked together to bring codetermination closer to implementation in the United States, experimenting with its introduction in Bolivar, Tennessee (Harman), and Jamestown, New York (Carborundum). In both instances, the experiments have been reasonably successful.[19]

It is ironic that while many in the management sector of the federal government, such as Sidney Harman and Commissioner Sackman, have spoken favorably of codetermination, it is the increased involvement of such individuals in labor-management relations, necessitated by the new system, that may well be the major negative aspect of the plan in the eyes of labor leaders. Based on experience in other countries, there is no doubt that the introduction of codetermination would, at least initially, mean increased government involvement in labor-management relations. It is generally accepted that more laws would be needed to govern the composition of these boards as well as their jurisdiction over traditional collective bargaining subjects, their relationship to stockholders, etc. The federal government's intervention to this extent in private-sector labor-management relations is outside the traditions and interests of the American labor movement. Most labor leaders would prefer to bargain with private employers than to wrestle with government bureaucrats.

The Management Perspective

From the perspective of American business owners and managers, industrial democracy represents both a threat and a promise. The perceived threat to managerial aims has been evidenced by more than a century of active struggle against organized labor. While steady inroads have been made into formerly management-determined conditions of employment such as employee benefits and health and safety, resistance to workers' sharing in planning and operations decisions has remained strong and effective. Decision making in the American workplace is still viewed as a management right.

Notwithstanding the threatening aspect of industrial democracy, its promise has received increasing emphasis as concern about worker productivity has risen. Several studies have indicated that worker participation programs often have been successful in raising productivity.[20] Such venerable strategies to increase worker participation as the Scanlon Plan and the incentive plans at Kaiser Steel and Lincoln Electric Company have been outdone in popularity by recent formulas for job enrichment, team projects, management by objectives, and other participative schemes. These latter attempts to involve American workers in the operation of the business do not envision participation in direction of the firm. The traditional role of management as paternalistic initiator has been altered very little. In fact, many strategies of industrial democracy have been motivated by management's desire to deny union representation or at least to limit its influence. In some instances industrial democracy and worker participation programs have been used as planned, preemptive tactics by such management representative organizations as the National Association of Manufacturers (NAM) against union organizing attempts.[21]

Codetermination, which represents the extreme form of industrial democracy - granting labor a formal voice in company decision making - is, of course, anathema to tradition-conscious American employers. It has been acknowledged as a threat in publications of the NAM.[22]

Summary

The fact that U. S. unions have not generally endorsed codetermination seems to preclude its receiving significant support in the political arena at present. Since the "red thread" referred to by Furlong is a specter that alarms union leaders as well as managers, it appears political capital could not be made by backing codetermination. That fact probably accounts for the evident lack of enthusiasm on the U. S. legislative scene. There is no pending legislation in either House of Congress addressing the topic.[23]

In view of the reservations about worker participation in company decision making, as expressed by American managers and labor representatives, it appears unlikely that any sweeping movement to include worker representatives in the management process is likely. No evidence of such a movement has surfaced in recent national political campaigns.

Since neither the legislative nor the electoral arena offers encouragement for proponents of codetermination in the United States, it would seem that the traditional political path to such a change is barred. Thus any near-term adoption of a codetermination strategy for worker participation in American firms will take place in individually negotiated cases. Single organizations may agree with their labor representatives to incorporate some features of the *Mitbestimmung* model. Even as such beachheads are established, there is little likelihood that codetermination will become a major force furthering employee participation in the U. S..

Endnotes

[1] Bettie, Jane, *Business Periodicals Index*, 3rd ed. (New York: The H. W. Wilson Co., January 1958, annual).

[2] Mintzberg, Henry, *The Structure of Organizations*, (Englewood Cliffs, NJ: Prentice-Hall, 1979), pp. 203-204.

[3] Furlong, James, *Labor in the Boardroom*, (Princeton, NJ: Dow Jones Books, 1977), p. 28.

[4] *Ibid.*, p. 5.

[5] Furlong, James, "Workers in the Boardroom," *The Wall Street Journal*, March 12, 1979, p. 18.

[6] "Codetermination in the Federal Republic of Germany," translation, *International Labor Organization*, Geneva (Bonn: Refererat Presse-und Offentlichkeitsarbeit, 1976), p. 18.

[7] *Ibid.*

[8] Furlong, *Labor in the Boardroom*, p. 19.

[9] *Co-determination: Worker Participation in German Industry* (New York: German Information Center, 1977), p. 13.

[10] *Ibid.*, p. 18.

[11] "Codetermination in the Federal Republic of Germany," p. 18.

[12] Furlong, *Labor in the Boardroom*, p. 74.

[13] Meade Paper Co., Eaton Corp., Carborundum Co., and Harman International Industries are a few companies with such schemes.

[14] *Labor News and Social Policy*, No. 3, June-July 1978 (periodical pamphlet issued by the Embassy of the Federal Republic of Germany, 4645 Reservoir Road, NW, Washington, DC).

[15] Seidman, Joel, London, Jack, and Karsh, Bernard, "Why Workers Join Unions," *Annals of the American Academy of Political and Social Science* 274 (January 1979), p. 84.

[16] Statement by Albert Zack, AFL-CIO Director of Public Relations, April 18, 1994, telephone conversation with author.

[17] Statement by Richard Calistri, Director of Public Relations, American Federation of Government Employees, April 16, 1994, telephone conversation with author.

[18] Statement by Bernard Henderson, Director of Public Relations, International Brotherhood of Teamsters, Warehousemen, and Helpers of America, April 14, 1994, telephone conversation with author.

[19] U. S. Department of Labor, Bureau of International Labor Affairs, *Industrial Democracy in 12 Nations*, (Monograph No. 2, January 1979), p. 4.

[20] Stokes, Bruce, "Answered Prayers," *MBA* 12 (December 1978 - January 1979), p. 22.

[21] *Industrial Democracy in 12 Nations*, p. 2.

[22] National Association of Manufacturers, *Codetermination: Labor's Voice in Corporate Management* (Washington, DC: 1975).

[23] Statement by Jeffrey E. Friedman, Office of the Subcommittee on Labor-Management Relations, U.S. House of Representatives, June 8, 1994, telephone conversation with author.

An Explanation of Management's Obligation to Bargain in "Good Faith" Under Labor Law

ABSTRACT

Today's manager is faced with an increasingly restrictive set of rules when dealing collectively with a labor organization. In an attempt to simplify certain of these obligations, this article gives an overview of what constitutes good faith bargaining under today's labor laws. By following the guidelines set forth herein, today's managers will avoid being accused of lacking good faith.

In 1935, the National Labor Relations Act (Wagner Act), while stating that the policy of the United States was to encourage collective bargaining, defined several management practices that were prohibited, and also established the National Labor Relations Board (NLRB) to administer the Act.

Five major types of management activity were defined as "Unfair Labor Practices":

1. to interfere with, restrain or coerce employees in the exercise of their rights to self-determination;
2. to dominate or interfere with the formation or administration of any labor organization, or contribute financial or other support to it;
3. to discriminate in regards to hire or tenure of employment, or any term or condition of employment, to encourage or discourage membership in any labor organization;
4. to refuse to bargain with the representative of its employees; and
5. to discharge or discriminate against an employee who files charges, or gives testimony before the NLRB with respect to alleged management violations.

As a result of the Wagner Act, labor relations in the U.S. became very one-sided. No restrictions were placed on the right of unions to strike, boycott, or picket employers, nor were unions compelled to bargain with representatives of management or held accountable for contractual violation. Management, however, was required as a matter of public policy to bargain with the union and to do so in "good faith."[1]

It is important for today's managers to understand their rights and obligations with respect to organized labor under the law. The first thing management should realize is that collective bargaining under the Wagner Act does not require them to actually reach an agreement with their employees' representatives. It merely obligates them to make a good faith attempt to reach such an agreement. If after numerous conferences and meetings, management and the union reach an impasse and cannot agree on the terms of a contract, the Board will not find management guilty of refusing to bargain collectively merely because they have refused to accept the union's demands. In other words, management is not required to enter into an agreement with a union if they cannot meet its terms. However, they must try their best to reach an agreement by bargaining back and forth - just as they would in negotiating with a business customer or supplier. Simply agreeing to recognize the union as the employees' exclusive bargaining representative and letting it go at that is not enough. Nor is it enough to meet with those representatives as many times as they wish merely to say "yes" or "no" to their terms. Even recognition *plus* such meetings does not constitute collective bargaining by management. The essential element is a *bona fide* attempt by the employer to reach an agreement with the union. It is that good faith effort to reach some kind of an understanding with their employees' representatives that is required of management by the Act's collective bargaining provisions. This good faith, or the lack of it, is something which the Board finds after looking at all the evidence. It cannot be defined simply in terms of a "state of mind," although that is important; but it can be analyzed by examining what facts and circumstances the Board considers evidence of good faith collective bargaining or evidence of its absence.

As already indicated, management is not required to bargain collectively with every labor organization or employee representative requesting recognition. Only those organizations or individuals who are not company dominated and who represent a majority of the employees in an appropriate bargaining unit are entitled to collective bargaining under the Act. If they represent just a minority of these employees, they need not be recognized. Management can legally refuse to have anything to do with a minority union, but has to make it clear that the refusal is because of their minority status and not because they are outsiders. If they refuse to meet with a minority union simply because they dislike unions or because they prefer individual bargaining to collective bargaining, they will find themselves in difficulty with the Board.[2] Such a refusal, while not a violation of collective bargaining provisions, is considered interference with labor organizing under Unfair Labor Practice No. 1. On the other hand, management must be just as careful not to recognize such a minority union when a majority representative is requesting recognition. Even if no majority union is present, management should not grant exclusive bargaining rights to a minority union. In such a case, the minority union can only represent its own members and cannot serve as a bargaining representative for all employees. Any ensuing agreements should be made to expire just as soon as a majority union appears on the scene and requests recognition. With this action, management effectively avoids any unfair labor practice charges under the Wagner Act's collective bargaining provisions and also avoids any breach of contract suits by the minority union.

Management's duty to bargain collectively with a union or individual representing a majority of their employees in an appropriate bargaining unit does not begin until that representative asks for recognition and negotiation. The mere fact that a union represents a majority of employees does not obligate management to seek it out for collective bargaining. That action is required only when the union requests recognition and a meeting. Then, however, management must agree to confer with the union at a time and place satisfactory to both. Refusal to do so is an unfair labor practice under Item Four of the aforementioned list. This does not mean, however, that management must immediately recognize the union as exclusive bargaining agent for their employees and proceed to negotiate a contract with it.

As stated earlier, there is no obligation to bargain with everyone claiming to represent a majority. Management has the right to, and they should for their own protection, ask the union to prove its majority at the very first meeting. If the union refuses to do so and insists on collective bargaining on its own claim of majority representation, management can then refuse to recognize it.[3] Even if it should later turn out that the union did represent a majority, management will not be found guilty of refusing to bargain collectively as long as the Board believes their doubt as to the union's majority or the appropriateness of the bargaining unit was genuine. "Reasonable doubt" as a defense will not work, however, when the union has recently been certified by the Board. Such certification is conclusive proof of its majority and the propriety of the bargaining unit, and it cannot be challenged by management. It is not given a specific duration by the

Act, but the Board usually recognizes such certification for about a year in the ordinary case.[4] After that time, management can challenge such certification.

Once a labor organization or individual has proven that it represents a majority of the employees in an appropriate bargaining unit, management's obligation to bargain collectively becomes inclusive and they cannot attach any conditions to this collective bargaining. For example, they cannot refuse to recognize and negotiate with the union until it organizes or signs contracts with their competitors, as such a condition constitutes a refusal to bargain collectively. This does not mean that they have to agree to terms which the union cannot or does not require of management's competitors. In other words, management may refuse to enter into a specific, proposed union agreement until their competitors do likewise.[5]

Similarly, management cannot refuse to bargain collectively with their employee's authorized representative because something illegal has been requested, such as a closed shop. They have the right to refuse that demand but cannot refuse to recognize the union and negotiate with it merely because they do not like its terms. Nor can they refuse to bargain collectively when the union in question has called a strike against them, which means management cannot refuse to negotiate unless or until the union abandons its strike. Their obligation to bargain continues during and after the strike so long as the union retains its majority. As a matter of fact, management must bargain with the union even if it loses its majority during the strike if such loss caused by management's refusal to bargain or any other unfair labor practice. Likewise, the fact that the union and its members engage in violence or other unlawful conduct during the strike does not excuse management from bargaining with them. Nor does a majority union lose its right to collective bargaining because it strikes in violation of its existing agreement.[6] Such violence or illegality in a strike may cost the union members their right to reinstatement, but it does not deprive them of their right to collective bargaining so long as the union retains its majority.

Additionally, management cannot simply meet with union representatives and deny everything they propose. They must offer counter proposals, if asked to do so by the union, when they reject its terms.[7] Nor can they insist that the union accept, without any modification, terms which they themselves have drawn up. To present such a contract on a "take it or leave it" basis is to refuse to bargain collectively.[8] Management must be willing to talk things over with the union and to discuss the proposals of both sides. After all, the whole question of good faith in collective bargaining is really a matter of evidence, since the Board looks at the entire record to see whether or not management engaged in good faith bargaining with the union. If management refused to make any counter offers, the Board will find them guilty of refusing to bargain in good faith. If, on the other hand, it finds that they made some concessions and offered counter proposals when they rejected union terms, it will not convict them of refusing to bargain collectively even though they fail to agree with the union's proposals. In other words, it is not the actions or statements of management on a particular demand that determines their good faith but their attitude and conduct during the entire negotiations.

Although counter proposals are a key test in the Board's determination of good faith, there are other factors that indicate its presence or absence in collective bargaining. For example, a management that announces or changes any term or condition of employment while the matter is still under discussion with a majority union will be found guilty of a refusal to bargain in good faith.[9] Any such unilateral action or statement of policy is not only the very opposite of collective bargaining but, according to the Board, also constitutes an attempt to undermine and discredit the union.

Furthermore, as long as their employees are represented by a union or other bargaining agency, management cannot go over the head of such an agency to deal directly with the employees. This again is lack of good faith and is particularly important during strikes. Management can be compelled to reinstate striking employees with back pay if the strike was caused or prolonged by such an unfair labor practice.

One example of a management tactic which falls under the preceding paragraph is the situation where management attempts to get the strikers to return to work despite the union's instructions not to.[10] If management offers to take them back or asks them to go back to work by appealing to them directly instead of negotiating for their return with their union, they are guilty of refusing to bargain collectively.[11] Any kind of refusal to bargain collectively before or during a strike will deprive management of their right to replace the strikers permanently and will force them to reinstate the strikers and award them back pay.

Additional examples of lack of good faith by management include:

1. making a misleading statement at the bargaining table;[12]
2. presenting a vague and uncooperative attitude toward union demands;[13]

3. refusing to consider a union demand;[14]
4. refusing to budge on checkoff provisions;[15]
5. retracting concessions previously granted;[16]
6. demanding additional concessions;[17] and
7. refusing to arbitrate bargaining differences.[18]

Because of the severity of the penalties for violations of the unfair labor practices and good faith bargaining provisions of the law, it is crucial that today's manager understand exactly what can and cannot be done. With an increasing number of unionized professional and white- collar employees, many managers who have never had to face this issue in the past will find themselves confronting it in the near future. Since it has long been established in this country that ignorance of the law is no defense, today's managers must familiarize themselves with these issues. Failure to do so could become a costly and inexcusable mistake.

Endnotes

[1] Dunlop, J. T., "Structure of Collective Bargaining," in G. G. Somers (ed.), *The Next Twenty-Five Years of Industrial Relations*, Madison, Wisconsin, Industrial Relations Research Association, 1973, p.174.

[2] *Berkshire Knitting Mills*, 10 NLRB No. 17.

[3] *Texarkana Bus Co. vs. NLRB*, CCA-8, April 30, 1941.

[4] *Whittier Mill Company*, 15 NLRB No. 47.

[5] *Aronsson Printing Co.*, 13 NLRB No. 799.

[6] *NLRB vs. Highland Shoe Co.*, 119 F.(2nd), 218.

[7] *NLRB vs. George P. Pilling & Son, Co.*, CCA-5, March 18, 1941.

[8] Roberts, H. S., *Roberts' Dictionary of Industrial Relations*, (Washington, DC: Bureau of National Affairs, Inc., 1971), p.312.

[9] *Inland Lime & Stone Co. vs. NLRB*, CCA-7, March 13, 1941.

[10] *NLRB vs. Lightner Publishing Co.*, 113 F.(2nd), 621.

[11] *Manville Jenekes Corp.*, 30 NLRB No. 60.

[12] *Rangaire Corp.*, 157 NLRB No. 62 (1966), 61 LRRM 1429.

[13] *Adler Metal Products Corp.*, 79 NLRB No. 33 (1948), 22 LRRM 1359.

[14] *V-O Milling Co.*, 43 NLRB No. 59 (1942), 11 LRRM 1392.

[15] *H. K. Porter Co., Inc., vs. NLRB*, U.S. Sup. Ct. (1970).

[16] *Tomlinson of High Point, Inc.*, 74 NLRB No. 127 (1947), 20 LRRM 1203.

[17] *Franklin Hosiery Mills, Inc.*, 83 NLRB No. 37 (1949).
[18] *Mechanical Contractors, Assn.*, 202 NLRB No. 1, 82 LRRM 1438.

The Plant Closing Issue Arrives at the Bargaining Table

Kenneth A. Kovach
Peter E. Millspaugh

During the last decade the United States has watched its economy undergo immense dislocations. Technological obsolescence, declining competitiveness in world markets, a severe recession, and other factors have combined to force drastic structural changes in many sectors, particularly in the heavy industries. Steel, automobiles, machine tools, textiles, and rubber have provided a strong foundation for the American economy for over half a century, but now some find that their very survival is at stake. Associated with these industries' efforts to adjust is the movement of capital in pursuit of new priorities and the consequent economic disruption associated with plant closings.

The Central Issues

Traditionally, organized labor and management in the United States have perceived their interests as opposed in relation to plant closings. Viewing plant shutdowns as a threat to job security, union membership, union territorial prerogatives, and wage and benefit achievements, organized labor has vigorously pressed for a voice in the closing decision. Management has just as vigorously resisted, contending that such decisions are management's prerogative and are necessary to the effective operation of a profitable business enterprise.

In recent years, a public interest dimension has been introduced into the plant closing debate. Greater recognition exists that a shutdown can injure those beyond the worker and their immediate family. Injury may also occur to the small businesses dependent on the plant, to the economic and social fiber of the community, and even to the viability of local government. All are now strongly promoted by a number of public interest groups.[1] Also gaining advocacy is the public interest thesis of corporate accountability which would place the responsibility for plant closing at the corporation doorstep.[2]

The Institutional Settings

The plant closing combatants are waging their struggle primarily within the framework of three institutions: the courts, the legislatures and the collective bargaining process.

The Courts

The federal judiciary has been engaged in the plant closing debate primarily due to labor's contention that the terms of the National Labor Relations Act (NLRA) bring management shutdown decisions within the ambit of mandatory bargaining.[3] Although the National Labor Relations Board appears to favor this interpretation, the courts have been considerably more cautious.[4] Through a small number of recent opinions, the Supreme Court has provided a degree of protection against mandatory decision bargaining in plant closing situations.[5] The Court's inclinations were reaffirmed in its ruling that management had no duty to bargain over an economically motivated decision to partially terminate a business.[6]

Sensitive to entrepreneurial freedom, the courts generally have given little indication that decision bargaining requirements about plant closings will be enlarged under NLRA interpretations in the foreseeable future. A partial judicial success can be reserved for labor, however, as the requirement for "effects" bargaining in plant closing situations under the amended NLRA appears now to be firmly in place.[7]

Over the years, judicial initiative in plant closing situations has been solicited on other grounds as well. For a brief interlude, the courts seemed to be on the verge of extending job protection after a shutdown, based on the theory that seniority rights established in a labor contract were "vested," thereby surviving termination of the agreement and following the job to a subsequent facility.[8]

The courts have also been asked to use interpretation of the terms of labor contracts to find an unwritten intent that worker job entitlements would continue beyond a plant closing.[9] Theories favoring the perception of a job as a legally protected interest, rather than a mere contract right, have also been advanced.[10] Even the public interest arguments of the corporate accountability lobby have appeared in the courtroom in opposition to plant closings.[11] One conclusion, however, is inescapable: no theory has succeeded in securing any significant judicial intervention in plant closing situations.[12]

The Legislatures

What then can be anticipated from the second institutional arena in which plant closing issues are being played out, i.e., the legislatures? In recent years, certain segments of organized labor, along with various public interest groups, have taken their case for plant closing relief to both the state legislatures and the Congress.[13] These groups have prompted the introduction of plant closing legislation in some twenty-one states as well as the U. S. House of Representatives and the Senate.[14]

Although the legislative proposals at the state level vary widely, requirements for pre-notification, severance benefits, and the establishment of a community action fund are the most universal.[15] A major stumbling block to the passage of such state proposals is the fear that such laws would create a strong disincentive to state economic and industrial development efforts.

Sweeping plant closing relief proposals have appeared at the federal level, generating considerable fact-finding activity through public hearings.[16] Ambitious requirements for governmental intervention before and after the closing decision, along with other controversial features, have thus far prevented federal proposals from gaining the support necessary for enactment. In addition, in light of a generally unfavorable political climate, the prognosis for a legislative response in the near term is not encouraging.

Collective Bargaining Developments

In contrast to the lack of responsiveness within the courts and legislatures, plant closing issues are gaining stature within the collective bargaining process. It can be argued that because the courts and the legislatures have failed to respond, the collective bargaining arena is showing activity. Whatever its cause, the emergence of plant closing issues in the bargaining process could be a driving force shaping labor-management relations in the future. This development is not, however, without ironies.

For half a century or more, management has resisted union involvement in the plant closing decision. Although required to "effects" bargain, management's discretion to close in the first instance has been practiced by the business community and has been largely protected by the courts.[17] Hard pressed to survive the forces of new economic order, management has necessarily intensified its interest in plant shutdown bargaining. Ironically, the management that is now more willing to bargain over the ultimate job security question is less able to guarantee the jobs in question. There is also evidence that although plant closing considerations are appearing at the bargaining table with increasing frequency, it is not at the pleasure of either party. As a result of such bargaining, labor must often agree to major "givebacks,"[18] while management surrenders a degree of entrepreneurial control and often must guarantee against future shutdowns.

The precise extent to which plant closing considerations have invaded the collective bargaining process can only be a matter of conjecture. Some indication of the extent to which they have penetrated specific industries in recent years, however, is demonstrated in Table 1.

Table 1

Plant Movement Limitations by Industry*

	Total Agreements		Agreements having plant movement limitations	
	Agreements	Workers (in '000s)	Agreements	Workers (in '000s)
Total, all unions	1,823	7,339.2	391	2,873.1
Total, 9 unions	764	3,615.0	271	2,277.3
Auto workers	118	995.2	39	738.2
Clothing workers	19	165.3	12	143.3
Electrical workers	110	295.8	16	29.0
Garment workers	42	257.0	36	242.8
Machinists	89	285.7	16	76.0
Meat cutters	50	142.8	19	66.7
Retail clerks	48	137.0	18	64.0
Steel workers	120	587.8	42	430.7
Teamsters	168	748.4	73	486.6
Other	1,059	3,724.3	121	595.8

* Because of rounding, sums of individual items may not equal totals.

Source: "Characteristics of Major Collective Bargaining Agreements," *Bureau of Labor Statistics Bulletin*, 2065, 1995. (Note that these figures reflect only "plant movement" limitations. This should be distinguished from an agreement pertaining to a plant shutdown where no relocation is contemplated.)

Conclusions

Unable to obtain legislative and judicial support for the increasingly serious problem of plant closings, labor unions are bringing the issue to the bargaining table. The influence of plant closing considerations on the collective bargaining process may be shown to correlate with the business conditions under which the bargaining is conducted.

As a matter of national labor policy, the desirability of addressing plant closing problems exclusively within the collective bargaining process will surely be debated in the years ahead. There are those who contend that the bargaining process called for under the NLRA, as interpreted by the courts, provides the appropriate mechanism for resolving such an issue. They point to the recent plant closing bargaining developments to support their position. Others hold the view that the existing bargaining structure is weighted against union interests, and they will continue to seek legislative or judicial intervention to right the imbalance. However appropriate, adequate, or inadequate this bargaining response is, it appears that labor and management, within the limits of their own resources, have begun to grapple with the problem.

The advent of bargaining over spreading plant shutdowns raises related questions that only time can answer. The extent to which this development marks a watershed in the history of United States labor-management bargaining is uncertain. It is tempting to conclude that the contract innovations, reflected in the recent agreements, will usher in a new era of labor-management relations and that the former relationship will be irreversibly altered. Nevertheless, to conclude that future relations will soon embrace principles of codetermination and abandon their adversarial moorings would be unrealistic. It would be more prudent to suggest that some residue of the good faith and cooperation, forced on the parties by their distressed conditions, may survive the return to better times.

Footnotes

[1] Bluestone, B., and Harrison, B., *Capital and Communities* (Washington, DC: The Progressive Alliance, April 9, 1980); Green, M., Bernstein, J., Kamber, V., and Teper-Marlin, A., *The Case for a Corporate Democracy Act of 1980* (Washington, DC: Americans Concerned About Corporate Power, December 1, 1979).

[2] Nadar, R., *Taming the Giant Corporation* (New York: Norton Publishing Company, 1979); M. Green, et. al.

[3] This is based most frequently on the argument that the plant closing decision is a "term" or "condition" of employment by the Act's definition. See 29 U.S. Code 158(d) which characterizes collective bargaining as "the performance of the mutual obligation of the employer and the representative of the employees to...confer in good faith with respect to wages, hours, and other terms and conditions of employment..."

[4] The difference between the National Labor Relations Board and the courts in this area has been apparent for some time. See analysis in Schwartz, T., "Plant Relocation or Partial Termination: The Duty to Decision-Bargain," 39 *Fordham Law Review* 81, 86 (1970).

[5] Although the Court has required bargaining on a decision to subcontract work previously done by union employees in *Fibreboard Paper Products Corp. vs. NLRB*, 379 U.S. 203 (1964), the decision to terminate an entire business for whatever reason has been protected from bargaining in *Textile Workers Union vs. Darlington Manufacturing Co.*, 380 U.S. 263 (1965), as has an economically motivated decision to partially terminate in *First National Maintenance vs. NLRB*, 452 U.S. 666 (1981).

[6] *First National Maintenance vs. NLRB*, 452 U.S. 666 (1981).

[7] *NLRB vs. Adams Dairy, Inc.*, 350 F.2d 108 (CA-8, 1965), *cert. denied*, 382 U.S. 101 1 (1965). Acknowledged in *First National Maintenance*, "effects" bargaining, as the term implies, requires the parties to bargain in good faith over the effects of a management decision; in this case, the decision to shut down.

[8] *Zdanok vs. Glidden Co.*, 288 F.2d 99 (2nd Cir, 1961). This ruling was extremely controversial, little followed, and eventually overruled. For a critical analysis of the case see Aaron, "Reflections on the Legal Nature and Enforceability of Seniority Rights," 75 *Harvard Law Review* 1532 (1962); *contra*, see Blumrosen, "Seniority Rights and Industrial Change: *Zdanok vs. Glidden Co.*," 47 *Minnesota Law Review* 505 (1962).

[9] The *Zdanok* holding again provides an excellent example of the application of broad interpretation of the terms of a bargaining agreement to achieve this purpose. It has been argued that broader "contextual" interpretations are warranted, because the workers of today "are caught up in a system of industrial relations that transcends the immediate contracting situation." See Blumrosen, "Seniority Rights," p. 528.

[10] The perception of a job as a legally protectable property interest has had its advocates in this country for many years. See Drucker, P., "The Job as Property Right," *The Wall Street Journal*, March 4, 1980. This concept was explored in the major plant closing case of *United Steel Workers vs. U.S. Steel Corp.*, 492 F.Supp. 1 (1980).

[11] *United Steel Workers vs. U.S. Steel Corp.*, 492 F.Supp. 1 (1980), Brief *Amici Curiae*.

[12] Millspaugh, P., "Plant Closings and the Prospects for a Judicial Response," *Journal of Corporation Law* (Spring 1983).

[13] See description of these efforts in Bloodstone and Harridan, *Capital and Communities*, Note 1; Labor Union Study Tour Participants, Economic Dislocation; Plant Closings, Plant Relocation and Plant Conversion (Washington, DC: UAW, USWA, IAM, Washington, DC, May 1, 1979), a report on plant closing laws in Sweden, West Germany, and Great Britain with recommendations for similar laws in the United States.

[14] Bolle, B., "Overview of Plant Closings and Industrial Migration Issues in the U.S.," Economics Division, *Congressional Research Services of the Library of Congress*, May 15, 1980; Millspaugh, P., "The Campaign For Plant Closing Laws in the United States: An Assessment," *The Corporation Law Review* (Fall 1982).

[15] The contents of the legislative proposals, both state and federal, are examined in Millspaugh, *ibid.*

[16] Most of the public hearings on plant closing legislative proposals in recent years have been conducted outside of Washington, DC, in areas experiencing plant shutdowns. They have been held under the auspices of the Senate Committee on Education, Labor, and Human Resources, and the House Committee on Education and Labor, or a respective subcommittee.

[17] See "Major Collective Bargaining Agreements, Management Rights and Union-Management Cooperation," *Bureau of Labor Statistics Bulletin*, 1425-5, 1991, pp. 15-16.

Various clauses in labor agreements giving management specific rights to shutdown decisions have become quite standard, such as:

(1) Without intending by the language of this section to limit the functions and prerogatives of management, or to define all of such functions and prerogatives, it is agreed that the following are the exclusive functions of the employers...the right to decide the number and location of its plants, the creation of new departments and the elimination of existing departments in a plant...
(2) The union recognizes other rights and responsibilities belonging solely to the company, prominent among which is the right to decide the number and location of plants...
(3) It shall be the sole right of the company to diminish operations in whole or part, or to remove a plant from operation or business of same or any part thereof, to any location as circumstances may require.

[18] A term that connotes a union bargaining concession in the form of "giving-back" to management those contract rights that were previously secured.

The Case Against Litton Industries

Some time ago, lawyers representing a number of unions approached the National Labor Relations Board to ask that Litton Industries be treated as a single employer for purposes of unfair labor practice cases brought against the company.[1] Until that time, the Board had treated each individual Litton division as a separate entity on most labor relations matters, including unfair labor practice charges. The unions contended that this practice of the Board needed to be changed since the conglomerate had, in their opinion, a history of willful, repeated labor law violations that was not evident when each division was treated separately.

Litton Industries is a multinational conglomerate headquartered in Beverly Hills, California with ninety divisions and wholly-owned subsidiaries. Its products include business and office machines, data automation equipment, marine and aircraft electronics, medical and electrical equipment, machine tools, microwave cooking products, resource exploration, and shipbuilding. Litton has 77,000 employees, twenty percent of whom are unionized, in 80 major plants in thirty states. It has revenues of 4.94 billion dollars including 1.5 billion dollars in Department of Defense contracts.

Over the last twenty years, the NLRB has lodged over 50 major unfair labor practice charges against Litton; but since many include multiple counts of illegal activity, the actual number of violations of labor law runs well into the hundreds. The Board and/or courts have found Litton guilty on over twenty of these counts, with the company settling before trial by offering remedial action (reinstatement, back pay, etc.) in another twenty counts.

A case can be built, based on charges filed, that the company has systematically used plant closings, layoffs, and the threat of same to discourage future unionization and to rid itself of existing unions. For example, when the microwave factory in Minneapolis went union, the number of jobs fell from 1,400 to 300 as positions were shifted to a new plant in South Dakota. When union troubles started at the Jefferson Electric plant near Chicago, 500 jobs were suddenly shifted to Alabama. Ten plants have been closed, each after undergoing some form of organizing activity. In one case, by the time the NLRB ruled that Litton had to offer employees from a recently closed plant jobs at a new plant because the old one had been closed to "bust" the union, the new plant had been closed and the jobs relocated again.[2] As a further example, at the McBee Systems plant in Athens, Ohio, the company violated the terms of an NLRB ruling by initiating a decertification election against the Graphic Arts International Union.

The company has been found guilty on a number of occasions of intimidating and spying on employees, of unlawful refusals to bargain in good faith, and of eliminating health and medical benefits unilaterally. Four workers who were trying to organize a local of the International Union of Electrical, Radio, and Machine Workers at the Triad-Utrad plant in Indiana were fired for their part in the organizing activities. By the time they were ordered reinstated, the organizing drive had failed. After the Aluminum Workers' Union won a certification election at the Jefferson Electric plant in Alabama, the top organizers were fired. Other union supporters were moved to the dirtiest jobs in the plant, and two first-line supervisors who refused to harass union activists testified that they were fired for their refusal. For over two years after the Printers' Union won a certification election at the plant in Santa Clara, California, the company refused to bargain. Faced with an NLRB final order to bargain with the union, the company closed the plant. Finally, an eight-month strike resulted when the company demanded that the Machinists' Union surrender seniority rights and unilaterally attempted to set wage rates and eliminate or reduce health and medical benefits.[3]

Litton officials continue to insist that each division administers its own labor relations program without direction from headquarters, and that because of this, the unions' contention that the NLRB treat the company as a single entity for purposes of handling unfair labor practice complaints is inappropriate. These officials deny charges of anti-union bias and continually emphasize the fact that twenty percent of Litton's work force is organized and that in the last fourteen months, twelve new collective bargaining agreements have been signed without a work stoppage.

Sioux Falls Plant

Litton's labor troubles go back many years, yet the situation began to reach its present untenable position due to actions taken at the company's microwave cooking products plant in Sioux Falls, South Dakota. The majority of the company's microwave oven production had recently been moved there from Minneapolis after the latter had experienced union organizing activity. After a somewhat bitter organizing drive, the small, independent United Electrical, Radio, and Machine Workers of America union was certified at the Sioux Falls plant. After months of futile negotiations, the union filed an unfair labor practice charge with the NLRB charging the company with refusing to bargain in good faith. After investigating, the General Counsel saw fit to file a complaint with the Board charging Litton with seventy counts of unfair labor practices.[4]

The case was tried before Administrative Law Judge David L. Evans on 67 different dates. It produced the following examples of company violations of the National Labor Relations Act:

- Company officials violated Section 8(a)(1) of the Act five times by interfering with legitimate union-organizing efforts.
- Company officials violated Section 8(a)(3) of the Act five times by issuing improper warning notices to employees engaged in legitimate union business.
- and the Company refused to bargain collectively in good faith concerning wages, hours, and other terms and conditions of employment, specifically by:
  - having an overall intent not to reach an agreement;
  - refusing to negotiate on the issue of a checkoff;
  - insisting on an unusually harsh absence-control program;
  - providing false and misleading reasons for wage proposals;
  - taking unilateral actions concerning the length of breaks and lunch periods; and finally,
  - refusing to furnish required information to the union concerning the company's financial position and, in one instance, providing false information in this area.[5]

In this particular case, Litton received a recommended order from Judge Evans, subject to NLRB approval and court challenges. It required that Litton cease and desist from these unlawful practices, begin good faith negotiations, and post an NLRB notice stating what the company would and would not do to rectify the situation.

While the specific trouble at Sioux Falls, detailed above, is illustrative of Litton's overall labor policy, it at least appears headed for a satisfactory resolution. This particular situation, however, is most important in that it was the incident that galvanized union resistance to Litton's practices and forced the various unions at Litton to unite and seek a long-term, general resolution covering the conglomerate's company-wide labor policy.

Campaign Against Litton

The union campaign to stop Litton's unfair labor practices has consisted of two main thrusts. The first of these is the formation of a coalition of unions to oppose Litton's practices. The actions of Litton at Sioux Falls has caused the union there to seek a partnership with other unions representing different plants and/or divisions of the conglomerate based on a proven pattern in the company's actions that affects all unions.

Howard D. Samuel, President of the AFL-CIO's Industrial Union Department, has taken control of this union partnership and has begun directing the campaign against Litton. It is this coalition, presently consisting of eleven unions, that has asked the NLRB to declare Litton a single employer with a unified labor policy.

The success of the coalition in achieving this goal is crucial in the continuing fight against Litton. While getting the NLRB to declare Litton a single employer will not make unfair labor practices any easier to prove or cut down on company delaying tactics, it will provide for stronger and more far-reaching remedies covering the entire company rather than specific installations. From a union perspective, when dealing with an employer as large and diverse as Litton, such a situation is not only desirable but is, in fact, essential. However, given the present composition of the NLRB, it is by no means certain that the Board will rule in favor of the coalition of unions and declare Litton a single entity. (This should be taken as a simple statement of fact, not a value judgment as to what the Board's decision should be.) The coalition has also organized protests at various Litton plants, NLRB regional offices and at the annual Litton stockholders' meeting.[6]

The second thrust of the campaign against Litton is legislative. Legislation has been introduced in the House of Representatives that would bar consistent labor law violators from receiving federal contracts. This bill presently has over 130 cosponsors and has given rise to a similar bill in the Senate introduced by Senator Edward Kennedy. Called the Federal Debarment Bill, it would apply to companies or unions that establish a pattern of willful violations of final NLRB orders. Relief from debarment would only be granted upon affirmative corrective action or for national security considerations.

Litton would be especially vulnerable to such legislation due to its 1.5 billion dollars in Department of Defense contracts and its recent purchases of the Itek Corporation and the Laser Weapons Systems Division of Martin Marietta - both of which are involved in laser weapons development and production. In light of these recent purchases, Litton's present $1.5 billion in defense contracts may soon grow to a considerably larger figure. Hence, the company is vulnerable to this legislative thrust. As is to be expected, Litton is actively campaigning against the Federal Debarment Bill, claiming that thousands of workers could be severely hurt by a debarment action. The changing composition of Congress will go a long way toward determining the success of this legislative thrust against Litton.

The General Counsel of the NLRB has announced a plan to monitor Litton's subsidiaries as a group to determine if the parent company controls their labor relations. He has instructed the NLRB's thirty-three Regional Directors to identify all Litton subsidiaries in their regions and keep a list of all Board and court orders against them. The appropriate unions were informed that they had a right to name Litton in addition to the subsidiary when filing unfair labor practice charges. The General Counsel also established a special committee within the NLRB to review all charges against Litton subsidiaries.[7] While such actions are a necessary first step, as mentioned earlier, the composition of the Board itself (as opposed to its General Counsel) will determine the effectiveness of the union coalition and its influence on the Board.

Perhaps as a result of this action by the General Counsel, Mathias J. Diederick, chief labor negotiator for Litton, and James C. Allen, Director of Coordinated Bargaining, Industrial Union Division, AFL-CIO, have recently agreed to enter into a continuing dialogue to discuss all pertinent labor issues at Litton and to refrain from any future inflammatory statements.[8] (Sometimes you do not actually have to hit people over the head with a club; the threat of doing so is enough!)

On the legislative side of the issue, the House Debarment Bill was approved by the House Labor-Management Relations Subcommittee and is presently before the full House Education and Labor Committee. There appears to be a very good chance that the bill will pass the House, but it faces strong opposition in the Senate.[9]

Shortly after the debarment legislation was introduced, Litton Chairman Fred O'Green made a surprising public statement suggesting that the company and the union coalition enter direct talks, through a joint panel, to resolve the escalating labor disputes. While the statement caught the unions by surprise, a spokesman for the AFL-CIO's Industrial Union Department stated that the coalition welcomed the proposal.[10]

Conclusion

Although the final results are not yet in, the early returns show progress for organized labor in its confrontation with Litton Industries. The actions of the General Counsel of the National Labor Relations Board and the Congressional Subcommittee on the debarment bill both hold promise that Litton's lawlessness will not be allowed to continue indefinitely. However, the reader should take note that, in both instances, these are intermediate and not final steps. The full Board still has to act on the General Counsel's lead and issue appropriate decisions in cases involving Litton subsidiaries, and the full Congress still must act on the debarment bill before it really means anything.

In the case of the NLRB, the crucial battles are being fought in Senate confirmation hearings of Board members. In the case of Congress, much will be determined by the political party composition of both the House and the Senate.

The reader would do well to keep in mind the fate of the "labor law reform bill" in a Congress with a Democratic majority in both Houses. It also had a provision similar to the present Debarment Bill and went down to defeat by one vote in the Senate after passing the House.

The author would advise against undue optimism that either the Board will act on the General Counsel's groundwork or that Congress will send the Debarment Bill to the President. While an objective observer would conclude that Litton is systematically and willfully violating the law with direction from the top, it will probably be able to continue to do so for the foreseeable future. Nobody said life was fair.

Endnotes

[1] Lewin, Tamar, "Conglomerates: Test for Labor," *New York Times*, January 11, 1993, p. D2.

[2] Higgins, George C., "The Litton Campaign: Unions United," *America*, August 27, 1993, p. 85.

[3] Compa, Lance, "How to Fight a Union-Busting Conglomerate," *The Nation*, July 9-16, 1993, p. 40.

[4] "Testing a New Weapon Against Litton," *Business Week*, December 27, 1992, p. 32.

[5] *Litton Microwave Cooking Products, Division of Litton Systems, Inc., vs. United Electrical, Radio, and Machine Workers of America*, JD-77-84, pp.174-176.

[6] "Labor Escalates its Campaign Against Litton," *Business Week*, November 21, 1994, p. 47.

[7] *Ibid.*, p. 51.

[8] Telephone interview with James C. Allen, April 10, 1994.

[9] Telephone interview with Joseph Jerel, Legislative Assistant to Sen. Paul Simon (D-IL), April 11, 1994.

[10] Hayes, Thomas C., "Litton Asks Panel on Labor," *New York Times*, December 12, 1994, p. D14.

The National Labor Relations Board: Current Problems and Suggested Changes

The United States system of labor relations is the most legalistic in the free world today. Pressures applied to change national labor policy in the past can be expected to continue in the future. Implicit in these attempted changes is the basic issue of how the economy should function. The outcome of the battle will influence many of the basic economic decisions made in society - not only how the economy should function, but for whom. Positioned in the middle of this constant struggle is the National Labor Relations Board. To discuss its current influence upon labor-management relations and vice versa, one must briefly examine the roles played by management and labor and the role of the Board in implementing the National Labor Relations Act (Wagner Act) of 1935.

The National Labor Relations Board was created by Congress for the sole purpose of administering the Wagner Act in accordance with public policy. Public policy in 1935, as now, was declared to be: "to eliminate the causes of certain substantial obstructions to the free flow of commerce and to mitigate and eliminate these obstructions when they have occurred by encouraging the practice and procedure of collective bargaining and by protecting the exercise by workers of full freedom of association, self-organization, and designation of representatives of their own choosing for the purpose of negotiating the terms and conditions of their employment or other mutual aid or protection."[1] The achievement of this aim through even-handed administration and judicious interpretation and enforcement of the Act is the overall job of the Board. In its statutory assignment, the Board has two primary functions:

- to determine and implement, through secret-ballot elections, the free democratic choice by employees as to whether they wish to be represented by a union and, if so, by which one; and
- to prevent and remedy unlawful acts, called unfair labor practices, by either employers or unions.

The Board consists of five members appointed by the President for five-year staggered terms. Any three members may constitute a panel for the purpose of rendering a decision. The Board does not initiate cases. It must wait until a charge or petition is filed and certain other procedures are complied with before any disputes may come before it for a decision.

No other quasi-judicial agency exhibits to the same extent a separation of the powers of prosecution and decision. Judicial power resides in the Board proper, but the function of prosecution is lodged in the Board's General Counsel, an independent officer appointed by the President for a four-year term.

The functions of the General Counsel flow partly from the statute and partly from powers delegated by the Board. Under the statute, this officer's basic duties are:

1. to determine whether, when, and upon what basis, charges of unfair labor practices should be prosecuted. This determination is final with no appeal either to the Board or the courts permitted; and
2. to supervise all employees in the regional offices and all attorneys except those serving as Administrative Law Judges and legal assistants to the Board members.

With these powers and responsibilities in mind, this article will now examine some of the present problems with, and suggested changes to, the National Labor Relations Board.

Problems

Public policy toward organized labor has changed significantly over the years. Every law since the Federal Anti-Injunction Act has expanded the scope of government regulation of the labor-management arena. Legislative control over collective bargaining started in 1932 (the Norris-LaGuardia Act) when the judiciary was limited in the use of injunctions to deal with labor disputes. In 1935 (the Wagner Act), Congress was concerned primarily with restricting employer conduct. The legislative branch attempted to balance the scales in collective bargaining in 1947 (the Taft-Hartley Act), by placing limitations on union conduct. In 1959 (the Landrum-Griffin Act), it moved forward again by enacting legislation to deal with internal union affairs, with employee rights being the main issue. All of these changes in the nation's labor policy were brought into being by the introduction of new areas of labor-management relations, realignment of political power, public dissatisfaction with the power of employers and/or unions, serious economic problems, or marked alterations in the labor force. The Board, in its implementation of the above-mentioned acts, has acted as a barometer for legislative change in national labor policy.

It has become obvious to many parties that the Board has outlived some of its usefulness in regard to the most important areas of its unfair labor practice jurisdiction. These areas include contract interpretation, arbitration, racial and sexual discrimination, and relations between employees and their unions. Legislation and/or other agencies which have come into existence since the Board's formation have taken over these functions. The Board is still viable, however, in the area of traditional conflicts concerning efforts of employees and unions to organize, and permissible conduct during collective bargaining. It is these areas, where the Board is still the main force, that are most glaringly in need of procedural change.

Over the years, one major complaint made by unions against the Board has been the time lag involved from the date of filing petitions for representation elections to the actual holding of these elections. The essential element for labor unions is the ability to expedite election proceedings to sustain bargaining unit enthusiasm when voting for union representation. The theory of the law is that NLRB-conducted elections will be promptly held and, where the vote is for a union, employers will accept the majority decision of their employees. But under the protection of the Board and NLRA, an employer may challenge the validity of the pre-election investigation to determine, for instance, whether the employer's operations meet the Board's jurisdictional standards or which employees constitute the bargaining unit the union is attempting to represent. Either course of action can result in time-consuming delays before a Board decision is reached and an election held. In the mind of organized labor, this delay produces an unfair advantage to unscrupulous employers who could use this time to influence employees' attitudes through implicit threats of job loss or, more explicitly, by reprimanding or discharging union activists in hopes of swinging future election outcomes in their favor. These delays can be prolonged for periods of 200 days or more from the initial filing to final Board decision.[2]

It is a known fact that some employers practice these tactics to avoid elections and union involvement with coaching from consultants employed specifically to preserve non-union status in their companies. Delay is regarded as an employer weapon. The longer the period between initiation of an organization attempt and an election, the more discouraged employees become. Surely questions of Board jurisdiction and bargaining unit definition are valid ones and should be dealt with. Yet as one views the abnormally long delays within certain employer organizations, any rational person must wonder if the questions are raised out of legitimate concern or merely as a stalling tactic.

Another weakness of the Board is the enforcement of its decisions. Unions argue that remedies provided by the labor laws are inadequate to enforce the national labor policy. Unions prefer more severe penalties for flagrant violations of the national labor laws such as criminal prosecution, triple backpay, and withdrawal of governmental contracts from firms engaged in activities calculated to destroy unions. Yet it must be pointed out again that the Board does not act on its own motion in charges of unfair labor practices or petitions for employee elections. Injured parties must file their claim with one of the Board's 47 regional, sub-regional, or resident offices.

In handling unfair labor practice cases, the Board is concerned with the adjustment of labor disputes either by settlements or through its quasi-judicial proceedings. The Board has no independent statutory power of enforcement of its decisions or orders. It must seek enforcement in the U.S. Court of Appeals and herein lies what one side calls the "power of due process under the law" and the other calls "premeditated attempts at continued delay." An employer found guilty of an unfair labor practice may appeal the regional Board's decision to a Court of Appeals where the time involved in processing the appeal can result, according to NLRB statistics, in a median delay of approximately 365 days.[3] If an issue can be raised that calls for a decision by the full Board in Washington, DC, and not just an NLRB regional office, an even longer delay is guaranteed.

A good example of the ineffectiveness of Board decisions and the NLRA itself is the continued violations perpetrated by J. P. Stevens Co. on its employees and the union trying to represent them. Two decades of Stevens litigation questions the ability of the courts to make the provisions of the federal labor law work in the face of persistent violations. Simply stated, Stevens would rather incur the punitive measures passed down by the Board and courts than deal with unionism and collective bargaining.

These procedural delays are understandable when the rising number of cases filed with the Board each year and the increasing backlog pending at the end of each year are considered. The Board itself is naturally concerned about this state of affairs. As the Board chairman pondered in his State-of-the-Board Address:

> ...the basic question is how do we handle that volume of business in a way that does not, through delay, diminish the effectiveness of our administration of the statute? No one should ever be content

> with the time lapses that accompany our decisions, even when no criticism generated by it flourishes. No matter how fast disputes are resolved, room for improvement should always be explored. The best justice is the speediest, within the ambit of our jurisprudential heritage of fairness, of due process.[4]

Upon examination of the current caseload, one will notice new types of cases awaiting Board decisions, e.g., whether an employer must respond to a union's request for information in the EEO area or jurisdictional applicability in the health care and educational fields. A look at the time involved in processing these cases shows a need for more Administrative Law Judges at the regional level.

Changes

If all parties are aware of the problems with the current law and the inability of the Board to deal with the violators and injured parties involved, the question then becomes: "What is being done to relieve this pressure?" Recently, the Board took what the chairman termed "a significant step to speed election procedures"[5] under which workers vote by secret ballot to select or reject a union as their collective bargaining representative. The Board revised its rules to establish a "vote and impound" procedure enabling employee elections to be held on the date scheduled by an NLRB Regional Director. Previously, voting was postponed whenever the five-member Board in Washington, DC granted an employer's or a union's request to review a Regional Director's rulings. Under the new procedure, the election will be held as scheduled without regard to any challenges to the Regional Director's ruling, and the employee ballots will be impounded - to be tallied only after the Board disposes of the request for review. The chairman said the rules revision "provides an important procedural change - one which will enable parties to our elections to plan their campaigns with greater certainty and afford employees the chance to cast their ballots at a time when they are most familiar with the issues involved."[6]

Another change, in addition to the "vote and impound" revision, is the Labor Reform Act, the labor-backed bill that would amend the National Labor Relations Act by setting timetables for the holding of representation elections. The bill provides that where a majority of employees in a clearly appropriate bargaining unit petition for a representation election, the election would be held within 25 days. Where a petition presents issues of exceptional novelty, the time limitation before the election would be 75 days. These time limits would apply to decertification elections as well as certification elections.

The Act would also provide for double backpay to employees illegally fired during an organizing campaign, up to the time of the signing of an initial contract. Although labor forces were hoping otherwise, House opponents of the bill added an amendment to allow for deductions from the backpay period for wages earned in the interim. Included in the bill is additional authority for the Board, allowing it to seek an injunction to stop stranger picketing when it is in violation of a collectively-bargained agreement. Additionally, any person or company found to have willfully violated a final Board order would be barred from participation in Federal contracts for a period not to exceed three years, although the Secretary of Labor may use discretion in lifting the ban in cases of national necessity. The bill also requires that if an employer campaigns during working hours, the employees would be assured an opportunity to hear the union side in an equivalent manner.

Reaction to the House action ranged from statements that the legislation represents a "giant step toward justice and equity" to assertions that it represents an "outrageous demonstration of unchecked union power."[7] Despite the encouragement of former AFL-CIO President Lane Kirkland, who felt the bill will correct the "current imbalance in the nation's labor laws in favor of those employers who willfully and repeatedly violate the law," this legislation makes no proposals that would affect the Board's handling of collective-bargaining relationships, strikes, picket lines, boycotts, union security, or Section 14(b) of Taft-Hartley.

Another proposal for more drastic reform has been suggested in some corners. This is the establishment of a United States Labor Court whose jurisdictional powers would be all-inclusive, formed by the unification of several existing administrative agencies. This "unitary system" would give the new Labor Court jurisdiction to enforce rights and duties under several major federal statutes.[8] Principal functions would include the ability to pass judgment on unfair labor practice cases under Section 8 (NLRA), contract enforcement actions under Section 301 (NLRA), private secondary boycott actions under Section 303 (NLRA), and injunctions under the national emergency provision of Title 11 under the Labor-Management Relations Act.

The court would also claim jurisdiction currently exercised by federal district courts under the Railway Labor Act (RLA) and Title VII of the 1964, 1972 and 1991 Civil Rights Acts. Should the Court attain an acceptable level of performance, advocates would see its jurisdiction expanded to include decisions under the Labor-Management Reporting and Disclosure Act, the Age Discrimination in Employment Act, the Fair Labor Standards Act, the Occupational Safety and Health Act, and the Pension Reform Act. The administrative structure of the new Court would consist of three components:

- first, a board responsible for NLRA and RLA representation questions;
- second, a mediation agency providing conciliation and mediation under Taft-Hartley and the RLA; and
- third, a general counsel to investigate and prosecute under the NLRA, RLA and Title VII of the Civil Rights Act.

It is anticipated that the court's broad jurisdiction over both the collective bargaining process and the resultant contract would allow for more flexible and effective remedies and result in a less litigious and chaotic state of labor management relations.

In addition to the Labor Court, another proposal addresses the area of representation elections. It has been suggested that the NLRB need not supervise these elections. Based upon a study he conducted, Julius G. Getman concluded that neither the union nor the company is overly successful in changing workers' predispositions when voting time comes around.[9] Current NLRB restrictions on union and employer campaign speeches, as well as the Board's practice of rerunning many contested elections, could be eliminated under Getman's proposal. Getman questions the Board's long-held assumptions about workers' attitudes and how they are affected by an election campaign.

Currently, the Board can void an election for infractions of election procedures under the NLRA, but in doing so is working under the assumption that an "unfair" company or union tactic actually affected the vote. Until Getman's study, there was no empirical data to support this assumption. His study showed conclusively that the majority of workers were not attentive to the issues presented by either side in a campaign. This finding casts doubt on the necessity of NLRB supervision of every election.

Conclusion

While accepting the Board's important contributions and assets, everyone would like to eliminate its lengthy delays, its inadequate remedies, its multiple jurisdictional conflicts, and the recurrent changes in its members. However, unless this country were to experience chaotic changes such as economic depression or marked political realignments in the legislature, no sweeping Board changes are likely. Management and union organizations are shaped by economic markets and are only modestly affected by labor law. The Board and its administration of the National Labor Relations Act will continue to change only on an incremental basis to meet the need for refinements in national labor law and policy.

Are changes in the Board needed? Most assuredly, yes. Will the changes suggested herein come about? Not in the immediate future, and more than likely not in the foreseeable future.

Endnotes

[1] Taylor, Benjamin J., Whitney, Fred, *Labor Relations Law*, 1991, p. 217.

[2] *The AFL-CIO American Federationist*, September 1994, p. 13.

[3] *Ibid.*

[4] Bureau of National Affairs, Inc., *Labor Relations Reporter*, August 22, 1994, p. 95, LRR 382.

[5] *Ibid.*, p. 95, LRR 383.

[6] National Labor Relations Board, Release in AM Papers, October 7, 1994.

[7] Bureau of National Affairs, Inc., *Labor Relations Reporter*, October 17, 1994, p. 96 LRR 124.

[8] Morris, Charles J., "The National Labor Relations Board: Its Future," *Labor Law Journal*, June, 1992, p. 334.

[9] Getman, Julius G., "Do Representation Elections Need the NLRB?" *Business Week*, March 21, 1994, p. 54.

Should The Davis-Bacon Act Be Repealed?

Sixty-plus years ago Congress passed the Davis-Bacon Act in order to correct a serious labor abuse caused by two factors: a huge federal construction program and a chaotic labor market. Unscrupulous contractors were winning government contracts by employing itinerant bands of unskilled laborers and paying them exploitive wages. This widespread practice had two results: it took contracts away from local contractors, and it resulted in work of lower quality since the laborers were, at best, only marginally skilled. The Davis-Bacon Act successfully corrected this abuse.

Today, however, it is questionable whether the Act is viable and effective under current economic conditions; and a move is clearly afoot to repeal the Act or to amend it radically. The champion of the Act is organized labor - primarily the Building and Construction Trades Department of the AFL-CIO in tandem with the Department of Labor. The foes of Davis-Bacon are far more diversified and have made their views known through nine separate Government Accounting Office reports, an Office of Management and Budget report, and a report by the Congressional Budget Office, to name only a few.[1] As could be expected, management organizations such as the Association of General Contractors and the U.S. Chamber of Commerce are also quite vocal in their support for repeal. It is interesting to note that no professional economists have testified in favor of the Davis-Bacon Act.[2]

Ultimately, the fate of the Davis-Bacon Act will be decided by Congress, not necessarily as a result of a rational decision about what is right or wrong, effective or obsolete, but as a clear function of political power. Whether organized labor retains the political potency to stave off the demise of the Act remains to be seen.

The author would like to clarify the issue of whether the Davis-Bacon Act remains viable through a discussion of the historic need for the Act, its present administration, an exploration of some of the major problems attributed to the Act, and a critical evaluation of some of the recurring arguments favoring the Act.

Problems of Interpretation

Incongruous as it may seem, the very simplicity of the law has created problems of interpretation. The body of the law states simply that "contractors constructing any building for the United States that costs more than $5,000 must pay to all workers at least the rate of pay prevailing in the locality." An amendment in 1935 lowered the minimum cost to $2,000 and gave the Secretary of Labor the responsibility for determining the prevailing rate of pay. In ensuing years, some sixty statutes have come into being that effectively apply the Davis-Bacon requirements to almost any construction project where federal funds are used.

The Department of Labor has had to evolve a system for determining several factors which affect the rate of pay. They begin by making these three determinations:

- scope of the market area - how geographically far from the construction project the sample wage levels will be gathered
- classification of the project - ranging from heavy construction (highest wage rate) to highway, building, and residential construction (lowest wage rate)
- designation of job classification and job structure - what specific trade (such as plumber) and experience level are required

Once these steps are completed, the target group has been identified. The only thing that remains is to compare the wages of the individuals in the group and determine the prevailing wage for this specific project.

When at least 50 percent of the target group make the same wage (in both pay and benefits, to the penny), that becomes the prevailing wage. When 50 percent of the target group do not make the same wage, then the wage common to the largest group representing over 30 percent of the target group becomes the prevailing wage. If this requirement is not met, then a straight average of all wages prevails.

It does not take a profound intellect to realize that in most cases where 30 to 50 percent (or more) of a group earn exactly the same wage, it is because of a union contract. So today, instead of what the act originally intended - "to guarantee that Federal construction labor be paid the going rate for a particular locality" - prevailing wage has become synonymous with union scale. Even if 70 percent of a target group are earning less than union wage, the government will pay union scale to all those employed on its projects, be they union members or not. In fact, according to the Government Accounting Office (GAO), over one-half of the project determinations that they had reviewed were not even based on wage surveys. They were based on union-negotiated contracts![3]

Inflation and Price

The application of the Davis-Bacon Act artificially raises the cost of 22 percent of the construction projects undertaken in this country.[4] Quite simply, in those cases where the prevailing wage is in excess of the normal wage, costs are raised without a corresponding raise in productivity - a classic example of a cause of inflation. Estimates on the cost added by Davis-Bacon range from $400 to $900 million per year.[5] Basic administrative improvements could lower the rate of inflation by .3 percent.[6]

Side effects of Davis-Bacon have serious implications for non-union contractors working on private projects as well. The prospect of ending work on a public project and returning to the previous wage rate, which in many cases is half what the employees earn under Davis-Bacon, can be disastrous to employee morale. It also creates tremendous conflict within companies where only a part of the work force is on a public project. End results are that worker morale decreases, agitation to unionize increases, and pay must be increased to retain personnel. It is estimated that the "spillover" costs of Davis-Bacon to private construction firms are approximately $1.8 billion per year.[7]

The federal level is not the only level of government to suffer the inefficiency and inflationary impact of this law. Forty-one states have "little Davis-Bacon Laws" in effect - causing nearly every political subdivision in the country to be faced with the prospect of artificially high costs on any publicly funded construction project.[8]

An example will illustrate the magnitude of the cost/inflation problem. In Carson City, Nevada, a federal project required a painter. Department of Labor surveys found eleven similar projects with eight painters as follows:

2 @ $ 6.25 per hour (25%);
2 @ $ 7.74 per hour (25%);
1 @ $ 9.00 per hour (12.5%); and
3 @ $12.40 per hour (37.5%).

The latter becomes the prevailing wage. If the two painters who usually work for $6.25 per hour get the contract for the job, the government will spend $6.15 more per hour than is necessary to hire these workers. The price for this one small aspect of the project nearly doubles, and this does not account for the added administrative costs inherent in the Act. By far the most moving argument for repeal of this law is that we can ill afford to continue such an inflationary policy.

Local Contractors/Small Businesses

The effect of the Department of Labor's administration of the law has not been to protect local contractors (its original purpose) but to protect unionized contractors and unions.[9] Local contractors in non-metropolitan areas are used on 67 percent of private construction projects but on only 27 percent of public, Davis-Bacon projects. On Davis-Bacon projects, the contractors came from adjacent counties 40 percent of the time - and from even farther away the remaining 33 percent.[10] Since the Act was designed to aid the local contractor, it has obviously missed the mark.

In their zeal to find a prevailing wage in a non-metropolitan area, the Department of Labor has often expanded the area of the wage survey to unrealistic proportions (or until it covers a metropolitan area with a union scale). The resultant prevailing wage is totally unindicative of the local wage structure and consequently scares local contractors away from the bidding.

For example, the wage survey undertaken before hiring a steamroller operator in Cape May, N. J. (extreme southern end of the state) extended to Newark (extreme northern end) - the most heavily-unionized city in the State.[11] The wage more than doubled, the local contractor was not willing to pay it, the local town could not afford it, and the project was scrapped.

Studies show that the size of the survey area is inversely proportional to the population density. A rural area is five times less likely to have a local contractor than an urban area would be.[12] Would it not be logical to expect that in a town of 500 people the rate charged by the only plumber in the county is the prevailing wage?

The problem of morale discussed earlier is another reason that many small businesses choose not to bid on government contracts. This problem is compounded by administrative procedures that eliminate the local contractor who does bid more than 70 percent of the time.

Even if the law had no inflationary effect and did not hurt employee morale, the fact that it is doing the most harm to the very group it is designed to aid is more than ample reason to repeal Davis-Bacon.

Administration

The administrative nightmare that is Davis-Bacon boggles the mind. More than $200 million in administrative and compliance cost is incurred annually by both contractors and the Department of Labor. This cost is ultimately borne by the taxpayer.[13] Private contractors must adjust bids to allow for a 3 to 4 percent cost increase caused by regulatory overhead. This cost is particularly burdensome to small contractors who pay proportionately three to four times more than a larger firm. Once again, the greatest adverse impact falls on those whom the Act should be assisting.

Reactions to the administrative performance of the Department of Labor range from astounded to appalled. Consider the magnitude of the administration of the Act: 3,000 possible counties, nineteen trades, and four different types of construction making 228,000 possible combinations. What is astounding is that these determinations are made by less than thirty government employees, and they are done manually - the system is not computerized![14] Small wonder the Department opts for union scale so readily. The weekly compliance reports, required of all contractors working under the Act, are collecting dust in a warehouse. The forms are never reviewed unless some action is taken to draw attention to a specific contractor. This waste of manpower, funds, and resources is inexcusable.

Position of Organized Labor

Robert A. Georgine, former President of the Building and Construction Trades Department of the AFL-CIO, stated that organized labor:

> has no intention of permitting this law (Davis-Bacon) to be emasculated. Those who would repeal these laws would adamantly oppose restricting the profits of contractors, yet they propose to restrict the wages of workers. If cutting personal income is such

> an effective weapon in fighting inflation, let them start with some C.E.O.'s $1,000,000 a year salary. Start with those who have a lot before they nickel-and-dime workers to death.[15]

Three defenses of the Act appear frequently in organized labor's presentations in support of Davis-Bacon. They are that:

1. the law assures quality (union) work;
2. it prevents exploitation of women and minorities; and
3. it helps to protect local contractors by making them more competitive.

A fourth defense is that the law does not have any inflationary impact. But as already shown, this is an unrealistic response to empirical data which prove otherwise.

The concept that the quality of work is higher under Davis-Bacon poses an intriguing question: does the quality of work performed by the aforementioned Nevada painter increase if his wages go from $6.25 to $12.40 per hour? If we look at process theories of motivation, we see that this pay will have no effect on the work output since no desired behavior is being rewarded. And the content theories of Herzberg and Maslow agree that this wage jump will not motivate the worker. One can only wonder what new theories of motivation the AFL-CIO has discovered.

Claiming that Davis-Bacon prevents exploitation of women and minorities is an interesting way of defending the law, since it is probably most effective in keeping these two groups underemployed in the construction trades. The apprenticeship requirements in construction unions (that currently employ only 13 percent African American and Hispanics) - compounded by fixed ratios of skilled workers to journeymen that are as high as 14 to 1 - make it extremely difficult for minorities to benefit from this law. The situation of non-union contractors under Davis-Bacon is not much better. Employers who must pay such inflated wage rates will not hire marginally qualified or semi-skilled workers. The law also excludes minority-owned businesses because they are primarily small, non-union contractors who, as we have seen, do not benefit from the law's provisions.

Earlier parts of this article have already demonstrated that the law does not, in fact, protect local contractors. Arguments concerning the efficiency of small contractors relative to their large urban counterparts, or the social and economic desirability of awarding work to the former as opposed to the latter, can be discounted if most of the small contractors refuse to bid on Davis-Bacon projects.

The position of organized labor on Davis-Bacon is summed up in one sentence by the AFL-CIO: "If Davis-Bacon is weakened in Congress, it could well set off a chain-reaction assault by anti-worker conservatives upon the entire fabric of federal labor law."[16] Stripped of its rhetoric, this statement reveals the true reason for union support of Davis-Bacon. Organized labor cannot afford a political loss of this magnitude. The merits or faults of this law have little bearing on the stand of labor. Their considerations are purely political.

The Davis-Bacon Act was a remarkable success when first passed, but since then other laws have been passed that guard against wage losses, exploitation by employers, and adverse working conditions. Davis-Bacon has outlived its usefulness and is no longer serving the purpose for which it was intended.

Repeal is the most viable course to take in correcting the inequities of this law. Major administrative modification would go far to correct the problems with the Act, but the author has no confidence that improving some aspects of the law through administrative change will correct the fundamental problem for more than a short time. In a few years we will again have yesterday's law in today's economy.

Legislatively and politically, repealing Davis-Bacon will not be an easy course to take. There is sure to be some backsliding of union wages in the construction industry, but this should be a short-term problem. Several states have repealed their "little Davis-Bacon" laws, and to date there has been no tremendous collapse of the wage scale in those localities. Neither has there been a return to the chaotic, exploitive labor practices of the early 1930s.

The Davis-Bacon Act has proven itself to be neither necessary nor viable in today's economy. As it exists today, it is a law of organized labor, administered by the Department of Labor, for organized labor. The losers are taxpayers, consumers, non-union labor, and the unemployed. These groups have a lower average income than the beneficiaries, who are predominantly white and male. Davis-Bacon, therefore, not only shrinks the size of the economic pie, but it also redistributes slices to the 'haves' while denying the 'have-nots.' Davis-Bacon enriches a minority of high-income people with political clout and deprives lower-income people who have no political clout.

It is difficult to conceive of a more inequitable situation. The time to repeal Davis-Bacon was yesterday!

Endnotes

[1] "In Search of a Cure for Davis-Bacon," *Nation's Business*, July 1981, p. 60.

[2] Thieblot, Armond J., Jr., *The Davis-Bacon Act* (Philadelphia: The Wharton School, University of Pennsylvania, 1975), p. 27.

[3] U. S. Comptroller General, *The Davis-Bacon Act Should Be Repealed*, (HRD-79-18; Washington, DC: GPO, April 27, 1979), p. 4.

[4] *Ibid.*, p. 3.

[5] Committee on Small Business (U.S. Senate), *The Impact of the Davis-Bacon Threshold on Small Business Construction Contractors*, 99th Congress, 2nd session, (Washington, DC: GPO, February 2, 1982), p. 638.

[6] "Hidden Report Points Way to Wage Reform," *Nation's Business*, May 1981, p. 22.

[7] Committee on Banking, Housing and Urban Affairs (U.S. Senate), *Oversight Hearings to Examine the Administration of the Davis-Bacon Act*, 96th Congress, lst session, (Washington, DC: GPO, May 2, 1979), p. 171.

[8] "In Search of a Cure for Davis-Bacon," *op. cit.*, p. 61.

[9] Reynolds, Morgan O., "Understanding the Political Pricing of Labor Services: The Davis-Bacon Act," *Journal of Labor Research*, Summer 1982, p. 299.

[10] Bureau of National Affairs, "Small Business Spokesmen Attack Davis-Bacon," *Daily Labor Report* No. 22 (Washington, DC, February 2, 1983), E-1.

[11] Easterbrook, Gregg, "How Big Labor Brings Home the Bacon," *The Washington Monthly*, February 1981, p. 46.

[12] Gould, John P., *The Economics of Prevailing Wage Laws* (Washington, DC: American Enterprise Institute for Public Research, 1971), p. 19.

[13] Sheler, Jeffrey L., "Test for Unions' Waning Strength In Congress," *U.S. News & World Report*, October 19, 1981, p. 72.

[14] "In Search of a Cure for Davis-Bacon," *op. cit.*, p. 61.

[15] Schumer, Fern, "Fighting Words in Washington," *Forbes*, May 14, 1979, p. 93.

[16] AFL-CIO Issue Alert, "The Davis-Bacon Act Under Attack," *Fact Sheet* No. 3 (Washington, DC, March 5, 1982), p. 2.

An Assessment Of The National Emergency Strike Provisions Of The Taft-Hartley Act

ABSTRACT

The national emergency strike provisions made available to the President under the Taft-Hartley Act are one of the most vital parts of our labor legislation structure. In the absence of government imposed arbitration, they represent the "bottom line" in dealing with major labor disputes. As both the largest labor organizations and the employers they deal with continue to grow, the ramifications of unsettled labor problems among these parties permeate every sector of our society. It is, therefore, vital that we realistically assess our last line of defense against economic chaos caused by major labor problems - the emergency strike provisions of Taft-Hartley.

Introduction and Explanation of the Act

The Labor Management Relations Act, effective June 23, 1947 and amended in 1959, (known as the Taft-Hartley Act) provides the necessary machinery for the investigation of labor disputes, and hopefully, a mechanism to resolve them before they become a national emergency.

The machinery is put in motion whenever the President of the United States considers a threatened (or actual) strike or lockout within an entire industry, or a substantial part of it, to imperil national health or safety.

The first step the President takes is to appoint a Board of Inquiry, composed of a chairman and other members as deemed necessary. The Board has the power to act and conduct hearings anywhere in the United States, either in public or in private, as the occasion may warrant, to investigate the issues in dispute and to marshal relevant facts. The Board submits to the President a written report within a pre-established time, and includes statements from labor and management, but does not make any recommendations. The President files a copy of the report with the Federal Mediation and Conciliation Service, (known as the "The Service" in Taft-Hartley) and makes the facts available to the public.

After reviewing the report, the President may direct the Attorney General to petition the appropriate District Court of the United States for a 60-day injunction to prohibit or end the strike or lockout. If the court finds that a threatened or actual strike or lockout is of sufficient severity that it will imperil national health or safety, it will issue a temporary restraining order.

During the 60-day injunction, each party involved in the labor dispute has to make every effort to adjust and settle their differences with the assistance of The Service. Neither party, however, is under any obligation to accept all or any part of settlement proposals made by The Service or by the other party.

After the court order has been issued, the President reconvenes the same Board of Inquiry. If the dispute has not been settled by the end of the 60-day period, a 20-day extension is usually granted. During this time the Board reports to the President the positions of the parties, efforts made by each party for settlement, and the employer's "last offer" of settlement. This report is also made available to the public.

Within fifteen days after the 60-day period, the National Labor Relations Board (NLRB) takes a secret ballot of the employees involved in the dispute, questioning whether they wish to accept or reject the final offered settlement. Within five days thereafter, the results are certified and forwarded to the Attorney General. Following the balloting or settlement, whichever happens sooner, the Attorney General requests the court to terminate the injunction. When the termination is granted, the President submits to Congress a full and comprehensive report of the proceedings - specifically the findings of the Board, results of the vote taken by the NLRB, and presidential recommendations in the case.

Application of the Act

During the period since enactment of the Labor-Management Relations Act in 1947, almost every President has considered at least one labor dispute serious enough to require emergency action (totaling 34 disputes), and the Attorney General has submitted petitions for each injunction.

In large part, the act was passed in response to the industrial turmoil that occurred after World War II. Its necessity was dramatized when the national emergency provisions were used in seven disputes in 1948, a year after its passage. The use of the emergency section has varied considerably during the life of the act. Only the five national emergency disputes in 1971, involving grain elevators and stevedoring, neared the number in 1948.

Use of the Injunction

Since the passage of the law, the Attorney General has submitted 34 petitions for an-80 day injunction to the Federal District Court to prevent or end a strike, but only 29 have been granted. In 1971 the court rejected the government's contention that a strike of 200 Chicago grain elevator employees would "imperil the national health and safety," making it the first refusal to issue an injunction since the emergency provisions were enacted. Strikes occurred at some stage of the national emergency procedure in 29 of the 34 national emergency disputes. Where the 80-day injunctions were issued (with the exception of the 1949-50 bituminous coal dispute), the strikes were effectively halted or prevented in all of the 29 cases. In the case of the coal dispute the injunction was issued, but in contempt proceedings the union was found not guilty of ordering continuation of the strike.

The 29 stoppages affected 1.8 million workers who were idle for a total of 88 million work days. It is worth noting that a single 116-day steel strike involving more than half a million workers accounted for about one-half of the idle work days.

Industries Affected and Issues

The national emergency machinery is limited to strikes that affect an entire industry or a substantial part of one. The criteria for activating the national emergency provisions of the act are intended to limit its use. As a result, they have been applied to a relatively small proportion of the industries and establishments in the U. S. economy. Eight organizations involved in 13 strikes had fewer than 10,000 workers which indicates that the act is not used exclusively against large employers or industries employing a large number of individuals.

Former Presidents have decided that extended strikes in the following list of industries would have a drastic effect on the nation's health or safety if allowed to continue without some control:

	Number of Disputes	Number of Strikes
stevedoring	10	10
aircraft/aerospace	5	4
atomic energy	4	2
bituminous coal mining	3	2
maritime	3	3
nonferrous smelting	2	2
grain elevators	2	2
meatpacking	1	1
fabricated metals	1	1
basic steel	1	1
shipbuilding	1	1
telephone	1	0
TOTAL	34	29

The most frequent issue in dispute - 28 times - was wage rates. In a number of cases, wages, combined with other issues, caused an impasse. The national emergency provisions have also been invoked in disputes where the establishment of a union shop was one of the issues as well as disputes involving the scope of the bargaining unit, job security, seniority, severance pay, supplementary benefits, hours of work, and pension plans.

Shortcomings of the Existing Act

Though the emergency strike provisions of the Taft-Hartley Act were intended to serve the national interest, it is clearly recognized that there are inherent weaknesses in the existing law. In cases where an 80-day injunction was actually issued, the provisions have failed to resolve labor disputes in over half the instances (15 out of 29).

Probably the most widespread objection to the provisions is that they serve to postpone settlement and offer no assistance or pressure toward reaching an agreement before they are invoked. The provisions seem to ignore the fact that bargaining representatives for both management and labor usually compromise their positions only when confronted with a rigid deadline. Knowing that a strike will likely be postponed with the invocation of the emergency procedures, management and labor representatives often intentionally delay a settlement with the knowledge that they will be afforded an extra eighty days to bargain. It is unfortunate that the Act provides no pressure for either side to reach an agreement before the 80-day period. Neither does it provide for additional remedies after this period if no settlement has been reached.

There seems to be general agreement that the existing law should be amended to give the government increased power and effectiveness in handling labor disputes constituting a national emergency. The problem lies in moving beyond this point to that of adopting new provisions which would be acceptable to the concerned parties - labor, management, Congress, the administration, and the public. Over the years, several legislative proposals have been offered. However, it is inevitable that conflicts of opinion and interest concerning any public policy change would arise. In fact, it has been the political influence of labor and management that has proven to be a stumbling block to the adoption of legislative proposals amending the provisions.

Proposed Efforts to Amend the Act

The author admits that there is no easy solution. Lloyd G. Reynolds recognized this difficulty when he stated that:

> The objective of public policy is not just to prevent strikes in essential industries. The objective is rather to prevent strikes by methods which are orderly and uniform in their application, which involve a minimum of direct compulsion, which do not impose greater hardships on one party than on another, and which leave maximum scope for settlements to be reached through direct negotiations between the parties.[1]

Mr. Reynolds has suggested that anyone who could devise a policy within the above criteria would deserve a Nobel Prize for industrial peace.

However difficult the problem is, it seems inevitable that it will have to be confronted in the future. Let us then examine some major, existing proposals that have tried to be fair and reasonable to labor, management, and the American public.

The Administration's Proposal - S. 560

The administration's proposal can be found in a bill (S. 560) presently before the Senate. This bill would repeal Section 10 of the Railway Labor Act and put all transportation industries under the national emergency provisions of Taft-Hartley. Following the expiration of the present 80-day period, this bill would provide for either an additional 30-day cooling-off period, the appointment of an impartial three member special board to determine if a partial operation of the involved industry is feasible, and/or appointment of a panel to select and order binding the most reasonable final offer made by a party in the dispute.

The addition of these new options to the existing law has been referred to as an arsenal of weapons or choice-of-procedures approach. The uncertainty as to which procedure might be invoked and the unwillingness to risk the adoption of one of the other parties' offers in place of a negotiated settlement would likely lead to greater efforts by both parties to settle their differences through collective bargaining. The availability of these additional procedures to the executive branch would place tremendous pressure on both parties to seek a solution to their differences without resorting to a prolonged strike.

During the additional 30-day period, the President could order both parties not to make any additional changes in the terms and conditions of employment except by mutual agreement. Both sides would be required to continue bargaining with the Board of Inquiry mediating the dispute. The argument against such a cooling-off period is that if both parties were close to reaching an agreement they would be likely to agree to such an extension anyway. If they were far apart, the extension would be unlikely to effect an agreement.

The second procedure of the administration's proposal - partial operations - is quite complicated and gives rise to confusion in its terminology and interpretation. A special board of three impartial members would be appointed by the President. This board would determine if and how the partial operation of an entire industry could continue without imperiling national health or safety and if a partial strike would pose a serious enough economic burden on both parties to encourage them to seek settlement of their differences. If a partial operation were feasible, the board could present an order detailing the extent and conditions of operations to be maintained. The board could not present an order constituting a greater economic burden on any party than that caused by a total cessation of operations. If a decision were reached to permit partial operations, the parties would be required to proceed without a strike or lockout for a period not to exceed 180 days.

Those who support a partial operation procedure see it as a compromise between the right to strike and the public's right to receive essential goods and services. Though perhaps sound in theory, if partial operation is ordered, problems of implementation arise. These include questions concerning administration, enforcement and fairness. This procedure in its present form seems to provide a potential roadblock to effective settlement of emergency strike issues inasmuch as the particulars of what constitutes "partial" operation are especially troublesome, from both a theoretical and practical point of view.

The last provision of the administration's proposal calls for final offer selection. Each party would be directed by the President to propose two alternative offers to the Secretary of Labor, who would then make these offers available to both parties and mediate a five-day bargaining session. If no agreement is reached, the parties would be given two days to appoint a three member panel to select one of the final offers in its entirety. The President would appoint the panel in the event the parties cannot agree on its composition.

As guidelines to reaching their selection, the panel would be permitted to consider:

1. past collective bargaining and contracts between the parties;
2. wages, hours and conditions of employment in the industry;
3. security and tenure of employment with regard for the effect of technological changes on employment practices or on utilization of particular operations; and
4. the public interest and any other factors normally considered in the determination of wages, hours and conditions of employment.[2]

Unless found to be arbitrary and capricious by a reviewing court, the panel's decision would be final and would become the binding labor agreement between the parties.

Supporters of final offer selection argue that it would discourage an extreme position by either party, as both are trying to gain the endorsement of the panel. It would also encourage swift settlement of differences and provide a contract free from the influences of the arbitrators.

Those who argue against final offer selection say that it will be unfair and inflexible. They contend that each side will offer counterbalancing terms, that issues put forth by both sides should be considered and weighed carefully, and that a combination of the two would likely make up the best contract. It is also argued that the party who feels its offer will be accepted is likely to include minor advantages in its offer that could not be had through negotiation and arbitration.

Recommendations from the American Bar Association

A Special Committee on National Strikes in the Transportation Industries was recently appointed by the American Bar Association. Its purpose was to examine the present provisions of Taft-Hartley for dispute settlement and to make appropriate recommendations. The committee concluded that any amended legislation should include maritime, airline, railroad, and trucking industries. Their recommendations apply only to the transportation industry.

The committee recommended that upon notification by the National Mediation Board of an impending strike which would threaten an essential transportation service, the President would be authorized to appoint a presidential Mediation Board. During its 60-day life, the board would investigate the dispute and act as a mediator. Just prior to the expiration of this 60-day period, the board would recommend to the President one of four procedures for settling the dispute.

The first of these procedures is that the President direct the board to make public its recommendations for settlement of the dispute. With the release of these recommendations, an additional 30-day *status quo* period would be allowed in the hopes that public opinion would persuade the parties to settle their differences. In the event no such agreement could be reached within 30 days, the parties would be permitted to resort to the strike or lockout.

The second recommendation is the appointment of a presidential Arbitration Board. This board would be given authority to conduct an investigation of the dispute and issue a final award to be binding on all parties in the dispute. The following factors would be considered by the board in arriving at its award:

1. the public interest;
2. industry-wide comparison of wages, hours and conditions of employment;
3. nationwide comparison of wages, hours and conditions of employment;
4. security and tenure of employment with due regard for the effect of technological changes on employment practices and;
5. other normal considerations in determining wages, hours and conditions of employment.

The American Bar Association reluctantly included this procedure, while fully realizing the unfavorable connotations of such binding arbitration. It was felt that this, more than any other procedure, recognized the public interest.

The third and most controversial procedure presented by the American Bar Association is the presidential creation of an executive receivership of the carrier or carriers involved. The President would consider the public interest in deciding the length of time and conditions of the receivership. The government receiver would be allowed to adjust wage conditions during the seizure period but would be required to keep any adjustments to a minimum. The suspension of union security and checkoff arrangements was also recommended during this period.

Critics of this procedure argue that it is unconstitutional, that government operation is no guarantee against strikes, and that the procedure does not really pressure the parties to seek an immediate termination of the strike or lockout.

The final procedure recommended is that the board be dismissed and that no further governmental action be taken. It seems unlikely that this action would be chosen, considering the implications of a true national emergency. However, the board felt that this procedure would deter the parties from delaying implementation of their own emergency procedures.

The Kennedy Bill - S. 594

Under Senator Edward Kennedy's proposal, the President would appoint a Board of Inquiry whose purpose would be to recommend procedures for resolving national emergency disputes. The Board's report would be forthcoming before any injunction period. If an 80-day injunction period were granted, it would be done by a three judge District Court. Any appeal would be taken to the Supreme Court. If no agreement had been reached within 60 days, the President could issue an Executive Order detailing the procedures to be followed. This order would be effective only as long as an emergency was considered to exist. Congress could veto an Executive Order within 15 days. After 60 days of the injunction period, the President could direct the NLRB to take a secret ballot of the employees concerning the employer's final offer. Should the employees vote for the offer, the dispute would be resolved and the offer imposed on both parties.

Author's Proposed Change

The use of the emergency provisions of the Taft-Hartley Act in settling emergency disputes has failed nine times since the machinery was invoked in 1947, resulting either in a strike or lockout following the 80-day cooling-off period. In each of these cases, the President's personal intervention and use of invoked remedies failed to resolve the differences between the parties. The failure of presidential involvement, resulting economic losses, damages to other industries and services, and the suffering of tens of thousands who were not party to the dispute, call for more effective legislation.

In the context of the Taft-Hartley Act, the term emergency is used to describe the effects of a threatened or actual strike that would imperil our national health and safety. Prior proposals have not really effectively dealt with the heart of the issue: a timely settlement, in the interest of the public, to avert an emergency. There is no denying that the affected industries and labor unions have a great deal at stake in the event of a strike, yet the interest of the public must always take precedence. Collective bargaining is a fair and proper way to settle disputes, but when such bargaining is dragged on and on with little or no effort and/or movement toward an agreement, the government should be given the power to render a final and binding settlement upon the parties to the dispute.

The author would propose the establishment of industrial commissions upon recommendation and periodic review by a congressional arbitration committee. An industrial commission would be set up for each industry considered essential to national health and safety. The industries identified herein as having been involved with the emergency provisions in the past seem to constitute an acceptable list. The commissions would include high-level personnel from labor, management and government. Their task would be to give advance notice to management, labor, government and the public of any areas which might lead to serious disputes and the potential effect on the national health, safety, and defense if these disputes were to lead to an actual strike. They would also be required to submit to management, labor, the congressional arbitration committee, and the media, suggestions which might lead to an early solution of the problem.

As part of this recommendation, the author proposes the establishment of the aforementioned Congressional Arbitration Committee. One member from each of the House and Senate Committees involved in Labor, Agriculture, Defense, Commerce, and Manufacturing would make up the committee. This committee, with the assistance of the industrial commissions of each industry, would decide whether an actual emergency existed. If the committee concluded an emergency did in fact exist, it would then notify the President of all issues involved in the dispute. If the President concurred with their assessment, a 60-day injunction period would be granted. During this time, the parties to the dispute would be required to collectively bargain, with the Congressional Arbitration Committee sitting in but taking no active role in the negotiations. If no agreement could be reached within the 60-day injunction period, the parties to the dispute would be ordered by the President to prepare and submit a final offer to both the President and the Congressional Arbitration Committee. The committee would make these final offers available to each party and the media. The parties would then be given a final 25 days in which to collectively bargain towards an agreement. The committee would sit in on this bargaining also. If at the end of this period the parties had still not reached an agreement, the President would order a halt to any further negotiation. The committee would then be given 30 days in which to present to the parties and the President a final and binding contract. This contract would be a compromise of the issues of each final offer and the judgments of the committee. Upon favorable review and final approval of the President, this contract would be considered legal and binding.

This proposal allows management and labor sufficient time, in light of an actual emergency, to come to terms through collective bargaining. The threat of intervention by the Industrial Commission and the Congressional Arbitration Committee would provide pressure for the parties to bargain in good faith in hopes of reaching an early settlement. In the event no settlement could be reached through collective bargaining, the settlement imposed by the Congressional Arbitration Committee and the President would protect the public interest by not allowing the dispute to continue to drag on indefinitely. Under these circumstances, the final order would likely be as fair a representation of both sides of the issues as possible without actual settlement by the parties.

This proposal has necessarily been rather broad based, and the author fully realizes that many minute details would have to be ironed out before it could be put into practice. It does, however, offer a fair and equitable solution to a presently unacceptable state of affairs. As both employers (through acquisitions and mergers) and unions (through mergers) continue to grow larger, there may well come a time in the not too distant future when this state of affairs causes us to realize that some action must be taken to change the emergency provisions of the Taft-Hartley Act.

Endnotes

[1] Reynolds, Lloyd G., *Labor Economics & Labor Relations*, 4th ed. (Englewood Cliffs, N.J.; Prentice-Hall, Inc., 1964), p. 285.

[2] Woodley, Thomas A., *Saint Louis University Law Journal*, 47-106 (Fall 1982).

The Case for Government-Imposed Compulsory Arbitration

ABSTRACT

Under present law, the President can prohibit a job action for up to eighty days if it will imperil national health or safety. A case is presented for legislation providing for government-imposed compulsory arbitration to handle job actions not settled within the eighty-day period. Based on the growth in size of both employer and employee organizations and the increasing interdependence within the economy, this legislation is needed immediately.

Most lawmakers are of the opinion that laws should serve as deterrents to prevent dangerous or despicable acts by members of society. Labor laws, when they were enacted, were no exception. The Wagner Act was supposed to prevent the oppression of labor unions by employers who seemingly had the upper hand at the time. When unions, through the provisions of this statute, began to gain the advantage, the Wagner Act was amended by the Taft-Hartley Act. Finally, union members and society were protected from the unions' internal misbehavior by the Landrum-Griffin Act.

The history of labor relations is liberally sprinkled with protections like these. All were designed by well-meaning lawmakers to regulate the labor movement. Only one avenue remains unpoliced: crippling strikes or lockouts that could have a devastating effect on the country. A half-hearted attempt was made to provide such protection in the Labor-Management Relations Act of 1947, which gives the President the authority to ask, through the Attorney General, for a court injunction for a total of eighty days when a strike/lockout or threatened strike/lockout "...if permitted to occur or to continue, will imperil the national health or safety."[1]

The question then becomes: what happens at the end of the eighty day "cooling off " period? The parties involved are free to continue whatever it was they were doing to imperil the national health or safety prior to the injunction!

The President has seen fit to ask for a Board of Inquiry (the first step of emergency action) on thirty-eight occasions since the enactment of the Labor-Management Relations Act. On four of these occasions, the President did not request court injunctions after reviewing the Inquiry Board's reports. An injunction was requested for the other thirty-four and was issued in twenty-nine instances. On five occasions, strikes took place after the emergency procedures were in effect - once even after the injunction was issued.[2]

Although many individuals believe union leaderships are too responsible to permit any job action that might harm the majority of our citizens, on five occasions a difference of opinion has occurred between union leaderships and the President on what constituted peril to the health and safety of the nation. Thus, the question of labor leaders' responsibility is not the key consideration at all. A situation exists in this country where the most well-intentioned, public-spirited labor leaders may still, in the President's opinion, imperil the public health or safety because of the way they interpret the Taft-Hartley Act.

Under Taft-Hartley emergency provisions, the President does not have sole authority to issue an injunction. The President must first appoint a Board of Inquiry and review its report. If the Board of Inquiry's report indicates that the "health and safety of the nation is imperiled," the President may request that the court issue an injunction. The court has the option of denying the injunction request if it concludes no peril exists.

If such safeguards protect labor against arbitrary government action, why then is union leadership afforded the unchecked option of imperiling the nation after the expiration of the injunction?

The President may take only one action under the statute when an injunction has been discharged - a report, with recommendations for future action, to the Congress. Section 210 of the Labor-Management Relations Act states, in part, "... the President shall submit to the Congress a full and comprehensive report of the proceedings, including the findings of the Board of Inquiry and the ballot taken by the National Labor Relations Board, together with such recommendations as he (sic) may see fit to make for consideration and appropriate action."[3] The time between the implementation of this procedure and any appropriate action could prove lengthy even if Congress were in session at the time the injunction was discharged. Should Congress be in recess at the time, the delay would be that much longer.

One possible solution may be in the precedent set by actions taken under the Railway Labor Act. The emergency provisions of that act are virtually the same as those contained in the Labor-Management Relations Act. There is a similar cooling-off period after which the disputing parties are free to strike or to continue to strike. On three occasions, the President has asked the Congress to take legislative action after expiration of the cooling-off period. On all of these occasions, the Congress passed joint resolutions directing the parties to settle their differences through arbitration based on the President's recommendations. The question to be answered is whether similar action can and will be taken in industries other than the rails - in other words, under Taft-Hartley.

The author would propose three additional options to those already existing:

The first option would give the President the power to extend the court-imposed injunction. This would be used when the disputing parties were close to a settlement at the end of the eighty days.

Secondly, the President could opt to appoint a board to study the industry in question. The study would determine what portion of the industry would be allowed to continue operation to relieve the peril to the nation and which portion, if allowed to stop, would cause some hardships to management or the union. This may provide either management or the union with some leverage, depending on the particulars, but the country would be out of danger.

The third alternative would allow the President to invoke a procedure for final-offer selection. If invoked, each party would be given three days to submit one or two final offers to the Secretary of Labor. After five days of additional bargaining without settlement, a final offer selector group of three neutral members would select a binding final offer from those submitted by the parties.

The author is aware that the introduction of such government- imposed compulsory arbitration is extremely controversial. Yet the process of arbitration is firmly entrenched in the overall art of collective bargaining. The provision for arbitration as a method of resolving grievances is included in 96 percent of all labor-management contracts. It is an established and accepted practice in the industrial community.

The U. S. Supreme Court handed down decisions in the now-famous "Trilogy Cases" that eliminated any question as to the validity of imposed arbitration.[4] No reason is evident why this method of resolving grievance impasses cannot be equally effective if applied to collective job actions.

It is clear, however, that many would view such a legislative change as contradictory to our free enterprise system. There are those who voice (loudly) their opinion that compulsory arbitration as a method of resolving labor disputes is "undemocratic." There are also those who claim that compulsory, government-imposed arbitration destroys the collective-bargaining process. On this point, Seinsheimer stated:

> Almost everyone favors voluntary arbitration and almost everyone opposes compulsory arbitration. But seldom are feasible alternatives to compulsory arbitration in the public sector offered. Without denying that compulsion is less than an ideal state of affairs, the author argues that the alternative - depriving the public of vital services - is worse.[5]

To paraphrase Seinsheimer's words and twist them a bit, it might be said that the alternative - to imperil the health and safety of the nation - is worse. This altered quote could then be applied to both the public and private sectors.

Either the precedent set under the Railway Labor Act should be extended to all other industries under Taft-Hartley or the proposals made herein should be adopted. In either case, the provision for government-imposed compulsory arbitration must be included as an extension of the emergency provisions of the Labor-Management Relations Act of 1947. The power to impose arbitration must be delegated to the President, as a last resort, to protect this nation against arbitrary actions by either labor or management. As our management and labor institutions become bigger, and as a result our entire industrial society becomes more interdependent, the potential problems are worse than the cures proposed herein.

Endnotes

[1] *Labor-Management Relations Act*, 1947, Section 206, "National Emergencies."

[2] Taylor, B. J., and Whitney, F., *Labor Relations Law*, (Englewood Cliffs, New Jersey: Prentice Hall, Inc., 1991), pp. 478-480.

[3] *Labor-Management Relations Act*, 1947, Section 210.

[4] *United Steelworkers of America vs. American Manufacturing Co.*, 363 U.S. 564 (1960); *United Steelworkers of America vs. Warrior and Gulf Navigation Co.*, 363 U.S. 574 (1960); and, *United Steelworkers of America vs. Enterprise Wheel and Car Corp.*, 363 U.S. 593 (1960).

[5] Seinsheimer, W. G., "What's So Terrible About Compulsory Arbitration?" *The Arbitration Journal*, 26:44, 1981.

NLRA-Style Labor Relations in the Professional Services Sector

Kenneth A. Kovach
Peter Millspaugh

Litigation in the business world tends toward the routine and predictable. In most instances, little impact is seen beyond resolving the immediate dispute between the parties. Just the opposite result can be obtained, however, on occasion. The law and events can converge in such a way that the judicial resolution carries wide-ranging implications. Such an incident occurred when an ongoing dispute between Arthur Young and Company and the National Labor Relations Board came to a precedent-setting end in a federal appeals court.[1]

At issue were the disciplinary measures Arthur Young management took against three employees who persisted in complaining to their supervisor about wage disparities within their work unit, thereby encouraging fellow workers to do likewise. The employer viewed such conduct as disruptive of the work process and aimed at discrediting certain of its managers. The firm terminated two of the employees, issued a formal warning to a third, and adopted a management policy that prohibited congregation and association among employees for any purpose other than that required by their work.

The litigation and resulting decision arising from this incident assumes a certain star quality for a number of reasons. It provides a timely reminder that the long reach of the National Labor Relations Act's employee protections easily extends into today's non-industrial sector. The holding carries substantial precedential value for subsequent cases because of the near universality of the grievance (salary), the typical employee behavior it engendered, and the predictable employer response that followed. Also, the final settlement augments the legal formulation for delineating where the employer's right to enforce workplace discipline ends and employee's right to assert workplace grievances under the NLRA begins in a professional services work setting. And finally, the case establishes some important guidelines and crucial lessons pertaining to work-related employee grievances in the emerging post-industrial era.

It is important to bear in mind that the NLRA was enacted over sixty years ago during the Great Depression, under conditions of massive worker unrest bordering on civil strife.[2] The legislation's immediate goal was to defuse industrial turmoil between worker and owner. The legislative presumption of an on-going adversarial relationship between worker and employer, in which the worker was disadvantaged, prompted Congress to institute collective bargaining and extend statutory protection to employee self-organizational activity.

The Arthur Young litigation that will be examined herein transports a legislative scheme designed to tame the tumultuous industrial relations of the early American factory system into the orderly, well-appointed offices of the professional services firm of the present day. Whether the NLRA precepts of an earlier era can or should be applied to the diverse settings of the modern American non-industrial workplace is a subliminal issue at work here that makes the Arthur Young employee relations problem at once both difficult and significant.

This article will first delineate the circumstance that led to the Arthur Young litigation. The legal issues that arose from the employee's conduct and the firm's response will then be outlined and examined. In conclusion, the broader implications that the case holds for the non-industrial sector and the workplace lessons it offers for the professional services supervisor and Human Resource Manager will be explored.

Employee Complaints

The event in question transpired in the office document processing center of the prominent professional services firm of Arthur Young and Company in the last months of 1986 and the first two months of 1987. Although these events were troublesome to this firm of 800 partners, 900 employees, and 90 offices throughout the U. S., they were not atypical.

The firm hired two new proofreaders at wages higher than those of some of the employees already working in the proofreading section. Nina Bloom and Lisa Cohen, proofreaders with six and one years' seniority, respectively, at first complained between themselves about this wage disparity. On December 2, 1986, speaking for both, employee Bloom complained to the firm's Personnel Administrator. She was told to speak to the Processing Center Director to whom the proofreading section reports. The next day, employees Bloom and Cohen received written warning from the Center Director regarding past tardiness.

Some ten days later, Bloom and Cohen went together to the Personnel Administrator's immediate supervisor, the company Personnel Director, and complained about the wage disparity. They received assurances that the matter would be investigated. On February 18, some five weeks later, the Personnel Director called Bloom and Cohen to his office and defended the wage disparity on the basis of the experience of the newly hired proofreaders. During this period, Bloom and Cohen met with two of the other proofreaders at a restaurant after work hours and discussed the need to improve working conditions at the Processing Center.

On February 20, Cohen and fellow employee Debbie Graham complained to the Personnel Administrator that the Processing Center Director was "bullying" employees and that the immediate supervisor of the proofreaders abused them with the use of profanity. The following day, Bloom alone contacted the Personnel Administrator. On this occasion, she reiterated her concerns about the wage disparity and the verbal abuse inflicted on the proofreaders. She also complained that the employee work breaks had been eliminated at the Processing Center and that morale in the unit was worsening. During this period, employee Cohen was strongly urging other employees to take their complaints to management. As a consequence, one of the proofreaders complained to the Processing Center Director that Cohen and others were harassing her to join them in complaining.

Company Response

A meeting with the proofreaders was called by the Personnel Administrator and the Processing Center Director shortly thereafter. At the meeting, the Personnel Administrator made accusations that some of the proofreaders had complained about their immediate supervisors to higher management and characterized as not "proper" the efforts of some of the proofreaders to encourage their fellow employees to complain. The Administrator also noted that certain proofreaders had been seen whispering, congregating, taking notes, and harassing fellow employees. Such "union-like" tactics would not be tolerated by the company, the Administrator said. Several attempts by employee Bloom to raise the salary issue were dismissed with increasing irritation as "inappropriate" by the Personnel Administrator conducting the meeting.

The following day, the Processing Center Director met with a company partner and some other members of management, and the situation was discussed. The Processing Center Director requested permission to investigate the activities of Bloom and Cohen and then dismiss them. However, a decision to dispense with any investigation and discharge Bloom immediately was made by the company partner. It was decided that employee Graham would be issued a warning and that employee Cohen would also be terminated upon confirmation of her involvement in the suspect activities.

On the same day that the decision to terminate Bloom was reached and implemented, the Processing Center Director held a meeting with the remaining proofreaders at which the adoption of a "new guideline" was announced. Proofreaders were instructed not to associate among themselves except as required by their work. Specifically, it was stressed that the rule prohibited "socialization" and "people congregating at each other's booths." To complete the firm's response to this unpleasant personnel relations episode, employee Cohen was also terminated by the Processing Center Director four days later.[3]

Judicial Resolution

The legal implication of Arthur Young's disciplinary actions soon became apparent to the firm when former employee Bloom filed formal charges with the National Labor Relations Board (NLRB). This led to the issuance of a formal complaint in May 1987. Contesting the complaint, the firm was nevertheless found by the Administrative Law Judge to have committed an unfair labor practice. Despite appeals, first to the National Labor Relations Board itself and subsequently to a federal appeals court, the finding of a violation was upheld. The employer was ordered to cease the unlawful disciplinary measures in question and offer full reinstatement or equivalent positions to former employees Bloom and Cohen without prejudice to their seniority or other employment rights or privileges. The firm was to also compensate them for any financial losses in the form of lost earnings with interest and to expunge all references to the previous disciplinary action from their personnel records. Finally, the employer was ordered to post prominently, for a minimum of 60 days, a notice to all employees fully stating the requirements imposed on the firm under the NLRB's order.

From an employer's perspective, the Arthur Young experience poses a number of important questions. The first concerns what aspect of the firm's actions were considered illegal and why.

To answer, it is necessary to bear in mind that under the National Labor Relations Act, Congress sought to equalize an employee's bargaining power *vis-à-vis* that of his or her employer by bestowing upon employees the right to band together to seek improved terms and conditions of employment. To protect this employee right, the Act declares that any attempt by an employer to "interfere with, restrain, or coerce employees in the exercise of their rights" constitutes an unfair labor practice and will be punishable. In other words, it is a violation for an employer to discharge or take repressive measures against employees who attempt to exercise their right to self-organization.

Matched against these principles, three aspects of the Arthur Young incident became critical. The first centered on whether the employee conduct in question was the type Congress intended to protect. The second concerned the firm's claim that its fundamental managerial right to promote production and instill discipline in its workplace was being denied. The third dealt with the employer's motive in acting as it did and the legal significance of its motive. Each will now be examined in turn.

Protected Employee Conduct

From the beginning, Arthur Young contended that the proofreaders' activity amounted to nothing more than incessant griping and complaining that so disrupted the workplace environment and production as to be unworthy of statutory protection. The Supreme Court has stated, however, that the type of activity Congress intended to shield under the NLRA encompasses any effort to achieve better working conditions.[4] In some jurisdictions, protection has been extended even to the activity of a single employee if his or her purpose is to initiate, induce, or prepare fellow employees to act for their mutual aid and protection.[5]

Applying these legal principles to the efforts of employees Bloom and Cohen, the Board and the appeals court both found the activity to be protected. Certainly wages are a condition of one's work. Proofreader complaints of wage disparities, and also their subsequent complaints relating to supervisor abuse, constitute precisely the type of employee activity the lawmakers sought to protect. Even the individual efforts of Bloom and Cohen to enlist the support of fellow employees in bringing these concerns to the attention of management were considered to fall within the sanctuary provided by federal labor law. In sum, the employee conduct that Arthur Young management found to be so disruptive, union-like, and discrediting, was found to fall within the ambit of protected activity under the law.

Employer's Right to Workplace Discipline

By alleging that its actions were not taken to discourage employee self-organization but rather to enforce discipline in the workplace, the firm raised another important aspect of the incident. The Board and court were forced to reconcile the conflict between protecting Bloom and Cohen's activity on the one hand and allowing the employer the leeway to properly regulate and discipline its work force on the other. Arthur Young took the position that the two employees in question had lost any statutory protection because their actions disrupted work production at the processing center.

The general proposition is well recognized in common law and under modern interpretations of federal labor statutes that an employer may adopt rules to maintain worker discipline at its workplace. At the same time, however, the Supreme Court has specifically recognized the right of employees under the NLRA to communicate at the job site regarding self-organization.[6] Over time, the court has narrowed this employee right by recognizing a concomitant right of the employer to prohibit exercise of this employee right during working time.[7] During non-working time, however, the court has prohibited the employer from imposing any restrictions on employee self-organization "unless the employer can demonstrate that a restriction is necessary to maintain production or discipline."[8] Present law does not allow the employer to impose restrictions merely because the employee activity inconveniences or disrupts the workplace. Self-organizational activity by employees was held to be protected as long as it is not unlawful, violent, indefensible, or a breach of contract.[9]

These are the principles against which the legality of the new company guideline, restricting the proofreaders from any association among themselves unless directly related to work, was judged. The guideline was found to constitute a violation of the proofreaders' self-organizational rights. The court's rationale is instructive. Although the law recognizes an employer's right to impose restrictions during the employees' working time, the court noted that it is equally clear that this right ceases at the moment its employees enter upon non-work or free time such as work breaks, lunch hour, and the like. The court concluded that the firm's guideline was flawed because it could be interpreted as applying to non-working time as well as working time.

The court cited evidence introduced at the trial that after the new guideline had been imposed, the affected employees "kept to themselves" when there was free time, in fear of violating the new rules.[10] Arthur Young argued, nonetheless, that the rule was necessary in this instance to maintain production and discipline within a unit whose work product was crucial to the office. The court was unpersuaded, noting the fact that the rule encompassed non-working time and that no evidence had been produced to establish that production at the work unit had actually been disrupted. Further, the court concluded that "the timing of imposing the rule tended to indicate that its real purpose was not to spur production but to suppress the problematic employee self-organizational activity."[11]

Employer Motive

Employer motive has traditionally been an important factor in court deliberations concerning the legality of worker terminations in general as well as terminations that appear related to worker activity protected under federal statutes. The Arthur Young dispute was a case in point.

In 1983, the Supreme Court upheld a standard established by the NLRB for deciding the legality of those terminations allegedly based simultaneously on both lawful and unlawful reasons.[12] This mixed-motive standard simply provides that any termination motivated by a desire to restrict the exercise of protected organizational rights will be treated as a violation of the NLRA unless the employer can establish that the discharge would have occurred in any event based on a second motive that was proper and legal. Mixed-motive cases hold out the hope that management can legally justify a personnel termination that otherwise would be considered illegal.

As to the Arthur Young incident, the court concluded that one of the firm's motives in discharging Bloom and Cohen was retaliation for their self-organizational activities, and it was, therefore, illegal. The evidence upon which the court relied to support this finding is important. The firm's pattern of behavior from the beginning (of hostility toward employee efforts to make management aware of the grievances) was extremely damaging to management's defense. This was deduced from a series of employer actions ranging from the formal citing of employees for past tardiness the day after the first complaints were lodged, to rebuking employees in the company meeting for their alleged use of "union-like" tactics. It was further evidenced by the supervisor's angry suppression of employee efforts to discuss wage disparities during a work unit meeting. It was manifested ultimately in the discharge of two employees at the height of their self-organizational efforts. The circumstantial evidence of illegal company retaliation was strong.

If the powerful indirect evidence that the dismissals were in retaliation was insufficient, remarkably there was no shortage of direct evidence. Management references to the objectionable employee agitation to improve wages, documented in company memoranda as justification for the termination of employees Bloom and Cohen, make clear the firm's retaliatory motive. The company partner himself testified at trial that he instructed a supervisor that employee Cohen was to be fired if it could be ascertained that she had, in fact, encouraged other employees to complain.[13]

Even though the court concluded that one of Arthur Young's motives for the discharges was unlawful, the firm could nevertheless establish that the dismissals would have been undertaken in any event for a lawful reason, thus escaping culpability under the mixed-motive rule. As examined earlier, the firm's contention that the discharges were lawful - because by engaging in activities that severely disrupted work production the employees had forfeited their protection under the law - was discounted by the court.

The firm then advanced a second lawful motive argument. This was the contention that the dismissals were lawful because they were based in part upon unsatisfactory job performance. In support of this position, company management testified, and company memoranda were produced, that indicated that Bloom and Cohen had been "marginal performers." These allegations were effectively offset in the eyes of the court, however, by the countervailing evidence of past job-performance ratings received by the subject employees which showed that their work had been rated by the firm as "satisfactory" or higher.

Implications for the Business Community

Much can be learned on the managerial level from the Arthur Young experience. The case carries some broader implication for business in general, however, which should be noted first.

Among other things, the case serves as a timely reminder that practically every private sector workplace, industrial or non-industrial, unionized or not, ultimately remains subject to the policies of the NLRA. The appeals court decision in the Arthur Young case stressed that NLRA protections apply with particular force to non-unionized employees who "have to speak for themselves as best they can."[14] As a successful and leading firm in its profession, Arthur Young is indisputably a well-run enterprise. And yet, from a partner to proofreader supervisor, the firm struggled with the aroused assertiveness of two employees concerning certain working conditions, as though the Act had been repealed. The unsettling implication is that a level of insensitivity to federal labor law dictates may sufficiently pervade the professional services sector to make it vulnerable to similar unwitting violations in the future.

If insufficient sensitivity indeed exists, it is no doubt related in part to the late arrival of large institutional providers in the professional services field. In contrast to its industrial counterpart, the professional services sector has not experienced a long and contentious history of labor strife, which of necessity would have engaged it early on with the NLRA. Nor are present-day working conditions and employee relations in the professional services workplace generally unbearable to the extent that workers feel the need to organize against the employer. In point of fact, neither employer nor employee tend to view their relationship as adversarial. Working condition concerns are normally resolved through joint accommodation, smoothly and professionally. Both employer and employee are cautious to protect the positive and cooperative aspect of their relationship because of its subtle but direct bearing on the success of the firm. In light of the work environment, it is not surprising that a low management tolerance for adversarial employee behavior may have crept into the professional services sector.

Finally, the Arthur Young case represents potential synergism between the broad employee protections recognized under the labor statutes and the heightened scrutiny to which employee dismissals have been subjected in recent years. As an exponentially expanding population of employers can attest, the powerful assault on "wrongful discharge" over the last decade in this country, led by organized labor and a plethora of public interest groups, has enlisted lawmakers, courts, and a growing segment of the bar in its cause.[15] Although the new and fashionable dismissal prohibitions based on such factors as race, age, and sex command the attention of the moment, the unfair labor practice prohibition under the nation's labor statutes is destined to become increasingly important to this movement. Broad employee protections coupled with the well-established availability of reinstatement as a remedy under the NLRA provision make this a particularly attractive weapon against wrongful dismissal.[16] Embarrassing and costly litigation awaits those in the professional services industry who fail to recognize or miscalculate the potential applicability of NLRA restrictions to their employee relations practice.

Suggestions for Managers

The relevance of outmoded aspects of the nation's early industrial relations regulations to the diverse workplace settings of the modern non-industrial sector of today is of growing concern. But this is a temporal public policy paradox which can only be redressed by the lawmakers. In the meantime, the industrial relations system, with court oversight, churns on and must occasionally face the task of fitting the round pegs of the modern workplace into the square holes called for by an industrial age statute.[17]

Those in today's non-industrial sectors, such as the professional services industry, must guard against the impression, easily and unwittingly formed, that they are somehow immune from NLRA dictates. While the Arthur Young case strongly suggests this vulnerability, it also leaves a rich legacy of lessons from which present and future professional services managers can benefit. A succinct statement of each follows.

Don't Take It Personally

Managers should not take complaints personally. The NLRA contemplates and protects employee assertiveness pertaining to terms and conditions of employment. Employee dissatisfaction, however, can be properly based on his or her relationship on a *personal level* with a supervisor or manager. This is so because, from the employee's perspective, the personal dimension inherent in work relationships constitutes an integral aspect of the conditions under which the employee must perform. Equally important is the fact that employee assertiveness can easily appear to attack important personal attributes of the manager such as judgment and competence. Viewed by the manager as a challenge to his or her managerial effectiveness, the tendency to overreact is strong.

As the Arthur Young managers were to learn, the seemingly personal nature of the employee activity lodged against them did not warrant a response in kind. The complaints of Bloom and others were not disqualified from statutory protection simply because they appeared to be an attempt to "discredit" certain members of the firm's management hierarchy. The Act seldom distinguishes between the general interests of the employer and the personal interests of its managers. In other words, the manager, as an agent of the firm, is expected to take the heat from his or her employees as long as the employee activity is protected by statute from employer retaliation.

Presume Statutory Protection

When employee agitation appears, the most important preliminary decision the manager must make concerns whether or not the activity in question is self-organizational and, therefore, protected. The proper preliminary characterization of the proofreaders' efforts was missing in the Arthur Young response, and the firm paid a heavy price. In a non-industrial setting, self-organization activity may well take subtle forms and thereby mislead the harried manager who is often preoccupied with a myriad of other immediate and overriding concerns of the moment. If, as suggested, the busy manager can mischaracterize protected employee behavior, care should be taken to err on the side of safety. Prudence dictates that the busy manager guard against reflexive retaliation. Little is lost by indulging in a presumption, albeit temporary, that the behavior may enjoy statutory protection until such time as the matter can be fully investigated and carefully considered.

The one compelling reason, among others, for this deference to safety is the decidedly stern climate an employer's case of this nature will encounter should the dispute leave the firm and make its way into the legal system. As we have seen, in legal proceedings such disputes will be decided under a statutory regime whose overriding concern is with the enforcement of worker protections against the employer. The case is also likely to receive a reading most sympathetic to the employee in the forum of first impression, i.e., the NLRB. On appeal, it is apt to encounter the preoccupation of the day among many jurists with righting allegedly wrongful discharges that come before them.

Be Wary of the Mixed-Motive Defense

Once a decision to terminate has been made, the most natural and universal impulse of management is to buttress that course of action with as many justifications as can be assembled at the time. These are then memorialized in the summary memorandum carefully placed in the former employee's personnel file. The NLRA seems to encourage such practices in light of the mixed-motive rule allowing the employer to justify an unlawful discharge by establishing that it was based on lawful grounds as well. The open door seemingly afforded can be a cruel hoax, however, of which management must be extremely leery.

Arthur Young made a determined effort to convince the court that the dismissals of Bloom and Cohen were based on poor job performance as well as their wage disparity agitation. The attempt failed, for reasons that it behooves management to fully appreciate.

Between the lines of the mixed-motive rule lies an unwritten presumption: the employer's alleged lawful grounds are merely a pretext behind which an unlawful termination is being hidden. The burden of overcoming this hidden presumption has traditionally been formidable. Evidence advanced by the employer that a second and lawful motive existed will most assuredly be skeptically scrutinized by the courts.

The court's disposition of Arthur Young's inadequate job performance contention was classic on this point. The firm was unable to overcome the silent presumption of pretext because its job performance allegations were considered largely unsupportable and because the proximity in time between the height of employee agitation and the dismissals suggested naked retaliation by the employer. Consequently, a mixed-motive justification is seldom the place for the employer to make a stand and should be used only in those rare instances where:

1. the lawful reason preceded or was contemporaneous with the termination;
2. the lawful reason would have brought about termination ultimately of itself; or
3. these conditions can be compellingly argued to a skeptical tribunal. Otherwise, the rule is a false prophet regarding disciplinary action.

Non-Work Time Not Suitable for Regulation

Rules that restrict protected activity cannot be imposed on employees during non-working time unless they are unarguably necessary to maintain production or discipline. Arthur Young failed in its contention that the firm's new guidelines were necessary for production and employee discipline, because the supporting evidence that either problem existed was inadequate. At the risk of stating the obvious, the employer's burden required to carry the day in the name of either "production" or "discipline" as defined and practiced in the professional workplace is always formidable when placed in opposition to the worker's rights protected by federal statute.

Two further aspects of the Arthur Young guideline that made its legality suspect in the eyes of the court carry significant management ramifications. The first concerned the type of intercourse to which the new guideline applied and the time periods during which it was operational. As promulgated, the employees' understanding was that the guideline essentially prohibited *any* discussion between them that was not related to work - both on and off the job. The key is that work rules such as this are often evaluated from the perspective of the worker. To the court, the rule was flawed because, as interpreted by the workers themselves, it was significantly broader and more restrictive than was necessary.

The second stumbling block the guideline encountered was the inescapable appearance that illegal retribution was the motivating purpose for its issuance in the first instance. Most convincing to the court was the evidence that, in fact, work production had not been interrupted during the period in question, as alleged. Further, the court found that the rule was invalid because it could be interpreted to encompass the employee's non-working time as well as working time. The close proximity in time between the rule's promulgation and the terminations of Bloom and Cohen was also troublesome.

In sum, to sustain legal scrutiny, workplace rule restrictions applicable to the professional services setting must be precisely delineated in order to place the operational time periods and the nature of the activities to be circumscribed beyond challenge. As if this standard were not sufficiently daunting, the employer must also be scrupulous in avoiding any hint of unlawful motivation. The employer's alternative, as noted earlier, is to take on the nearly insurmountable burden of establishing operational necessity for the rule in the interests of discipline or work production.

Plan for Prevention

When the Arthur Young Personnel Administrator warned the office proofreaders that "union-like tactics" would not be tolerated, her stance was understandable; and such a posture may well be preferred within the employee relations exigencies of the modern professional services workplace. Critics of measuring the legality of professional services employee relations practices against the presumptions and policies of a sixty year old industrial relations model are on the rise. Until such time as federal labor statute reforms are instituted, however, the professional services community, among others throughout the non-industrial sector, would be well advised to avoid formal engagement under the NLRA provisions whenever possible. With vigilance, those scattered and relatively infrequent incidents of aggressive protected activity can be identified early and, if adroitly managed, can be resolved without major incident. A deliberate effort to prevent the escalation and subsequent impasse that leads to litigation suggests itself as a simple but prudent strategy for managing this type of problem under today's controlling law and legal climate. Many provisions of the NLRA can be ill-fitting and unfriendly in the modern professional services workplace.

Modern mangers in non-industrial settings would do well to heed the lessons discussed above when dealing with employee activities such as those encountered at Arthur Young. This case is only the beginning of legal intervention in this area. The personal and corporate penalties for ignorance of the developing trend are frightening.

Endnotes

[1] *Arthur Young and Company v. NLRB*, No. 88-3640 (4th Cir. Aug. 28, 1989).

[2] Heilman, M. J., "The National Labor Relations Act at Fifty: Roots Revisited" *Duquesne Law Review* 1959 (Winter 1985).

[3] *Arthur Young and Company*, 291 NLRB No. 6 (Sept. 28, 1988), pp. 1-6, 1988-89 CCH, NLRB 15,191.

[4] *NLRB v. City Disposal Systems, Inc.* 465 U.S. 822,831 (1984), 100 LC 10,846.

[5] *NLRB v. Waco Insulation, Inc.* 567 F. 2d 596,599 (4th Cir. 1977), 82 LC 10,254.

[6] *Beth Israel Hospital v. NLRB*, 437 U.S. 483, 491 (1978), 84 LC 10,655.

[7] *Republic Aviation Corp. v. NLRB*, 324 U.S. 793, 795-803 (1945), 9 LC 51,199.

[8] *NLRB v. Babcock and Wilcox Co.*, 351 U.S. 105, 113 (1956), 30 LC 69, 911.

[9] Cited above at note 5.

[10] Cited above at note 1.

[11] *Ibid.*

[12] *NLRB v. Transportation Management Corp.*, 462 U.S. 393 (1983), 97 LC 10,164.

[13] Cited above at note 1.

[14] *NLRB v. Washington Aluminum Company*, 370 U.S. 9, 14, (1962), 45 LC 17, 637.

[15] Shepard, P. Heylman and Duston, R., *Without Just Cause: An Employer's Practical and Legal Guide on Wrongful Discharge* (Bureau of National Affairs: Washington, D.C., 1989).

[16] Sockell, D., "The Future of Labor Law: A Mismatch Between Statutory Interpretation and Industrial Reality," 30 *Boston College Law Review* 987 (1989).

[17] Sclossberg, S. and Fetter S., *U. S. Labor Law and the Future of Labor-Management Cooperation* (Department of Labor: Washington, D.C., 1986). Millspaugh, P., "America's Industrial Relations Experiment: Legal Scholarship Assesses the Wagner Act," 32 *St. Louis University Law Journal* 673 (1988).

Comparable Worth Moves into the Private Sector

Kenneth A. Kovach
Peter E. Millspaugh

Pay equity has been an issue of considerable discussion in the United States for decades. This discussion has led to such legislative and judicial initiatives as the Equal Pay Act of 1963, the Bennett Amendment to Title VII of the 1964 Civil Rights Act, and the *Gunther* and *State of Washington* court cases. Comparable worth is the most current area of pay equity to be addressed, yet major concerns have been expressed over the practicality of implementing this concept. The validity of such concerns is now being tested in the province of Ontario, Canada. For the first time in this hemisphere, an aggressive comparable worth law has been enacted which is applicable to both the public and private sectors. All Ontario employers are now attempting to achieve compliance. To say that proponents and opponents of comparable worth are watching the unfolding drama with intense interest would be a drastic understatement. The implications of the success or failure of this pioneering legislation are self-evident and enormous. Practical support for the validity of proponent or opponent arguments will emerge, and such support may well prove crucial in determining the future course of comparable worth in the U.S. and elsewhere.

Overview

Simple economic justice dictates that wages in the workplace be the same within similar jobs for both men and women. Legislation in pursuit of this ideal was first content to strive for equal pay for equal, or substantially similar, work as it took form in the United States. In recent years, however, strong advocates have urged that wage equity between the sexes not be confined just to similar jobs performed by both, but expanded to include jobs that are dissimilar, but of comparable value. This extension of the pay equity concept has gathered a considerable following over the last two decades in this country and become widely identified as the theory of "comparable worth."

An imposing literature has evolved over the years addressing the subject of comparable worth pay equity from diverse perspectives. Although there have been applications of comparable worth theory through legislation in the United States, these have been confined to state and local jurisdictions, and applicable to only the (government) public sector work places. There have been no instances where a political jurisdiction has imposed the application of comparable worth policies on its private sector employers. Canada has likewise exhibited the same reluctance to move comparable worth dictates into the private sector, until the province of Ontario stunned many observers by breaking ranks.

This article will explore the implications of this Canadian initiative by first sketching the evolution and applications of comparable worth policy in the U.S. The pioneering Canadian law will then be carefully examined from the broader setting from which it emerged to its final configuration and requirements. In conclusion, it will explore the broader implications of this type of legislation and offer some observations as to its applicability in the U.S..

I. Comparable Worth Policy: The United States Setting

The importance society is attaching to pay equity and gender corresponds to the emergence of women as a factor in the labor force. The rise of the feminist movement and the increasing percentage of working women have been the two major factors driving the concern for wage comparability. Demographic changes reflected in the modern American work force, in particular, are instructive.

The Demographic Underpinnings

The stereotypical family unit of a generation ago, with the male breadwinner, the female housewife and one or more children, applies to only 15% of U.S. families today.[1] While the vast majority of unmarried women have traditionally worked, at present in the U.S. nearly 50% of married women with children under two-years old are working, with 62% of all mothers working outside the home. These figures have doubled since 1973, and there is every indication that the trend will continue. In the near future, over 80% of all mothers with children at home will be working.[2]

Part of this increase comes from women seeking self-fulfillment through careers - the feminist influence mentioned earlier. The rest is the result of economic necessity. From 1960 to 1973, family income increased every year, but the level achieved in 1973 has not been matched since, despite the rapid increase in dual-income families resulting from women entering the labor force.[3] One reason for this can be found by looking at sex-segregation markets that confine women to a limited number of low-paying jobs. For example, according to the last U.S. Census, women constitute 44% of all workers, but fill 81% of clerical, 97% of private household and 61% of other service occupations.[4] Other reasons include the average number of years of professional preparation (male 4.2, female 0.4) and average years of job seniority (male 12.6, female 2.4), both of which depress the wages of women and confine them to lower paying jobs.

The earnings from jobs such as those mentioned above, now being filled by an increasing percentage of married women, are not enough to offset the decrease in their husbands' real wages caused by inflation and the technologically forced shift from manufacturing jobs to lower paying service jobs. Thus, the decrease in real family income.

Proponents of comparable worth argue that one of the reasons the above-mentioned occupations, as well as individual, stereotyped "female" jobs, e.g., elementary and high school teachers, nurses, librarians, etc., are paid at their present low level, is because most of the positions are held by women. The same proponents contend that a fairly applied standard of comparable worth would raise the wages associated with these jobs and drastically alter many of the demographic patterns evident in today's workplace.

Legislative History

Congress first addressed the problem of gender pay equity through an amendment to the 1938 Fair Labor Standards Act (FLSA). In 1962, a bill was introduced to amend FLSA requiring equal pay for jobs of "comparable worth." First the House, and subsequently the Senate voted to narrow the concept to require equal pay for "equal work." This resulted in the passage of the Equal Pay Act (EPA) of 1963. Its provisions applied to those workers performing closely related jobs, not different jobs - even though they demanded the same degree of skill, effort, and responsibility and had the same working conditions. Exceptions were recognized to allow for merit and seniority systems along with the quality of the work product.

The following year, Congress passed the Civil Rights Act. Under the language of Title VII, discrimination in employment decisions based on sex was outlawed. When concerns were raised about potential conflicts between the sex discrimination provisions of Title VII and the wage equality guarantees of the Equal Pay Act, Senator Wallace Bennett advanced an amendment designed to eliminate the perceived problem. Ultimately enacted, this amendment stated that an employer may differentiate on the basis of sex in determining pay under Title VII, if the differentiation is authorized by a fair reading of the Equal Pay Act of 1963. By limiting gender-based wage discrimination under Title VII to EPA standards (equal work, not comparable), the Bennett amendment seemed to eliminate the statutory authority necessary to advance wage discrimination claims based on the theory of comparable worth.[5]

This question was later settled by the U.S. Supreme Court in *Gunther v. County of Washington*,[6] which ruled that claims of sex discrimination in compensation under Title VII were not necessarily limited to equal work situations. A claim of discriminatory pay, the High Court instructed, is not barred under Title VII simply because the type of work associated with the jobs being compared is not identical.

Judicial sentiment for comparable worth as a viable legal doctrine was further tested in the celebrated case of *AFSCME v. State of Washington*.[7] Responding to a comparable worth pay discrimination complaint, the State of Washington ordered a study to identify female-dominated job classifications that had salaries falling below male-dominated classifications of comparable skill and responsibility. This study, the first of its kind in the United States, found numerous such classifications.

Breaking new ground, the District Court recognized the plaintiff's comparable worth arguments and ruled in their favor. This decision was subsequently reversed by the Ninth Circuit Court of Appeals. A settlement between the parties prevented an opportunity for Supreme Court review, but this widely followed litigation symbolized the substantial moral sentiment, public opinion, and interest group pressure in promoting the comparable worth approach to pay equity.[8]

In 1984, Congress enacted the Pay Equity and Management Act reflecting the federal government's interest in the comparable worth theory as it might be applied to the government work force. The Act requires that outside experts conduct a study of pay and job classifications of federal employees to determine if gender based wage discrimination is present. In 1987, the U.S. Federal Employee Compensation Equity Study Commission Act examined and further attempted to promote equitable pay practices within the federal work force. In search of ever greater levels of sophistication, the Congress enacted the Federal Equitable Pay Practices

Act of 1988 to determine the extent that wages are affected by gender alone, across the board, and the role this may play in the formation of wage differentials between male and female-dominated occupations.

This flurry of federal activity has been matched by numerous state government actions as well. A recent survey indicated that some thirty-one states were formally examining their work forces for gender based pay equity. Twenty states had specifically enacted legislation or adopted policies aggressively implementing comparable worth standards in the state and civil service. Ten states simply enacted legal prohibition against unequal compensation rates for comparable jobs within their civil service ranks.[9]

Alongside the federal and state government activity must be placed similar actions by thousands of local governments throughout the country. Despite a lack of data as to the precise extent, it is clear that comparable worth pay policies are deeply penetrating the personnel systems of cities, countries and school districts around the nation today.[10] The comparable worth approach to combat gender based wage discrimination is clearly gaining acceptance in the public sector.

Despite considerable public sector acceptance and experience to date, the merits of comparable worth as a matter of broad public policy remain highly controversial in the United States. While proponents argue for the concept based on its inherent fairness, its moral underpinnings, and its impact on wage-based discrimination against women, opponents cite its lack of consideration of market forces, its impact on labor supply and demand, and the seemingly impossible task of consistent, objective and fair enforcement. These opponents contend that market forces such as inflation rates that dictate higher real wage rates for those most recently hired in a particular job, the hazardous or unpleasant nature of certain tasks within a job or group of jobs, geographic location, location-specific inflation rates, and the level of competition for labor within a particular area all make implementation of comparable worth on a wide scale impractical.

Opponents further argue that even if these problems did not prevent implementation, they would cause major labor force movements with no relation to supply and demand of labor. How then are employers to entice applicants to jobs not favored in a comparable worth system? By paying more and thus upsetting the balance again? Finally, who is to administer and enforce such a system on a nationwide scale? Few in the private sector doubt what the answer will be, but even fewer look forward to government intervention to the degree seemingly required.

Although those opposed fiercely disagree, the proponents of a comparable worth approach to pay equity contend that it is necessary not only in the public sector but also in the private sector. For this and many other reasons, the recently enacted Ontario private sector comparable worth law will be followed closely by opponents and advocates of greater pay equity. Its implications for eventually moving an aggressive comparable worth policy into the private sector in the United States need to be carefully examined.

II. The Canadian Comparable Worth Initiative

Canadian public policy concerning gender based wage discrimination has undergone the same evolution as in the United States. Defined initially as comparisons between substantially similar jobs, the working definition of "equal pay" is gradually being expanded to jobs which may be dissimilar, but of comparable value. Unlike the United States, Canadian pay equity legislation has not been confined only to the public sector.

Equal Pay Laws: Legislative Background

Equal pay legislation in Canada first began to appear in the provinces and territories some four decades ago. Following the lead of Ontario in 1951,[11] subsequently enacted legislation in all provincial jurisdictions generally mandates that women be paid the same as men for equal or "substantially similar" work.[12]

At the national level, the principle of equal pay is addressed in careful detail in the Canadian Human Rights Act. Enacted in the mid-1970s, evidence of the Canadian evolution toward a comparable worth view of pay equity appears in the language of this statute. Under the title of "Equal Wages," the legislation clearly states that wage differentials between male and female employees are illegally discriminatory if both are performing "work of equal value." This law and the provincial pay equity laws throughout Canada are enforced by the Canadian Human Rights Commission, provincial departments of labor, or human rights agencies, separately or in combination.

Despite long standing pay equity provisions in Canadian law, survey data in the 1980s suggested that a substantial wage gap between men and women persisted. For example, female average occupational earnings as a percentage of male average earnings was 59.4 percent, a full seven years after the Human Rights Act was passed, with a range across occupations of 46 to 68 percent.[13] Even comparisons between the same occupations within the same firm reflected wage disparities between 10 to 20 percent.[14] Reasons advanced to explain the lack of sufficient progress under existing pay equity law included the prevailing narrow interpretation of the laws and the extent of their enforcement. Despite the support for a comparable worth approach to attaining pay equity on the part of a growing number of lawmakers and public policy advocates, existing laws were being interpreted to apply only to the same or similar jobs within the same firm. Enforcement was found to be lacking, because most laws were passive or essentially reactive in posture - merely declaring a general prohibition against gender based wage discrimination. Cited also were impediments to meaningful litigation in the courts, such as the unavailability of class actions and a specific-intent burden-of-proof associated with enforcing some of the prevailing statutes.[15] It is largely the disappointing results experienced under the old regime that are fueling support for today's aggressive, proactive pay equity legislation utilizing comparable worth standards.

The Ontario Experiment: Proactive Comparable Worth Pay Equity

Before its daring new comparable worth law took effect, Ontario's long-standing pay equity statute carried the title "Equal Pay for Equal Work" and predictably set up a standard prohibition against gender based wage discrimination between "substantially the same kind of work in the same establishment, the performance of which requires substantially the same skill, effort and responsibility, and which is performed under similar working conditions..." [16] Impatient with the marginal results this traditional approach had produced over the years, the government began work on pay equity legislative reform in the fall of 1985.

Drawing on legislative ideas already emerging in Manitoba, Ontario first proceeded on the notion that two separate statutes would be necessary - one for the public sector and the other for the private sector. Through a lengthy two year process that enlisted the participation of the Province's citizenry and organized interest groups, the legislative provisions applicable to both sectors were ultimately combined into a single law.

Secure in its determination and expertise to write legislation for its own employees, the provincial government concentrated on an approach best suited to private sector regulation. To stimulate public discussion on the proposition of extending an aggressive comparable worth law to cover the province's private economy, the Ontario government issued a document entitled "Green Paper on Pay Equity."[17] A panel of distinguished citizens was then appointed which conducted public hearings on the proposition all across the province, gathering ideas and gauging public sentiment. At the same time, advisory groups from business and organized labor were appointed to advise the Premier and senior government officials at regular intervals as the legislation was being developed.

The result was the enactment of the Pay Equity Act of 1987 by the Ontario Legislative Assembly, with its provisions enforced as of January 1, 1988. This precedent setting law defines male and female job classes, establishes evaluative criteria, mandates equality of pay between classes of comparable worth in both the public and private sectors, and creates two permanent government agencies to insure its enforcement. A close look at each of the law's five major parts is instructive.

Part I: Definitions and Purpose

The act's singular purpose is "to redress systemic gender discrimination in compensation for work performed by employees in female jobs" (Sec. 4(1)). Discrimination in this form is identified by comparing each male and female job class in an organization in terms of compensation for the work performed and its value. Female job classes are defined as those comprised of 60 percent or more female members, while male job classes are considered to be those with 70 percent or more male members (Sec. 1(1)).

The formulation employed to place a value on each designated job class specifies the applicable criterion. The criterion is described as "a composite of the skill, effort and responsibility normally required in the performance of the work and the conditions under which it is normally performed" (Sec. 5(1)). Nowhere in the law is it specified how the skill, effort and responsibility are to be evaluated. Thus far, most firms are using the point system of job evaluation to assess the level of each factor.

Once job class valuation has been completed, if the employer's work force contains a trade union, only job classes contained within the bargaining unit may be compared. The same rule holds for compar-isons of job classes established within that segment of the work force falling outside a bargaining unit (Sec. 6(4)).

The act specifically prohibits employers from reducing the compensation of any employee or position to meet the new pay-equity requirements (Sec. 9 (1)).

Part II: Implementation: Public Sector and Large Private Sector Employers

Where wage discrepancies appear, employers are required to prepare and post their pay equity plans in the workplace. The employer with a segment of its employees within a bargaining unit and the remainder without, must prepare a separate plan for each (Sec. 14(1)). Employees not part of a bargaining unit have 90 days from posting to suggest changes in the employer's proposed plan. Whether these are incorporated or not is left to the discretion of the employer (Sec. 15(4)(5)).

The pay equity plan and wage adjustment posting deadlines under the new law are summarized in the following table:

Pay Equity Plan Requirements[18]

Location	No. of Employees	Mandatory Posting	Wage Adjustment
Public Sector	All	January 1, 1990	January 1, 1990
Private Sector	500 or more	January 1, 1990	January 1, 1991
	100-499	January 1, 1991	January 1, 1992
	50-99*	January 1, 1992	January 1, 1993
	10-49*	January 1, 1993	January 1, 1994

*Employers with 10 to 99 employees *may elect* to post a pay equity plan.

If an employer and the employees cannot agree on a plan, the Pay Equity Commission is to be notified (Sec. 15 (7)). A review officer is then assigned to investigate and effect a settlement. Failing a settlement, the review officer is empowered to choose the plan and order it placed into effect. Objection from either party to the review officer's disposition can be filed with the Commission within 30 days, in which case a tribunal (discussed below) shall make a final resolution of the matter (Sections 16, 17).

Part III: Implementation: Small Private Sector Employers

Formal pay equity plans for employers of more than nine but less than 100 employees are optional (Sec. 19). Should the employer choose to establish a plan, however, it would then be subjected to the same posting, amending, and formal objection requirements established for mandatory plans (Sec. 20).

Part IV: Enforcement

The creation of a formal Hearings Tribunal and a discussion of its powers are found in this section. Among the powers allocated to the Hearings Tribunal are the authority, when necessary, to order a review officer to prepare a pay equity plan for an establishment (at the employer's and the bargaining agent's expense), to order reinstatement of an employee's job and previous pay level, to order back pay and wage adjustments, and to order revisions in an employer's pay equity plan (Sec. 25 (2)). Failure to comply with any provision of the act or any order issued by the Hearings Tribunal can result in fines of up to $2,000 in the case of individuals, and up to $25,000 in the case of firms or bargaining units.

Part V: Administration

This section describes the various institutional arrangements referred to briefly in the proceedings parts of the statute. For example, the creation and establishment of a "Pay Equity Commission of Ontario" is to consist of two sub-agencies, the "Pay Equity Hearing Tribunal" mentioned above, and the "Pay Equity Office" (Sec. 27 (1) (2)).

The Hearings Tribunal is similar in concept to the Industrial Tribunals introduced into British industrial relations in the mid-1960s. Pay Equity Hearing Tribunals are to be comprised of a presiding officer and deputy officer, and include representatives from employers and employees in equal numbers (Sec. 28 (1)).

The Pay Equity Office is conceived as a permanent provincial agency responsible for the ongoing enforcement of the provisions of the Act and the orders of the Hearings Tribunal (Sec. 33 (1)).

Finally, the pay-equity review officer, as the foot-soldier of the statute's implementation and enforcement programs, is granted unsettling powers by current United State's standards. In pursuit of investigatory authority, the review officer is empowered to enter any premises at any time, request the production of relevant documents, remove those documents for purposes of making copies, and to interrogate persons (subject to their right to have counsel or another present) (Sec. 34(3)).

Employer Experience To Date

The preceding table showed that the first group to comply did not have to take any posting or wage adjustment actions until January 1, 1990, so it is now possible to look at the experiences from those companies who were first required to meet the law's provisions.

The two large employers who are further along the road to compliance than any others are Warner-Lambert, the Canadian arm of the Morris Plains, N.J., pharmaceutical company, and T. Eaton Company, the Toronto based retailer. At Warner-Lambert, an eight factor point system was used to determine comparable jobs. The plan was posted for employees to see and there was almost no negative feedback. Donald Henley, Director of Employee Relations, attributes the ease with which the plan has advanced to the lack of labor organizations within the company. The company is pleasantly surprised at the amount of positive employee feedback from those whose jobs were not directly affected.

T. Eaton Company has 15,000 employees in 580 jobs within Ontario and in the past, had used a different evaluation system at each of three organizational levels. To comply with the new legislation, the company went to a computer scored version of the Weighted Job Questionnaire, modified specifically for T. Eaton. According to William E. Robinson, Compensation Manager, completion of this task required four full-time employees, and the results continue to cost the company "quite a few million dollars annually" in equity adjustments. On the other hand, he notes benefits of increased internal communication including a monthly bulletin devoted solely to company actions relative to the law, and an awareness of compensation inequities that had gone undetected in the past.

In at least one heavily unionized sector, all major employers have come together in an attempt to achieve compliance. In the retail food industry where all employers deal with the United Food and Commercial Workers' Union, the industry has bargained as one with the union in an attempt to arrive at one overall plan. Here again, the point system is being used, but major problems have arisen in reaching agreement about points assigned within each job factor for particular jobs. If this one situation is any indication of what lies ahead, large unionized firms or industries are going to have severe problems.

Wyatt Company, a Toronto-based consulting company, is presently working with over fifty firms on compliance with the law. Sizes range from 200 to 20,000 employees and include many U.S. subsidiaries. The major problem Wyatt clients are encountering is similar to that in the food industry - that is, reaching agreement with bargaining agents over details of the plan. Those clients of Wyatt who are still struggling with formulation of their plan are those who have labor forces represented by automobile, steel and hotel workers' unions. To date, the Pay Equity Commission has received over eighty formal complaints from unions under the Pay Equity Act according to Nanette Weiner, the Commission Research Manager. Some employers have deliberately let deadlines pass without complying. The rationale here is obvious when one considers that the maximum fine is $25,000, while the difference between the plans proposed by the employer and the union is often several hundred thousand dollars. The lesson here for the U.S. is that, if such legislation is enacted in this country, economic sanctions may not be enough, and if they are all that is available, the size of the fine should serve as a deterrent to even the largest employers.

III. A Canadian Model For The American Workplace

As the Ontario Pay Equity Act went into effect, attempts were undertaken to gauge its success. With accumulated experience, the statute's impact on the political, social and economic life of the province will become more clear. In turn, this outcome will bear heavily on the influence this legislation will exert on lawmakers in the United States. For the present, there are certain particular features of the legislation that should be noted and monitored.

Perspectives on the Ontario Law

The salient feature of this law distinguishes it from previous United States and Canadian laws: its proactive imposition of comparable worth wage scales on the private sector. Less obvious, but of equal importance, is its focus on jobs, as opposed to individual employees. The evaluations and comparisons called for by the statute pertain to job classes, not the workers themselves. Because the law represents a crusade against discriminatory wages paid to female-dominated job classes, it is only these jobs which can be affected. Therefore, the workers who stand to benefit are confined to those employed in female-dominated job classes found to be underpaid in comparison with a comparable male-dominated class within the same establishment.

It is an intriguing irony that the structure of this approach to pay equity inevitably boosts the male worker minority, as well as female workers, in those female-dominated classes where wage adjustments will be required under the law. Disappointedly, the same structural limitations prevent the law from reaching those female employees who suffer from gender based wage discrimination, but fall outside a female-dominated job class. Because of these design limitations, the present Ontario legislation can never be said to ensure fair compensation for all female employees, let alone employees of both genders.

Another obscure but important feature of the law pertains to the mechanics of evaluating job classes. Beyond the statutory requirement to take the criteria of skill, effort, responsibility and working conditions into consideration, the precise type of job evaluation scheme is left to the employer's discretion. This represents an area with potential for ongoing conflict between the Pay Equity Commission and the provincial employers it must regulate. Its implementation could be extremely thorny and will bear watching.

Of far-reaching consequence is the statutory role envisioned for labor unions. In essence, implementation of the act, as it pertains to union members, is made largely a subject and function of collective bargaining. Presumably, this allows critical aspects of how the law is to be applied to this segment of the work force to be negotiated between unions and employers. Permitting key determinations of what constitutes a single "establishment" or "gender dominance" to be made through negotiation seems to put the employee who is a union member on a footing different from that of a non-union counterpart. In many respects, this feature of the new law would appear to benefit the unionized employee by virtue of the leverage which collective bargaining affords. One can argue that organized labor lobbying may have come into play here. Were glaring discrepancies in the statute's application to begin appearing between the unionized and non-unionized employee, the credibility and full acceptance of the new law would be seriously impaired.

The final feature of this legislation which should not be overlooked pertains to the surprisingly broad categories of exempted wage discrepancies. Until some experience is gained, it is difficult to estimate the size of the hole that the exemption for wage differentials based on seniority, merit, temporary training, etc., will put in the overall legislative scheme. It is unlikely that employers will seek wholesale refuge in these exclusions, but the incentive to move in this direction is certainly present. Whether or not the exceptions ultimately overrun the rule, the swath they cut is certain to be wide.

The Ontario Law's Adaptability to the United States

The adaptability of the Ontario legislative scheme to federal or local jurisdictions in the United States seems highly unlikely for the foreseeable future. Opposition to comparable worth policies remains vocal and well organized among business organizations and others. The aggressive scheme adopted by Ontario might be more palatable in the U.S. if confined to the public sector where comparable worth measures are gaining some degree of acceptability. Private sector mandates such as these, however, would predictably encounter stiff opposition in this country.

Private sector commercial interests opposed the Ontario legislation in its initial form. This caused Canadian lawmakers to accommodate a number of the business communities' concerns in the design and language of the legislation. Fully cognizant that moving comparable worth dictates into the private sector would raise problems unequal to the public sector's, the matter was studied intently.[19] The statutory accommodations to business interests ultimately adopted are particularly instructive to American policy analysts, since comparable worth critics in the United States cite essentially the same objections.

The Ontario framers contemplated the concern that employers may be unable to afford the required wage adjustments and that higher wages would lead to higher consumer prices and reduce much of the competitive advantage enjoyed by provincial employers. The lawmakers' response was to phase in pay equity requirements starting with those sectors most easily able to make the adjustment, i.e., the public sector and large private sector employers, followed by private firms of decreasing size. It was felt that the smaller firms could benefit with more time to learn from the experiences of the larger firms preceding them. Also, private-sector employers were not placed under a calendar-date deadline for full compliance, as long as a minimum of one percent of the previous year's payroll was devoted to wage adjustments annually.

To offset concerns that the law would intervene in labor markets as it standardized wages across the entire province, the law limited wage comparisons geographically to single establishments, even though geographically dispersed establishments may share the same ownership. Wage comparisons were also limited to prohibit the matching of union with non-union jobs, or the matching of job classes between different unions whenever possible. Wage control and standardization were further relaxed by allowing pay equity plans and their implementation for unionized employees to be worked out through collective bargaining. Also, the statutory exemptions for established practices, e.g., seniority preferences and merit pay, can be viewed as an attempt to preserve certain wage setting prerogatives important to the private sector.

IV. Observations and Conclusions

A private sector experiment with mandatory comparable worth standards has now been instituted in the Canadian province of Ontario. The neighboring province of Manitoba is preparing similar legislation. Drawn with elaborate care in an attempt to accommodate private sector interests, the Ontario legislation still carries liabilities which would be considered unacceptable by contemporary U.S. standards. These shortcomings can be briefly summarized:

1. The problems which have long plagued the comparable worth theory of pay equity have not been overcome through this legislation. A meaningful and practical definition of "job worth" remains elusive, as does the basis for job class comparison with the requisite precision. The problems applying these amorphous concepts in the private sector will only magnify as employer, employee and bargaining agent pursue advantage, while provincial review officers and hearing tribunals attempt to mediate and enforce.
2. The scale of intervention into labor markets and managerial operating prerogatives would be considered unnecessarily heavy handed from a United States perspective. Only less intrusive means could hope for acceptability.
3. The benefits sought are unlikely to outweigh the costs. The direct and indirect costs associated with employer compliance would not likely be viewed as appropriate, since the legislation achieves only marginal rate adjustments in a relatively small subsegment of the labor force.

It is certain that this controversial legislative experiment undertaken by our neighbors to the north will be closely followed by both the advocates of comparable worth pay equity standards and its detractors. The prospects of similar laws rooting in the United States will inevitably hinge to a certain extent on the success or failure of the Ontario initiative. With case studies in process, perhaps the debate concerning the efficacy of comparable worth policy in the private sector can be joined once again. To be sure, the Canadian laboratory is, at best, a rough approximation of conditions in the United States. Much can be extrapolated from the Canadian effort, however, that will inform the debate in the future. All serious followers of comparable worth would be well-advised to become familiar with, and to follow the progress of, this piece of Canadian legislation. It may well be the most important development to date in the area of comparable worth.

Endnotes

[1] "Job Protection Guarantees for Workers," *Congressional Quarterly*, June 14, 1986, p. 1361, and Samuelson, Robert J., "Uncle Sam in a Family Way," *Newsweek*, August 11, 1986, p. 40.

[2] Giraldo, Z.I., *Public Policy and the Family: Wives and Mothers in the Labor Force* (Lexington Books, DC: Heath and Company, 1990), p. 31.

[3] Mann, Judy, "Families Need These Bills," *The Washington Post*, July 3, 1987, p. D13.

[4] Patten, Thomas J., *Fair Pay* (San Francisco: Jossey-Bass, 1988), p. 31.

[5] Patten, *op. cit.*, pp. 40-41.

[6] 452 U.S. 161 (1981).

[7] 578 E Supp. 846 (WD. Wash. 1983), 770 E 2d 1401 (9th Cir., 1985).

[8] Hunter, E.C., *Equal Pay for Comparable Work: The Working Women's Issue of the Eighties*, (New York: Praeger, 1986).

[9] Patten, *op. cit.*, pp. 74-81.

[10] Patten, *op. cit.*, pp. 97-102.

[11] *Ontario Female Employees Fair Remuneration Act*, 1951.

[12] Abella, R.S., "Employment Equity," 16 *Manitoba Law Journal* 187 (1987).

[13] Statistics Canada, unpublished data from *Survey of Consumer Finances*, 1983, cited in Abella, *op. cit.*, note 12, p. 186.

[14] Gunderson and Morley, "Work Patterns," *Opportunity For Choice: A Goal For Women in Canada*, ed. A. Cook (Ottawa: Statistics Canada, 1988), p. 120.

[15] Abella, *op. cit.*, p. 189. See Nieman, L., *Wage Discrimination and Women Workers: The Move Toward Equal Pay for Equal Value in Canada*, Bureau Series A: *Equity in the Workplace*, No. 5 (Ottawa: Labour Canada, Women's Bureau, 1984).

[16] *Ontario Employment Standards Act*, 1981, Part IX.

[17] Ontario, *Green Paper on Pay Equity*, (Toronto: Queen's Printer, 1985).

[18] Pay Equity Commission, *Pay Equity Implementation*, Series 3:1, March, 1988.

[19] Discussed by the Assistant Deputy Minister of the Ontario Women's Directorate in Todres, E.M., "With Deliberate Care: The Framing of Bill 154," 16 *Manitoba Law Journal* 202 (1987).

State And Local Public Employee Labor Relations

Introduction

State and local public employees today constitute one of the fastest growing groups in the American labor movement. While unionization grew dramatically in the private sector during the late 1930s and early 1940s, much slower growth followed in the state and local government sectors. The last two decades have been the period of the most rapid growth in the latter two sectors, primarily for the following reasons:

1. The expanding demand for public service has resulted in a dramatic increase in public employment.
2. Public employees began to question their exclusion from the protections afforded private employees by the National Labor Relations Act.
3. A younger, more militant influx of personnel sought to mobilize the public sector to realize the same benefits afforded public sector employees in other countries and private sector employees in this country.
4. The traditional grants of prevailing wages extended to government employed construction workers and others under the federal and state Davis-Bacon type laws stirred the desire of non-covered public employees to achieve wages and working conditions matching those in the private sector.
5. The granting of limited collective bargaining rights to federal employees was interpreted by state and local government employees as a mandate for protesting the historical denial of such rights on the state and local level.
6. The demonstrated success of initial illegal strikes became powerful proof that the power to strike was of far greater relevance than the right to strike. As long as some employees obtained improvements from the strike, others recognized it as a useful vehicle for their protest as well.[1]

Because of their decreasing membership, one objective identified by national unions has been the extension of union membership into the public service. To date, too little attention has been given by the citizenry and elected representatives in our government to public employee unionization. The complexity and magnitude, diversity and size of public employment has frustrated the citizen's understanding of labor relations in the public sector. One reason why it took so long for union activity in the public sector to gain a foothold was the historic tendency of American citizens to believe that the government, as sovereign, could not negotiate with its own employees.

These citizens also believed that the civil service system was equitable in its compensation system, projecting as part of its image to both the employee and the public the assurance of equal employment opportunity and merit promotion. The civil service concept also placed heavy emphasis on the individual and on the rights and benefits of the individual and not on group action or decision. Additionally, there was a belief for many years that an incompatibility existed between collective bargaining and the civil service concept. This belief held that standards of individual merit would clash with collective bargaining and membership practices of the union.

The new presence of labor organizations within the state and local public sector is going to mean considerable loss of legislative control over budgets, tax rates and other government programs and projects. Yet the fact remains that public employees are using labor organizations to realize an increasing degree of success in achieving their demands. Without legislation, some organized public employees (fire fighters, police officers, school teachers, etc.) have been able to achieve formal, highly effective bargaining conditions with public officials, and legislation has just trailed along to give official approval to current practice.[2]

Public Employee Unions

Public employee organizations are of several types (See Table 1). Some have exclusively public employees and some have a membership that includes employees in private industry. Among these "mixed unions" are the Service Employees International Union (SEIU), the Laborers' International Union, the International Brotherhood of Teamsters, and 25 others.[3]

The American Federation of State, County, and Municipal Employees (AFSCME) is the fastest growing and most influential union in the municipal service with approximately 750,000 dues-paying members and a representation that includes approximately 1.5 million workers. AFSCME evolved out of the Wisconsin State Administration Association in 1932 with a membership of less than 100. Under the leadership of its founder, Dr. Arnold Zander, it affiliated with the American Federation of Government Employees (AFGE) and extended AFGE's jurisdiction to include state, county and municipal employees. This affiliation was to be a brief one, however. AFSCME was granted its own charter by the AFL in 1936, and by 1950 it had a membership of 68,000. Organized into locals, usually grouped into larger district councils, AFSCME primarily operates on the municipal level, giving extensive autonomy to its locals.

During the first decade of its existence, AFSCME stressed support of the merit system and civil service legislation, relying heavily on lobbying to achieve its goals. But with the assumption of leadership by Jerry Wurf in 1964 (after a bitterly contested election), AFSCME questioned the adequacy of merit systems, proclaimed its right to strike, and escalated both its political and collective bargaining roles. Within two years of Wurf's election, membership had risen by 50,000 and there was growing militancy among the organization's members. In July 1966, AFSCME got an important collective bargaining law passed in Wisconsin which affirmed the right of public employees, except law enforcement officers, to strike. In 1968, the union played an important role in the Memphis, Tennessee, sanitation workers' strike. In 1971, Wurf was elected to a position on the AFL-CIO Executive Council, giving increased significance to AFSCME's growth and also recognition to the importance of public employee unions.[4] Today AFSCME is the second largest union in the AFL-CIO.

In the field of public education, the most important unions today are the American Federation of Teachers (AFT), the United Federation of Teachers (UFT), and the National Education Association (NEA).

Early teacher strikes were mainly over economic issues and were evidence of the great discontent among teachers over the way they had been treated for years by city school administrators and Boards of Education. Among the early teacher unions were the Teachers' Union of New York City, founded in 1916 by a group of progressive teachers who believed that trade unionism was compatible with high professional standards. The first teachers' associations dealt mainly with professional problems, with very little concern given to the handling of complaints and grievances.

During the 1920s, communists infiltrated certain sectors of the labor movement, and Local No. 5 of the Teachers' Union in New York City (affiliate of AFT) became dominated by the communists. The noncommunists within the local organization split and formed the Teachers' Guild in New York City, replacing the Teachers' Union as the affiliate to the AFT. This new guild immediately began merging with other teacher organizations and in 1960 formed the United Federation of Teachers (UFT), the organization that represents most New York City teachers in bargaining today. Today UFT's interest is centered on such issues as teacher safety, pension rights, promotion, endorsements of local and state political candidates, higher wages, welfare and benefit packages, the length of workdays and lunch periods, the number of pupils assigned to different types of classes, and the conditions under which a teacher can transfer to another school.

The National Education Association has over one million members, 50 state affiliates, and approximately 8,000 local associations, with public school teachers constituting over three-fourths of its membership. The American Federation of Teachers, with over 200,000 members, is primarily a trade union for classroom teachers, excluding supervisory personnel from membership. AFT stresses the use of collective bargaining, including strikes, whereas NEA opposes these. This and other basic philosophical differences between AFT and NEA has led to keen competition between these two educational associations for members.[5]

The International Brotherhood of Teamsters (IBT) is a very strong competitor of the AFSCME. IBT has long been engaged in public employee organization as an independent industrial union, taking all classes of workers including clerks, sanitation workers, laborers, correction officers, sheriff's deputies, police officers, and fire fighters, as well as school principals, nurses, and physicians. The Teamsters' size (1.6 million) and powerful image have helped them attract many state and local employees. IBT has organized approximately 75,000 public blue-collar employees into 170 separate locals - 70 percent in towns, cities, or villages, 20 percent in special municipal authorities, and 10 percent in state-wide units.

The Laborers' International Union was established in 1903. Like the Teamsters, it organizes all types and classes of workers but concentrates mostly on blue-collar workers and is also competitive with AFSCME for state and local members.

The Service Employees' International Union is an AFL-CIO affiliate which organizes both public and private sector workers. It has 600,000 members, approximately 160,000 of which are public employees - mostly maintenance, upkeep, cleaning, and service workers.

An example of the independent associations involved in public sector organizing are the numerous Civil Service Employees Associations (CSEA) which exist in some 37 states, with memberships ranging from a few hundred in Florida to 170,000 in New York (where CSEA was founded in 1910). These associations stress their independence and claim they have freedom of action without interference or supervision from an international union. Most of these associations admit supervisory/management officials into membership and are regarded by the affiliated public service labor unions as "company unions." Most of these types of state and local associations are now members of a loose confederation called the Assembly of Government Employees (AGE).

Professional unions and associations are also an important factor in the public sector. An example of this type of organization is the International Association of Fire Fighters (IAFF), which includes in its membership over 90 percent of the nation's uniformed fire fighters.

Another example of professional associations in the public sector is police labor organizations. In recent years, we have witnessed a marked increase in police unionization through employee organizations or labor union affiliations. Police officers have organized to achieve economic improvements and resolve job-related problems. Police unions have concentrated on issues such as increased wages, shorter hours, uniform allowances, roll-call pay, premium pay for overtime, health and welfare plans, and other improvements in the terms and conditions of employment. Parity between police officers' and fire fighters' wages has also become a principal issue in police bargaining. At present, the largest police unions are the Fraternal Order of Police, the International Brotherhood of Police Officers, and the International Conference of Police Associations, which serves as the Washington, D.C., representative of local police organizations.[6]

Union Security

Most state laws grant public employees the right to join or not join a union. As a result, union security provisions that would require an employee to belong to a union (union shop, modified union shop, etc.) as a condition of employment are generally not permitted. Recently, however, the U. S. Supreme Court gave agency shops in the public sector a boost when it upheld the right of government employee unions to require non-union employees to pay a fee to defray the costs of union representation and contract enforcement. Negotiation of union or agency shops is now authorized in 15 states. In the eight states below, these laws apply to both state and local employees:

Alaska	Montana
Hawaii	Oregon
Massachusetts	Washington
Minnesota	Wisconsin

The Connecticut and Rhode Island laws cover only state employees, and the Michigan and Vermont laws cover only local employees. A Kentucky law is limited to fire fighters, while a California law applies only to school employees, and a Maine law applies only to university employees.[7]

Municipalities have been the pacesetters on questions of union security. In 1984, 30 percent of AFSCME's agreements contained union security provisions, while four years later, the figure had risen to 40 percent. By 1994, AFSCME had negotiated approximately 1,100 agreements. Forty-two percent had union security provisions. Twenty percent called for a union shop or modified union shop, 10 percent for maintenance of membership, 10 percent for an agency shop, and 90 percent for exclusive recognition.

The most widespread and least controversial union security provision is the dues check-off. In 1992, AFSCME reported that a check-off of employees' dues had been authorized in 38 states and that more than 80 percent of AFSCME members paid their dues in this manner. Since this time, additional states and municipal jurisdictions have either legally authorized the check-off or permitted it in practice. From 1992 to 1995, 16 states enacted statutes granting check-off to recognized or certified employee organizations.

New York's Taylor Law granted the check-off but provided that it could be suspended for up to 18 months if unions struck in violation of the statute. The impact of this provision was apparent in the 1987 strike of the New York City UFT. The union resorted to a private computer service to bill teachers directly when the check-off was suspended, and the estimated cost to the union for the first 8 months of operation was $500,000.

The check-off has several advantages for public (as well as private) employee organizations:

1. it insures a steady income on a year-round basis;
2. it provides for collection of dues from employees without pressure, coercion or resentment;

3. it eliminates the much larger expense of direct collection by the union itself;
4. it reduces the likelihood of membership withdrawal; and
5. union stewards are given more time for other more important union activities.

While the union shop is favored by most public employee unions, the chief legal barrier to its implementation in public employment is the traditional concept of unrestricted employment in the public service sector. However, modified union shop agreements have been negotiated with municipal governments. Philadelphia's modified union shop agreement with AFSCME District Council No. 33 covers approximately 20,000 of the city's 30,000 employees. An AFSCME affiliate in Hartford, Connecticut, negotiated in 1994 for a union shop clause for labor and trades employees. Modified union shops exist in locations such as Lansing, Michigan; Paducah, Kentucky; and Vernon, Connecticut.

Because of the resistance, legal and political, to the union shop in the public sector, many unions have concentrated on the agency shop concept in which a worker must pay either dues or a fee for union services but need not join the union. The advantages of the agency shop to unions are many. It eliminates "free riders," the union's financial position is strengthened, and an overall increase in union security is gained. There is also an increased incentive for non-members to join the union, since they already are paying a fee and are thus more likely to develop an interest in the organization's activities.

Opponents of the agency shop in the public sector say that it introduces new, non-merit factors into the employment process.[8] Here again one hears the previously stated argument that public employees do not need the same protection and benefits characteristically accorded unions in the private sector. Whether one agrees or disagrees with this contention, the fact is that the agency shop is becoming a more prevalent form of security for state and local employee labor organizations.

Collective Bargaining

Collective bargaining at the state and local level is at the same stage of development that collective bargaining was in the private sector in the late 1930s and the federal sector in the early 1960s. Like the private and federal sectors then, the state and local level is beset today with a growing militancy and a considerable uncertainty over the future. It is the author's opinion that the path travelled by state and local employees in this area will closely parallel that travelled by their private and federal counterparts previously. Many similar trends are already evident. Virtually all of the state statutes provide that public employees have the right to join unions and bargain collectively, yet some have no unfair labor practice provisions nor do they have established administrative machinery to implement the rights granted such employees. The determination of the appropriate bargaining unit is made by the agency that administers the comprehensive state acts (in each state), in accordance with criteria set forth in the statute or in the rules and regulations set up by that administering agency. If one reviews the history of private and federal unions in this area, they will find that a similar state of affairs existed when those sectors were at a stage of development similar to state and local employee unions today.

The scope of bargaining in the public sector is not as broad as in the private sector. In the public sector most state statutes provide that the parties negotiate in good faith "with respect to grievance procedures and conditions of employment," whereas under the NLRA, private employers and unions are required to bargain in good faith with respect to "wages, hours, and other terms and conditions of employment."

Collective bargaining in the public sector has been recently expanded to include mandatory subjects (wages, hours, fringe benefits), voluntary subjects (joint employer-union recommendations to amend or change civil service or educational laws, promotional opportunities, and/or other personnel changes), and prohibited subjects (such as union shop provisions and members-only contracts providing benefits for only members of the union).

Virtually all of the state legislation concerning public employees establishes procedures to resolve collective bargaining disputes. The most prevalent provides for mediation, followed by fact-finding with non-binding recommendations. This approach has been adopted by at least 12 states, including Connecticut, Michigan, New Jersey, New York, and Wisconsin. Additionally, despite the considerable resistance to compulsory arbitration for resolving disputes, an increasing number of states have enacted compulsory arbitration statutes, especially for employees who provide essential services, e.g., police and fire fighters. Four states (Pennsylvania, Michigan, Rhode Island, and South Dakota) provide for compulsory arbitration of interest disputes (i.e., disputes over what the basic agreement should contain) for both fire fighters and police officers. Vermont and Wyoming have similar legislation covering only fire fighters.

There are now 20 states which meet the AFSCME's criteria of a "comprehensive broad scope law which mandates collective bargaining of wages, hours, and conditions of employment for state and local government workers." These are Alaska, Connecticut, Delaware, Florida, Hawaii, Iowa, Maine, Massachusetts, Minnesota, Montana, Nebraska, New Hampshire, New Jersey, New York, Oregon, Pennsylvania, Rhode Island, South Dakota, Vermont, and Wisconsin. Washington allows a limited form of collective bargaining for state employees. Michigan, Nevada and Washington have mandatory, comprehensive collective-bargaining laws for local employees. California and Kansas have mandatory meet-and-confer laws covering state and local government employees. In addition, many states have statutes which apply to certain employees, such as teachers or police.[9]

Strikes

The strike issue is probably the most controversial, urgent and misunderstood problem of labor relations in the public sector. Generally, strikes by public employees have been considered to be illegal by common law. At present, only four states (Alaska, Hawaii, Illinois and Pennsylvania) allow strikes by public employees, while an additional four (Minnesota, Montana, Oregon and Vermont) have granted a limited right to strike.

The author would raise the question as to whether it is sound public policy to guarantee workers the right to strike in the most vital sectors of private industry yet deny that same right to all public employees regardless of the importance of their function or the impact the stoppage might have on the public. Is it not possible that strikes by certain categories of state and local employees could be tolerated, while acceptable alternatives to a strike (similar to the Emergency Provisions of Taft-Hartley for the private sector or the Federal Service Impasse Panel for the federal sector) could be found for those employees not in these categories? The author realizes that if the states lift their ban on strikes by public employees and no such alternative is provided, the public cannot be protected when such strikes interrupt services vital to their health, safety and welfare. Thus, some neutral agency must be formed as the final authority when a strike threatens a sector whose services are continuously needed (police, prison guards, etc.). Under existing, all-encompassing legal bans, public employees have no realistic protection against an arbitrary employer who uses sovereign rights to implement personnel policies unilaterally or paternalistically. Anyone who would argue, as stated earlier, that their protection is the public service system itself, with its stated assurance of an equitable reward system based on merit, is totally ignoring the facts of the last twenty years.

It is obvious from past experience that without the right to strike these employees have no way to pressure officials to negotiate in good faith. Thus, strikes could and should be permitted for certain employees, e.g., those who perform a service that could be interrupted for a limited period of time and those performing functions with which the community could continue for an extended period of time without serious effects - (not all public employees perform essential services).

Regardless of the prohibitions on striking, the number of strikes by public employees continues to increase every year. The new militancy of professional and other specialized workers, one of the most notable developments in local government labor relations, is the biggest single contributory factor. During the last few years, virtually every municipal service has suffered strikes. Public school teachers led the way with a variety of strikes, ranging from a one-teacher school in Maine to a massive statewide strike conducted by Florida teachers of the NEA and UFT. Sanitation workers, with almost 200 recent strikes, have followed the educational workers lead. Other instances, too numerous to mention here, provide ample proof that strikes by state and local employees are here to stay.

Conclusion

The basic question facing state and local public employee unions is whether or not labor relations in this sector should be patterned after those in the federal or even the private sector. With each new state or municipal regulation, with each new "job action" by public employees, with each self-approved change in the bylaws of a public employee union, this question is being answered. Indeed, present trends make the answer clear. Labor relations at the state and local level are being patterned after those of the federal sector, which in turn (with a 40 to 50-year time lag) are being patterned after those in the private sector. Any serious student of labor relations who carefully examines the historic (in the private) and present (in the federal, state, and local) trends and makes a rational comparison can arrive at only one conclusion. All three groups are headed down the same path, although they are at different points along the way. The reader is urged to analyze any of the areas discussed in this article -

the right to organize, strikes, dispute settlement, etc. - and see if this is not the case.

Whether such an occurrence is good or bad is a value judgment each reader must make individually, but the fact that it is indeed the case cannot be denied.

Table 1

List of Employee Organizations With Public Sector Members

AFGE	- American Federation of Government Employees
AFSCME	- American Federation of State, County and Municipal Employees
AFT	- American Federation of Teachers
AGE	- Assembly of Government Employees
ANA	- American Nursing Association
CSEA	- Civil Service Employees' Association
FOP	- Fraternal Order of Police
IBPO	- International Brotherhood of Police Officers
IAFF	- International Association of Fire Fighters
IBT	- International Brotherhood of Teamsters
ICPA	- International Conference of Police Associations
IUOE	- International Union of Operating Engineers
LIU	- Laborers' International Union
NEA	- National Education Association
NFFE	- National Federation of Federal Employees
PBA	- Patrolmen's Benevolent Association
SCMWA	- State, County and Municipal Workers of America
SEIU	- Service Employees' International Union
SSEU	- Social Services Employees' Union
TWU	- Transport Workers' Union
UAW	- United Automobile Workers
UFA	- Uniformed Firefighters' Association
UFOA	- Uniformed Fire Officers' Association
UFT	- United Federation of Teachers
UPWA	- United Public Workers of America

Table 2

Full-Time State Employees
Who Belong to Employee Organizations*

Rank by % of all full-time state employees	Members
1. Hawaii	25,379
2. Rhode Island	13,569
3. Alaska	9,661
4. Pennsylvania	91,175
5. Maine	11,151
6. Connecticut	25,778
7. New York	119,012
8. Vermont	5,444
9. California	114,134
10. Minnesota	25,827
11. Oregon	15,780
12. Michigan	53,760
13. Montana	7,063
14. Wisconsin	23,336
15. New Jersey	31,939
16. New Hampshire	5,531
17. Massachusetts	30,624
18. Delaware	6,210
19. North Carolina	52,691
20. Idaho	5,864
21. Illinois	44,585
22. Nevada	3,841
23. Washington	23,291
24. Maryland	26,668
25. Ohio	34,620

Table 2

Full-Time State Employees
Who Belong to Employee Organizations*

Rank by % of all full-time state employees	Members
26. South Dakota	3,830
27. Colorado	14,413
28. Utah	8,907
29. Wyoming	2,532
30. Arizona	9,746
31. Alabama	16,506
32. Indiana	17,202
33. Virginia	23,508
34. South Carolina	13,490
35. Iowa	6,154
36. Texas	32,784
37. Missouri	11,563
38. Louisiana	12,829
39. South Dakota	2,085
40. New Mexico	3,674
41. Kansas	5,010
42. Arkansas	3,674
43. Nebraska	2,729
44. Georgia	7,151
45. Kentucky	5,248
46. Tennessee	5,199
47. Oklahoma	1,663
48. West Virginia	1,130
49. Mississippi	940
50. Florida	530

*Source: Bureau of the Census, U.S. Department of Commerce.

Endnotes

[1] Zagoria, Sam, ed., *Public Workers and Public Unions*, (Englewood Cliffs, NJ: Prentice-Hall, Inc., 1992), pp. 101-102.

[2] Marx, Herbert L., Jr., ed., *Collective Bargaining for Public Employees*, (H. W. Wilson Co., 1989,) Vol. 41, No. 5, pp. 1-23.

[3] *The Municipal Yearbook 1994*, The International City Management Association, 1994, p. 162.

[4] Billings, Richard N., and Greenya, John, *Power to the Public Worker*, (Washington - New York: FACT Research, Inc.), 1974, pp. 1-21.

[5] Taft, Philip, *United They Teach - The Story of the United Federation of Teachers*, (Los Angeles, CA: Nash Publishing, 1984), p. 26.

[6] *The Municipal Yearbook 1994, op. cit.*, pp. 162- 163.

[7] *State Government News*, The Council of State Governments, Washington, D.C., October 1994, p. 6.

[8] Capozzola, John M. and Spero, Sterling D., *The Urban Community and Its Unionized Bureaucracies - Pressure Politics in Local Government Labor Relations*, (New York: Dunellen Publishing Co., Inc., 1973), pp. 150-157.

[9] *State Government News, op. cit.*, pp. 2, 6.

Federal Employee Unionism: An Overview

ABSTRACT

An overview of the history, current status and trends in federal employee unionism, and the laws relating to bargaining in the federal service are presented.

Introduction

The field of public employment is today's new frontier in the realm of labor-management relations. *Business Week* has characterized the tremendous potential of this field as the real "growth stock" of the trade-union movement. But as recently as the 1950s, the subject of labor relations in public employment could not have meant less to more people - both in and out of government. It was a time in which public employees at all levels were excluded from the protection of our national and state labor relations laws. The reason for this is not clear. The United States Supreme Court and a New York court have ventured the following explanations:

1. public employees were so well taken care of by the governmental parent they served that they did not need to band together to achieve better working conditions; and,
2. collective bargaining was not shown to be as necessary in public employment as it was in private industry.[1]

These explanations no longer hold true. The past few years have brought changes at a rapidly accelerating pace. Louder and more persistent employee demands, increased employee organization and better employee leadership, public awakening and governmental enlightenment, social contagion, and perhaps even political expediency have all played their part in fostering and shaping new relationships.

Progress in the federal field has been marked by two separate phases. The first made fundamental policy and provided machinery for the enforcement of this policy, i.e., officially defining the rights of public employees and how those rights would be enjoyed. In the second phase, government assumed the direct role of employer. It applied its new policy to itself by attempting to establish and maintain what is, in essence, a collective bargaining relationship between itself and its own employees.

Legal Framework for Federal Employee Unionism

In the late 1800s, the Post Office became the most heavily organized of all the government agencies. With this growth came an increase in the activities in which the unions engaged, particularly the "lobbying" or petitioning of Congressional members on behalf of security and better working conditions for union members. The petitioning of Congress was necessary because the Pendleton Act, passed in 1883, gave Congress the right to regulate federal employees wages, hours, working conditions, and other terms of employment. This lobbying activity, which was to become the hallmark of federal employee unionism for decades to come, was the cause of a series of "gag orders" issued by President Theodore Roosevelt in 1902 and made more restrictive by President Taft in 1909. These orders followed closely an order issued by Postmaster General Wilson in 1895 forbidding postal employees from visiting Washington, D.C., for the purpose of influencing legislation.[2]

It was through the culmination of a successful protest campaign against the restrictive and constitutionally questionable provisions of these gag orders that the Lloyd-LaFollette Act was passed in 1912. This act gave federal employees the right to petition and to furnish information to Congress. It gave postal employees the right to belong to employee organizations for the improvement of working conditions and the right to petition Congress. This was all provided such organizations did not assist in or impose upon their members an obligation to strike against the government.[3] By implication, this right to organize was interpreted by the workers as applying to all federal employees and led to the formation in 1917 of the National Federation of Federal Employees and in 1932 to the American Federation of Government Employees - two of the major federal unions existing today.

In 1947, the second piece of important legislation affecting federal employee labor relations was passed. The Taft-Hartley Act, although excluding the federal government as an employer from the provisions of the act (as did the Wagner Act of 1935), laid down a strong anti-strike policy providing for mandatory loss of job and civil service status regarding federal employees.

The 1950s were marked by frequent and sometimes bitter clashes between government and union leaders - particularly the postal unions and the Eisenhower Administration. In 1955, Public Law 330 was passed and superseded Section 305 of the Taft-Hartley Act. It made striking against the government a felony punishable by fine and imprisonment and provided that anyone thus striking could not "accept" or "hold" any position in the federal government.

Also during this time, the American Federation of Labor repeatedly attempted to introduce a bill into Congress that would have provided for union recognition, consultation, binding arbitration, and union grievance handling for federal employees. This bill never attained either administrative support or a congressional majority. It did, however, cause President Kennedy, early in 1961, to appoint a task force on Employee-Management Relations in the Federal Service, chaired by Labor Secretary Arthur Goldberg and including Postmaster General Day, Civil Service Chairman Macy, Defense Secretary Robert McNamara, Budget Director Bell, and White House Counsel Theodore Sorensen. The task force report noted that although 33 percent of all federal employees belonged to national employee organizations, membership varied greatly among agencies. It also stated that there existed within the executive branch no general policy on employee-management relations, and that the result was wide variation among agencies in their dealings with employee organizations.

The main recommendations of the task force report submitted in November 1961 were incorporated into Executive Order 10988 issued by President Kennedy on January 7, 1962. The main provisions of this Executive Order are listed below:

1. Federal employees were granted the right to form, join, and assist any employee organization or to refrain from such activity. No union or closed shop provisions were permitted.
2. Three types of union recognition were established for the first time, based upon the extent of employee membership within an appropriate unit. Informal (less than 10 percent membership with the right to present petitions to be heard), formal (at least 10 percent membership, but less than 50 percent, with right to be consulted, and exclusive (at least 10 percent membership, and

designated by the majority of employees in a unit as a representative for all, with the right to bargain collectively.

3. Management officials were required to grant appropriate recognition, to meet and negotiate at reasonable times, and if an agreement was reached, to execute a written contract.
4. Exclusive unions had to represent everyone in the bargaining unit.
5. A strong management-rights clause was included giving agency officials the right, without any negotiating requirement, to direct employees; to hire, fire, promote, suspend, assign, and demote employees; to relieve them from duty for lack of work; to determine methods, means, and personnel by which operations were to be conducted; and to take whatever action was necessary in emergency situations.
6. Privileges of the order were not to be extended to any organization that asserted the right to strike against the government, advocated its overthrow, or discriminated in membership on racial or religious grounds.
7. Impasses of negotiable issues, i.e., working conditions, promotion standards, apprenticeships, training, job classification, and safety, were to be settled by means short of arbitration.
8. Establishment of a negotiated grievance procedure was authorized, with provisions for advisory arbitration of grievances, as well as disputes relating to interpretation and application of agreements.
9. No unit for bargaining purposes could be established that included both managerial and supervisory, as well as rank-and-file employees, in the same units. Advisory arbitration for unit determinations and representation disputes was authorized.
10. The head of the government agency had to approve each local agreement.[4]

In May 1963, President Kennedy further supplemented E. O. 10988 with the issuance of a "Standards of Conduct for Employee Organizations" and a "Code of Fair Labor Practices." The standards called generally for the maintenance by employee organizations of certain democratic internal procedures, equal treatment of members, periodic elections, and due process. The code prohibited both management and labor from engaging in specified practices that tended to thwart free choice of individuals in the determination and selection of employee unions to which they might wish to belong (similar to unfair labor practices of other federal labor laws).

Significantly, it also prohibited employee organizations from calling or engaging in work stoppages, slowdowns, or related picketing which was engaged in as a substitute for such activities.

Also in 1963, the Comptroller General issued a ruling in response to a request from the administration that enabled the Civil Service Commission to issue regulations authorizing the voluntary withholding of dues for employee organizations under a check-off arrangement, the administrative cost of which was to be defrayed by a small service charge.

Despite the acknowledged success of E. O. 10988 in promoting union membership and collective bargaining, employee organizations voiced criticism of it in five major areas.

The first was the bargaining impasse. Critics suggested that there was a greater need to develop mediation and fact-finding procedures and also to expedite referrals to higher authority within a governmental agency.

The second area of criticism was the scope of mediation. Some employee organizations had been against the use of mediation and advisory arbitration provisions to determine grievances and to deal with adverse actions by the agencies (an adverse action being an action in violation of the Code of Fair Labor Practices). These organizations wanted such issues decided solely by the two parties without outside intervention.

The third area of criticism was agency review and delegation of authority. The unions complained that agency heads were overly restrictive in delegating sufficient local authority to permit meaningful negotiations.

The fourth area was lack of binding arbitration of adverse actions. The unions complained that the use of federal agency hearing officers to determine alleged violations of unfair labor practices was in itself unfair, for agencies would not be objective in evaluating their own compliance, and the tendency would be to approve the actions of supervisors.

The fifth area was the scope of collective bargaining. Despite necessary limitations on issues subject to negotiations, unions felt there was far more room for bargaining than most agencies permitted. Obviously, the fifth and second problem areas were closely related.

Shortly after his inauguration in 1968, President Nixon appointed a study committee under the leadership of Civil Service Chairman Hampton to conduct an extensive review and evaluation of these criticisms and of the overall federal labor relations program. This study determined that E. O. 10988 had produced some excellent results but that several important changes were needed. These changes were made by President Nixon in October 1969 in Executive Order 11491. Major provisions included:

1. Establishing a Federal Labor Relations Council, consisting of the Secretary of Labor, an official of the Executive Office, and the Chairman of the Civil Service Commission, responsible for administering the order, deciding major policy issues, prescribing regulations, and entertaining appeals.
2. Prohibiting supervisors from acting as union officers or representatives.
3. Establishing a Federal Service Impasse Panel of three members to assist in resolving, or to actually resolve, negotiation impasses.
4. Giving the Assistant Secretary of Labor for Labor-Management Relations the authority to decide "administrative" disputes and to order and supervise elections.
5. Establishing a separate system for consultation with associations of supervisors.
6. Eliminating informal and formal recognition.
7. According exclusive recognition only on the basis of secret ballot elections.
8. Adding rules for settling disputes on negotiable issues.
9. Prohibiting union shop, agency shop, and maintenance of membership clauses.
10. Permitting a single negotiated grievance system, eliminating advisory arbitration, and substituting binding arbitration on a cost-sharing basis.
11. Limiting agency headquarters' authority to disapprove locally negotiated agreements.
12. Authorizing full Federal Mediation and Conciliation Service participation to assist parties.
13. Adding financial reporting and disclosure requirements for unions and transferring enforcement responsibility in this area from agencies to the Assistant Secretary of Labor.
14. Making it an unfair labor practice for a labor organization to punish a member for his work performance, to condone a strike or prohibited picketing by failing to take "affirmative action" to stop or prevent it, or to refuse to consult or bargain as required.
15. Authorizing managerial and supervisory organizations to participate in voluntary dues withholding.
16. Continuing to exclude from bargaining wages, hours and terms of employment.

E. O. 11491 also contained a provision that required the establishment of a panel to study the effects of the order. The changes found by this panel to be needed were incorporated into E. O. 11616. These changes included:

1. Professional employees were allowed to join regular employee unions.
2. Responsibility for enforcement in code and unfair labor practice cases was transferred from agency heads to the Assistant Secretary of Labor for Labor-Management Relations.
3. A grievance procedure was required to be included in each agreement.
4. The agency requirement to cover its expenses in check-off provisions was changed to a negotiable issue.[5]

These executive orders were, however, still inadequate to meet the demands for full-scale collective bargaining by postal employees, and a strike involving some 200,000 postal employees occurred in 1970. As a result of that strike, the executive branch engaged in direct collective bargaining with heads of the major postal organizations and ultimately reached agreement on wage increases, wage progression schedules, fringe benefits, and endorsement of the Postal Reform Act. Congress confirmed the bargaining decisions reached, which included arbitration of contract terms as a substitute for the prohibited right to strike and arbitration of interest disputes and grievances. This postal law is still in effect and is based on private sector principles set forth in the Wagner Act.

The Unions Themselves

Contrary to popular knowledge, public employee unionism has a very long and honorable tradition within the federal government dating back to the early 1800s with craftsmen in the Navy shipyards, to the 1860s with workers in the Government Printing Office, and to the latter third of the nineteenth century with letter carriers in the Post Office Department. Historically, three major classifications of unions have existed in federal employment:

1. unions organizing solely in the post office;

2. unions composed primarily of employees in private employment but also organizing blue-collar workers in federal employment; and,
3. unions restricting their membership to federal employees but not those employed by the post office.

Beginning with the earliest postal union when the letter carriers in New York City organized in 1863, unions in the postal service have continuously grown. Today there are about a dozen, with the American Postal Workers' Union (membership 360,000) and the National Association of Letter Carriers (membership 224,000) as the two largest.

Blue-collar unions currently affiliated with the AFL-CIO Metal Trades Department have a long history of organization in federal employment dating back to the 1830s in the Navy yards. These unions presently have the bulk of their membership in the Department of Defense, and Metal Trades Council representation is presently 58,629. Total blue-collar coverage is now over 400,000.

The first of the unions that restricted their membership solely to federal employment - excluding postal employees - was the National Federation of Federal Employees (NFFE). Jurisdiction over federal employees not covered by any craft unions was given to the NFFE in 1917 by the American Federation of Labor (AFL). In 1931 the AFL, at the instigation of craft unions having members in federal employment, went on record opposing the report of the U. S. Personnel Classification Board because the board had recommended the extension of the classification principles to all federal employees including the skilled crafts. NFFE, which strongly favored the classification principle for federal white-collar employees, left the AFL in protest over the fact that they were not consulted concerning the AFL's position on this issue. To cover this jurisdiction, the American Federation of Government Employees (AFGE) was chartered by the AFL on August 18, 1932, with about two thousand former members of the original NFFE in thirty-nine lodges. For many years the NFFE was by far the larger of the two unions, but, partially as a result of its isolation, the NFFE has now dwindled in size and is presently the representative of 136,071 federal employees.[6]

By the mid-1960s, the AFGE had grown into the largest of the unions representing federal workers, and today it represents over 670,000 federal employees. The AFGE's growth was aided by the jurisdiction allotted them in their charter by the AFL, which includes all civilian employees of the United States government and the District of Columbia, excepting those over whom jurisdiction has been granted to other national or international unions by the AFL-CIO.

Along with wide jurisdiction for the AFGE came jurisdictional disputes with other AFL-CIO unions. The most significant involved the AFL-CIO's Metal Trades Department and the International Association of Machinists. These disputes arose, in large part, from the organizing techniques used by the unions. The AFGE was classified as an industrial union belonging to the AFL-CIO's Industrial Union Department. However, organizing did not take place on strictly industrial lines. Rather, a free form of organization developed whereby the union issued charters to virtually any unaffiliated group that showed a willingness to belong to the organization. In other words, craft or industrial locals were formed on the basis of the wishes of those applying for charters. The union, however, was industrial in the sense that all workers within the general jurisdiction outlined above were accepted for membership, not just those in a particular craft.

The area in which the AFGE differs most drastically from other AFL-CIO public employee unions is strategy and tactics. It is generally believed that public employee unions have two basic weapons at their disposal. These are passage of legislative acts improving the circumstances of employment and direct collective bargaining. The AFGE Constitution emphasizes legislative action. Article 11, Objectives and Methods, Section 2, states that "the Federation shall strive to promote efficiency in the governmental service, and shall advance plans of improvement to be secured by legislative enactment through cooperation with governmental officials and other lawful means."

In 1973 the AFL-CIO executive council recognized the growing importance of public employee unionism by creating the Public Employee Department. The two million member department, which is equivalent to the AFL-CIO's Industrial Union Department, Building and Construction Trades Department, and eight similar bodies, is made up of 24 unions with public employee membership. Its major roles are to serve as lobbying and collective bargaining agent and to persuade people on government payrolls that unionization is the wave of the future.[7]

Virtually all federal employees have their pay determined by congressional action. Similarly, Congress has jurisdiction over basic employee benefits such as annual and sick leave, insurance, and employer contributions to health and welfare plans. Until Congress relinquishes authority over these areas, the best way that unions representing federal employees can secure increased pay and improved benefits is to use legislative tactics.

Union Growth

Just as employee-management relations in private industry were revolutionized some sixty years ago, employee-management relations in the federal sector underwent drastic changes in the 1960s - changes that are continuing today. One such change is the tremendous growth in representation of federal employees by unions. In the last five years, agreements have been negotiated in 227 additional recognition units. Overall, 2,704 units (75%) are now covered by agreements. Employees covered by negotiated agreements are at a record level of 1,083,017, encompassing 90 percent of all employees under exclusive recognition. Of the entire non-postal federal work force, 61 percent are presently covered by agreements. A total of 1,200,336 non-postal federal employees are represented by unions. When postal and non-postal data are combined, the total coverage under exclusive recognition becomes 1,799,340, or 68 percent of total federal employment (See Tables 1, 2, and 3).

Table 1

Total Federal Employees in Exclusive Units and Covered by Agreement, 1984-1994

	Total Employees in Exclusive Units		Employees Covered By Agreement	
Year	**Total**	**%**	**Number**	**%**
1984	230,543	12	110,573	6
1985	319,724	16	241,850	12
1986	434,890	21	291,532	14
1987	629,915	29	423,052	20
1988	797,511	40	556,962	28
1989	842,843	42	559,415	28
1990	916,381	48	601,505	31
1991	1,038,288	53	707,067	36
1992	1,082,587	55	753,247	39
1993	1,086,361	56	837,410	43
1994	1,142,419	57	984,553	49

Source: *Civil Service News*, Office of Personnel Management, Washington, D.C., 1995.

Table 2

Exclusive Recognitions and Agreements by Major Unions in Federal Sector, November 1994 (Excluding Postal Workers)

Union*	Recognition Units	Employees Represented	Units Under Agreement	Employees Covered	Percent Covered
AFGE	1,724	670,029	1,223	589,613	88
NFFE	690	136,071	521	116,465	86
NTEU	101	83,868	100	83,778	100
NAGE	333	77,878	236	72,134	93
MTC	51	58,629	49	58,560	100
IAM	96	32,859	90	32,193	98

*** Column definitions:**

AFGE - American Federation of Government Employees
NFFE - National Federation of Federal Employees
NTEU - National Treasury Employees' Union
NAGE - National Association of Government Employees
MTC - Metal Trades Council
IAM - International Association of Machinists

Source: *Civil Service News*, Office of Personnel Management, Washington, D.C., 1995.

Table 3

Growth in Exclusive Recognition, By Major Unions

	Number of Units			Employees Represented		
Union*	1994	1993	Change	1994	1993	Change
AFGE	1,724	1,627	+ 6	670,029	650,038	+ 3
NFFE	690	672	+ 3	136,071	125,234	+ 9
NTEU	101	89	+13	83,868	65,417	+28
NAGE	333	328	+ 2	77,878	74,127	+ 5
MTC	51	48	+ 6	58,629	58,366	--
IAM	96	94	+ 2	32,859	30,166	+ 9

*** Column definitions:**

AFGE - American Federation of Government Employees
NFFE - National Federation of Federal Employees
NTEU - National Treasury Employees' Union
NAGE - National Association of Government Employees
MTC - Metal Trades Council
IAM - International Association of Machinists

Source: *Civil Service News*, Office of Personnel Management, Washington, D.C., 1995.

Several conditions have led to the increased unionization of government employees. The substantial growth in federal employment made inevitable the emergence of a federal employee group consciousness that led to group organization. When many employees are working at the same kind of job, they are bound to be drawn together when disputes with management arise. Formal organization gave these employees a voice for expressing grievances and making demands.

Moreover, the growth of organized labor in the private sector during the 1950s and 1960s impacted on the federal sector. Employee organizations in the federal service are usually found in large cities and industrialized areas where industrial unions have flourished. This affords federal employees the opportunity to view firsthand the benefits of unionization for the individual employee in large organizations. In addition, the civil service system, originally conceived to protect federal employees from the spoils system, has tended to create hostility toward the federal administration among some employees. Those who cannot advance under the merit principle of promotion seek other means of improving income and maintaining their self-respect. Employee organizations furnish both a method of challenging the rules of advancement under the merit system and a route toward self-satisfaction when advancement is stymied.

But perhaps the most specific reason for the growth of government unionism is the executive orders issued by Presidents Kennedy and Nixon. E. O. 10988 issued by President Kennedy in 1962 was as clear and unequivocal in its support of federal unionism as the Wagner Act of 1935 had been in its support for unions and collective bargaining in the private sector. Executive Orders 11491 and 11616 issued by President Nixon took this one step further by favorably responding to most of labor's criticisms regarding E.O. 10988.

Summary

The advent of employee organizations and collective bargaining in the federal sector is the most significant development in the industrial relations field in the last forty years. In addition to the more obvious implications for employees, federal officials, and the art of government, it may have important effects on the labor movement and on labor- management relations in the private sector.

Trade union membership in the United States has not been keeping pace with the growth in the labor force, and union members as a percentage of the work force dropped from 22.7 percent in 1970 to 16.8

percent in 1995. This has been due largely to the relative employment decline in industries where unions have been strongest, and the failure of trade unions to appeal to the growing technical and white-collar segment of the labor force.

The opening of federal employment to trade unions may change this. Government employees could provide a source of enough new recruits to reverse the decline in trade union membership. Government employees who join unions could also change the image of the labor movement to make it more acceptable to white-collar employees and technicians in private industry.

But whatever the effects of federal unionism on these areas, the road ahead is not apt to provide smooth sailing. In the sense that federal employee unions are essentially political organizations, and they must be, given present legislation, they will interject into the daily routine of the federal official substantial and sometimes startling changes. The basic conclusion must be reached, though, that no defensible reason exists for denying to federal employees this right to self-organize and collectively bargain over a wider range of issues than is presently permitted. The formation of employee organizations flows from deep-seated human needs. They will continue to be formed, and they will grow stronger. As legislation, with a certain time lag, reflects public opinion and human necessity, it will sanction this growth. It is only a matter of time. Get used to it.

Endnotes

[1] Kruger, D. H., *Collective Bargaining in the Public Service*, (New York: Random House, 1969), pp. 10-11.

[2] Ulman, L., *Challenges to Collective Bargaining*, (Englewood Cliffs, NJ: Prentice-Hall, Inc., 1967), p. 69.

[3] Murphy, R. J., *The Crisis in Public Employee Relations in the Decade of the Seventies*, The Bureau of National Affairs, (Washington, DC, 1970), pp. 1-2.

[4] Kaye, S., *International Manual on Collective Bargaining for Public Employees* (New York: Praeger Publishers, 1973), pp. 16-19.

[5] Nelson, R. R., "Collective Bargaining Agreements in the Federal Service," *Monthly Labor Review*, November 1972, pp. 51-53.

[6] *Civil Service News*, Office of Personnel Management, Washington, D.C., February 18, 1993, p. 2.

[7] "Public Workers Test Their Clout," *Business Week*, November 16, 1994, p. 103.

Federal Sector Labor Relations: A Legal Perspective

The right of employees to bargain collectively has a long history in the United States. A part of this history has been the quest for collective bargaining by public employees, including those in the federal sector. It is only in recent history, however, that genuine progress has been made in bringing this part of the labor force into the American collective bargaining process.

The problem with collective bargaining by federal employees first appeared back in the 1830s during the presidency of Andrew Jackson. Government employees belonged to the same craft unions as private employees, and the government claimed no special status over them, resisting and yielding to union demands the same as any private firm. It was not until the late 1880s and 1890s when the postal workers began to organize that the government began to oppose labor activity in the federal sector.

The first executive action taken against organized postal employee activity came in 1885 with an order by Postmaster General William L. Wilson which forbade any (postal) employee under "pain of removal" from visiting Washington, whether on leave, with or without pay, for the purpose of influencing legislation before Congress.[1] During the Theodore Roosevelt administration, union activity by federal employees was considered to be an interference with executive authority and a violation of the political neutrality of the civil service. In his famous "gag" order issued on January 25, 1902, Roosevelt forbade federal employees from "either directly or indirectly, individually or through association, soliciting any increase in pay or the influence of any other legislation except through the head of the department."[2]

This major barrier to federal employee unionism was removed on August 24, 1912, with the passage of the Lloyd-LaFollette Act which outlawed the presidential "gag" orders and gave postal workers the right to lobby, to organize, and to affiliate with outside organizations. The Act did, however, impose an obligation not to strike against the government. Following passage of this act, it became more practical for the postal workers to join Samuel Gomper's American Federation of Labor (AFL), which they did as soon as Lloyd-LaFollette had been ruled legal by the courts. The act itself was not limited to postal employees but gave all employees of the civil service the right to collectively or individually "petition Congress or any member thereof" - a right which was not to be interfered with or denied. This piece of legislation, though not looked on with much favor by the executive branch, gave rise to the formation of a number of postal employee unions and remained the major piece of legislation dealing with federal labor-management relations until President Kennedy's Executive Order (E.O.) 10988 of 1962.

The Executive Orders

In 1961 approximately 33 percent of all federal employees were unionized,[3] yet the federal government still had no effective labor-management relations policy.

Prior to the passage of E. O. 10988, there had been growing criticism of the government's lack of direction and cohesiveness between federal management and employee organizations. Since 1912 and the Lloyd-LaFollette Act, numerous employee organizations had sprung up, and the various government agencies dealing with them had each developed their own labor relations policy.

Shortly after his inauguration in January 1961, President Kennedy appointed a task force headed by Secretary of Labor Arthur J. Goldberg to look into the question of labor-management relations in the federal service. The task force, which presented its report to the President in November 1961, concluded that "labor organizations were capable of contributing to the more effective conduct of the public business by insuring the positive participation of employees in the formulation and improvement of federal personnel policies and practices."[4] The task force also concluded that there were fundamental differences in employment conditions between the public and private sector, making it undesirable to pattern federal labor-management relations after those in private industry. While the task force agreed that important matters relating to federal employees fell within the jurisdiction of Congress, thus making it difficult to subject them to collective bargaining, it saw no conflict between its recommendation concerning the desirability of labor organizations and the Civil Service merit system.

The recommendations made by the task force were as follows:

1. Federal employees were to have the right to join or not to join *bona fide* employee organizations, and where there was sufficient desire

to do so, the government should express a willingness to enter into such relationships.

2. All organizations not discriminating against individuals because of race, color, creed, sex, or national origin, who were free of corruption, and who did not advocate strikes against the government or the overthrow of the government of the United States, were to be recognized. Such organizations were to be granted informal, formal, or exclusive recognition depending on the extent to which they represented a unit or activity within a government agency.

   Informal recognition was to be given to an organization whose membership was less than 10 percent of the employees in a unit or activity. In this case the organization had a right to be heard in matters pertaining to its members but placed an agency under no obligation to consult with that organization.

   Formal recognition was to be given to an organization whose membership comprised 10 to 50 percent of the employees in a unit or activity and where no organization had been given exclusive recognition. In this case, the agency had to consult with the organization in matters pertaining to its members.

   Exclusive recognition was to be given to organizations chosen by the majority of employees within a given unit. This status gave the organization the right to bargain collectively on behalf of its members. Collectively bargained agreements could not conflict with established federal law, agency regulations, government personnel policies, or the authority of Congress.

3. The scope of consultation and negotiation was to depend on the form of recognition given the organization and could concern working conditions and personnel policies within the limits of the law and in consonance with the principles of the merit system.
4. Impasses between federal agencies and employee organizations given exclusive recognition were to be settled by means other than arbitration, devised on an "agency-by-agency" basis.
5. All agreements with organizations granted exclusive or formal recognition were to be in writing and the effective dates kept within reasonable time limits.
6. Some of the "do's" and "don'ts" recommended by the task force were:
   a. Bulletin boards could and should be provided to the employee organizations.

b. Officially approved or requested consultations with employee organizations should take place on official time.
c. An agency could require that negotiation with an employee organization granted exclusive recognition take place on employee's time.
d. No internal business of the employee organization could be conducted on official time.
e. Voluntary dues withholding (check-off) could be granted to an employee organization.

7. Employee organizations were to have a recognized grievance procedure. Advisory arbitration, which the agency did not have to abide by, could be provided by agreement between an agency and an employee organization granted exclusive recognition.
8. Union shops and closed shops were declared "inappropriate" to the federal system.
9. Technical services required to implement the program were to be provided by the Department of Labor and the Civil Service Commission. The program, when enacted into law, was to be administered by the Civil Service Commission.

These recommendations were accepted by President Kennedy and formed the basis for E. O. 10988. The above, of course, is a very general and broad description of what was contained in the order. The actual provisions of the order are numerous and much more specific. For instance, Section 6, paragraph (b) stated that while an employee organization granted exclusive recognition could negotiate with an agency on matters pertaining to employees' interests and working conditions, it could not negotiate on matters pertaining to "the mission of an agency, its budget, its organization and the assignment of its personnel, or the technology used for performing its work."

Section 13, paragraph (b) established a President's Temporary Committee on the Implementation of the Federal Employee- Management Relations Program to consist of the Secretary of Labor (who was to be the Chairman), the Secretary of Defense, the Postmaster General and the Chairman of the Civil Service Commission. Section 16 stipulated that the order did not apply to such agencies as the CIA, FBI, National Security Agency and other intelligence and investigatory agencies.[5] The reason for this can be readily surmised.

While E. O. 10988, as originally adopted, remained on the books only a short time (8 years), it nevertheless provided the first major guidelines and thus led to a considerable expansion of labor organizations within the federal system. During the period it was in effect, representation of employees in exclusive bargaining units expanded from two agencies with 29 units covering 19,000 employees to 35 agencies (including the Post Office Department) with 2,305 units covering 1.4 million employees. This constituted 52 percent of the federal work force.[6]

On September 8, 1967, President Lyndon Johnson appointed a President's Review Committee on Federal Employee-Management Relations, known as the Johnson Review Committee. Its purpose was to review the program and determine its accomplishments, deficiencies, and needed modifications to insure "its continued vitality in the public interest." This committee was almost identical to the 1961 Kennedy Task Force. Again it was chaired by the Secretary of Labor, Willard Wirtz, and included John Macy, Chairman of the Civil Service Commission and Robert McNamara, Secretary of Defense. Although this committee did present to the President a completed review, with recommended changes of the program in general and E. O. 10988 in particular, no action was taken on this report before President Johnson left office in January 1969.

When President Nixon took office, he appointed another study committee with the same charge as its predecessor under President Johnson. The Nixon committee included the Civil Service Commission's Robert Hampton, the Defense Department's Melvin Laird, Labor Secretary George Schultz, Postmaster General Winton Blount, and Budget Director Robert Mayo. This committee relied heavily on the study conducted by the Johnson committee and, in fact, adopted many of the recommendations that the Johnson committee had proposed.

There were six major changes to the Kennedy order proposed by the Nixon committee which were accepted and incorporated into E. O. 10988 and reissued as E. O. 11491, signed October 29, 1969, to become effective January 1, 1970. The changes recommended were as follows:

1. The Kennedy order had given each agency head autonomy in the implementation of the order while E. O. 11491 provided for one central authority to administer the order. This central authority was the newly created Federal Labor Relations Council (FLRC) (Section 4). This council was made up of the Chairman of the Civil Service Commission (later changed to the Director of the Office of Personnel Management) who chaired the Council, the Secretary of Labor, and originally a member of the President's Executive Office to be appointed by the President. The third member, however, was

later changed to the Director of the Office of Management and Budget under the provisions of Executive Order 11616 of August, 1971. The functions of the council are to oversee the entire federal labor-management relations program, to interpret the order and rule on its provisions, to decide on policy issues, to hear appeals made on the decisions of the Assistant Secretary of Labor for Labor-Management Relations, to resolve unfair labor practices, to arbitrate grievances, and to make periodic reports to the President on the status of the program.

2. E. O. 11491 also provides for several third-party processes differing from E. O. 10988. For example, E. O. 10988 stated that the head of each agency was to settle labor-management disputes. E. O. 11491 changed this and provided four basic third-party processes for settling disputes. The first gives the Assistant Secretary of Labor for Labor-Management Relations authority to decide on questions regarding the appropriateness of awarding a unit exclusive recognition (Section 6). Empowered to supervise and certify all elections, the Assistant Secretary can decide on unfair labor practice complaints including violations of the standards of conduct for labor organizations. In cases involving the Labor Department, this authority is transferred to the Chairman of the Civil Service Commission (later changed to the Director of the Office of Personnel Management).

   The second process is the provision that the Federal Mediation and Conciliation Service should extend its services to include the federal sector and provide the same mediation assistance it offers the private sector.

   The third process is the creation of the Federal Service Impasse Panel (Section 5). This panel is an agency of the Federal Labor Relations Council charged with providing additional assistance when all other efforts, including the services of the Federal Mediation and Conciliation Service, are unable to settle a dispute. The panel relies heavily on the technique of fact-finding and resultant recommendations.

   The fourth process is binding arbitration. E. O. 10988 had provided that agencies did not have to abide by arbitration while the employee organizations did. Under E. O. 11491, the FLRC is empowered to make decisions on issues submitted for arbitration that are binding on both sides.

3. Another change to the labor-management relations program made by the Nixon order was to do away with two of the three forms of recognition provided for under E. O. 10988 (i.e., informal and formal) and limit recognition to exclusive units only (Sections 7 and 10). It also expanded the criteria for determining a unit's appropriateness to be given exclusive recognition to include not only "community of interest" but also that "it promote effective dealings and efficiency of agency operations" (Section 10). Another provision added was for national consultation rights (Section 9). Agencies are required to give such a right to labor organizations when they represent a substantial number of employees in a given agency. This provision gives the organization the right to consult and make recommendations on personnel policies affecting its members. However, an agency is not obligated to follow through with such recommendations.
4. Under E. O. 10988, the right of supervisors to join labor organizations was vague and confusing, since there was nothing in the order that really specified their role other than the "rights of management" in Section 7 (2). E. O. 11491 clarified the status of supervisors in Section 2 (c), Section 10 (b)(1), and Section 24 (2). The former two define the terms "management official" and "supervisor" and prohibit exclusive recognition of units containing such personnel. The latter states that the order "did not preclude" granting exclusive recognition for units of management officials and supervisors represented by organizations which "historically and traditionally represented the management officials and supervisors in private industry." Otherwise, a unit which included such personnel could not be granted exclusive recognition [Section 10 (b)(1)].
5. Another major change brought about by E. O. 11491 had to do with the negotiation of agreements. While the Kennedy order was rather vague on this subject, 11491 originally addressed the issue in seven separate sections (Sections 11-17, with Section 14 later revoked). It expanded the scope of negotiation to permit negotiations on shifts, overtime, the effects on the work force of technological changes, and it provided more specific procedures for handling negotiable disputes. The FLRC was authorized to decide to what extent a proposal was negotiable, or non-negotiable because it might be contrary to statute or regulations outside the agency or the order itself (Section 11). It also specified that review of an

agency's approval of agreements was limited to the agreement's conformity with the law, agency policies and regulations, and the regulations of authorities outside the agency. It further provided that an employee who represented a recognized labor organization could not do so on official time (Section 20).

6. Finally, one of the most significant changes to the Kennedy order was to specify what were to be considered unfair labor practices, both on the part of management and labor. These were spelled out in Section 19.

Briefly summarized, these unfair labor practices stated that *management* could not:

a. Interfere with employees' rights to join a union
b. Encourage or discourage union membership by discriminating in regard to hiring, tenure, promotion, or other conditions of employment
c. Discipline or discriminate against an employee who testified under the order
d. Refuse to recognize an organization qualified for such recognition
e. Refuse to consult, confer, or negotiate with a labor organization as required by the order

On the other hand, *labor* could not:

a. Interfere with an employee's right *not* to join a union
b. Attempt to induce agency management to coerce an employee against exercising employee rights under the order
c. Attempt to interfere in an employee's effort to discharge their responsibilities as an employee of the United States government
d. Call or engage in a strike, stoppage or slowdown, or picket any agency in a labor-management dispute, or fail to take appropriate action to prevent such activities
e. Discriminate against an employee because of race, color, creed, sex, age, or national origin. (This, as mentioned previously, was also stipulated in Executive Order 10988.)
f. Refuse to consult, confer, or negotiate with an agency as required by the order[7]

Thus E. O. 11491 was simply a reissuance of E. O. 10988 with the six changes detailed above. E.O. 11491 has itself undergone some major changes, having been incorporated into the Civil Service Reform Act, but its provisions remain intact and serve to govern labor-management relations in the federal sector today.

Conclusion

While many will disagree, federal labor-management relations, administered through the Executive Order system and the Civil Service Reform Act, are presently in an acceptable state. Certainly there is room for improvement in the system, and both management and labor, as well as the executive branch and the Congress, continue to seek ways to improve it. In fact, the United States House of Representatives' Subcommittee on Manpower and Civil Service recently held hearings to look into the status of federal labor-management relations with the aim of introducing legislation that would bring such relations more in line with the provisions of the National Labor Relations Act. These hearings produced no major revisions in the present system, for, as stated by the Director of the Office of Personnel Management in testimony before the subcommittee, "there has been no compelling evidence that the proposals before this committee would provide a better or more balanced program."[8]

If one reflects on the fact that Executive Orders directed at federal labor relations have only come about in the last thirty to forty years, and that the Civil Service Reform Act is less than twenty years old - and then looks at the state of labor relations in the private sector in the same period after passage of the National Labor Relations Act - the situation in the federal sector is put into perspective. Labor relations problems of the type discussed above are complex ones that cannot be solved simply by the passage of a directive. The long, slow process of interpretation and administration is necessary before any resolution can be achieved. The federal sector is now in the middle of the process. With each amendment to the Civil Service Reform Act, with each ruling by the FLRC, FSIP, or any other administrative agency, it will move closer to a clear definition of its own labor relations policy. Given the history of the private sector in this regard, it is obvious that despite the standard criticism of some concerning the speed with which the federal government moves, progress is being made, and will continue to be made as rapidly as can be expected given the complexity of the issues.

Endnotes

[1] Nesbitt, Murray B., *Labor Relations in the Federal Government Service*, (Washington, DC, 1976), p. 6.

[2] *Ibid.*, p. 7.

[3] *Report of the Federal Labor Relations Council*, January 1, 1970-December 31, 1976, (Washington, DC, 1977), p. 3.

[4] *Ibid.*, p. 4.

[5] Executive Order 10988: Employee-Management Cooperation in the Federal Service, (Washington, DC, 1962), p. 6.

[6] *Report of the Federal Labor Relations Council, op. cit.*, p. 9.

[7] Executive Order 11491: Labor-Management Relations in the Federal Service as Amended, (Washington, DC, 1969), p. 16.

[8] *Federal Service Labor-Management Legislation Hearings*: House of Representatives, May 21, 22, June 5, 12, 13, July 16, 25, 1994, (Washington, 1994), p. 18.

Federal Employee Unions: Blessing or Curse?

The desirability of labor unions for federal employees is an issue which clearly divides public opinion. Many outside the federal service do not see the need for such organizations, espousing the theory that civil servants are to be tended to by a benevolent public. Yet the drastic increase in the number of federal workers who have joined these unions over the past 10 years is clear evidence that those inside Uncle Sam's walls feel the need for such organizations.

No one argues with the assertion that one of the basic goals of unions is to increase the compensation their members receive for their work. As unions in the federal sector exert their increasing influence to push compensation rates higher, it stands to reason that careers in the federal service will attract an increasing number of applicants. With a larger pool to choose from relative to the number of openings, higher qualifications can be demanded for entrance into the federal sector. The higher compensation, caused in part by union demands, will attract better-qualified individuals to the federal job market.

While it is true that the federal payroll will increase as a result of unions, the American public should not be upset. Typical resentment toward the size of the federal payroll is directed at its perceived waste. If the taxpayer gets a top-notch employee for the money instead of the "do-nothing bureaucrat" believed to haunt the halls of government agencies, such resentment will fade. In the words of the old axiom: "You get what you pay for."

Some present public servants who entered when competition for such jobs was less severe will, in fact, be overly compensated as a result of union-supported wage increases. This is a short-term problem that will solve itself as these individuals leave the federal payroll. Their "free ride" is a small price to pay for the long-term overall improvement in personnel.

In addition to the increase in payroll size, another often heard argument against federal employee unions is that labor organizations use job security for their members as a cornerstone of their foundation. That is, many feel that unions cover their members with a blanket of job security so thick that it is nearly impossible for employers to increase efficiency by weeding out non-productive or less productive employees. While this argument has merit in the private sector, one must be careful to differentiate between private and federal employment. True, a private sector employer whose labor force is newly unionized may notice this growing restriction on authority to replace, or even transfer, personnel. In the federal sector, however, such restrictions are already in place to such an extent that it is hard to imagine what labor organizations could do to increase them.

Also to be remembered is that the establishment of unions is usually accompanied by a greater specificity in requirements for appointment and promotion to certain jobs. In the federal sector, this may well reduce the number of instances where political connections are a factor in personnel decisions and, as such, would be a welcome change.

Thus while short-term factors like the increase in payroll size, the number of free riders, etc., may cause many to argue against the desirability of federal employee unions, these factors are more than outweighed by the long-term results of these unions.

Federal employee unions are, in the long run, a blessing.

Cases

Employer Dismissal of a Union Official

During recent negotiations for the renewal of the contract between a federal agency and the union representing the agency's employees, some discontent developed on both sides because of different ploys used by the parties in attempting to gain an advantage at the beginning of the negotiations. One member of the union negotiating team, who was also a shop steward, appeared to interpret the "jockeying for position" by the management team as a personal affront to his intelligence and integrity and was most boisterous in his criticism of management's "good faith" bargaining tactics.

On a day when the steward was working (because an impasse had been reached in the negotiations), he slipped on a wet spot in the men's restroom and slightly injured his wrist. The wet spot was caused by a leaky water pipe, and several attempts had been made in the recent past to repair it. The numerous unsuccessful attempts to repair the pipe had become a standing joke in the building, and the hazardous condition was known to all, including the steward.

One day after this accident the men's restroom was vandalized shortly before quitting time. A porcelain basin was pulled from the wall and broken, overhead fluorescent lights were smashed, and paper towels, toilet paper, and broken mirrors were strewn all over the floor.

Management was able to determine that five employees had been in the restroom at the time the vandalism occurred but was unable to determine which of the five had actually taken part in the destruction. One of the five employees was the shop steward who had previously been injured in that same restroom.

The employees were counseled individually, but while each admitted that the vandalism occurred while they were in the restroom, they all said they did not know who was responsible, because it was dark without the lights. Management told the employees that they had until the next day to reveal the offender(s). When no one came forward with any information, management gave three-day suspensions to all five of the employees.

The union filed a grievance claiming that management's action was unjust, since none of the five were observed committing the acts of destruction. It further argued that it was unfair to discipline up to four innocent people simply because management was unable to uncover the real offender(s). The union also implied that management's action was highly suspect in view of the fact that one of the five was the shop steward.

Questions

1. Was management's mass discipline justified? Was there a viable alternative?
2. What would be the consequences of not disciplining anyone since the actual offender(s) could not be identified?
3. Did management violate any labor laws in suspending the shop steward when there was no real proof of his participation in the vandalism?

Union Organizing: What Can and Cannot Be Done

A small suburban manufacturing plant employed 500 production personnel and 50 office personnel. Of the 50 office personnel, 15 were management and 35 were professionals or clerical support staff. Fifteen of the 35 non-management employees were classified as secretaries and three of the 15 secretaries were differentiated as executive secretaries. Each of the three executive secretaries worked exclusively for one of the three company officers: the President, the Vice-President of Production, and the Vice-President of Finance. The secretary to the President was also his wife, and any confidential or sensitive company information (whether relating to personnel, finance, or production), was processed by her and hand carried directly to the appropriate department head in a "for eyes only" sealed folder.

The company distributed its product line through a network of manufacturer's representatives. Positions in marketing, personnel, accounting, etc., were all middle-level management positions. Each section had a secretary that supported not only the manager but also the manager's first-line supervisors, professional staff, and non-typing clerical support staff.

During the company's ten years of operation there had been no attempts at, or talk of, unionization. The company officers were also the three major stockholders of the company and had operated under a paternalistic form of management that equated dissent with disloyalty. There was no formal system for voicing complaints. There was, however, an informal discipline procedure. Usually an oral warning was issued and also documented in the employee's personnel file. The succeeding steps included a written warning and, if necessary, discharge. Previous discharges had occurred for infractions of stated rules, non-compliance with established company procedural precedents, or for such nebulous reasons as not being suited for a particular type of work, or company disloyalty.

Recently, on several occasions union representatives from a national industrial union had contacted production employees and talked with them concerning the advantages of unionization. Management had become aware of these contacts through "old timers" who felt it their duty to warn management of the union interlopers. Through chance overhearing of a management discussion concerning the production employee/union situation, the executive secretary to the Vice-President of Production became aware of the union overtures to production personnel. She then began to promote the idea of unionization among the office clerical and professional staff.

Management, viewing unionization attempts as betrayal by their employees, was adamant in its opposition to recognition of any union. A bulletin was posted stating that there were to be no union organizing activities on company time, and that employees engaging in such activities would be discharged. Managers were instructed to conduct meetings with their subordinates (both office and production) and warn them of the negative aspects of union membership. They were also to infer possible reprisals for those employees who advocated unionization. Each of the department secretaries, including those of the two Vice-Presidents, was called into their bosses' offices separately and warned that their participation in unionization efforts was, in the eyes of management, unforgivable company disloyalty.

Shortly thereafter, during a lunch break in the employees' lounge, the Production Vice-President's secretary announced a union organizing meeting for the office staff to be held that evening at a nearby motel. She further informed the other employees of information she had obtained from the union representatives as to employee rights to organize without management interference, including the fact that their jobs could not be taken away because of their union organizing activities. During that afternoon, the Vice-President of Production again spoke with his secretary concerning her pro-union activities, reiterating his distaste for her lack of judgment and warning her she was "skating on thin ice" since she had previously received a verbal warning for absenteeism and tardiness.

More than the required 30% of the production and office staff, including two of the three executive secretaries, signed cards requesting that a union election be conducted. The NLRB investigated to see if the proposed group of employees constituted an appropriate bargaining unit. The professional employees were polled separately and elected to be part of the unit with the production and clerical staff. The investigator met with management and reviewed working conditions, job descriptions, etc., in an effort to determine the appropriateness of the proposed unit.

During one of the management/NLRB interviews, one of the secretaries overheard the investigator being told that all of the executive secretaries had access to company confidential material. The story of what she had overheard spread throughout the plant, so it came as no surprise to the employees when the NLRB determined the appropriate bargaining unit to be all production and office personnel except the three executive secretaries.

A union election was held and the approved bargaining unit became an official local of a national industrial union. Within a brief period of time after the election, the Production Vice-President's secretary was given a written warning for absenteeism and tardiness and within the same month was discharged for "just cause." Her supervisor cited her poor attendance record, which was in fact excessive, and disloyalty to the firm. The production and office personnel began to picket the company in support of the discharged secretary, and threatened to walk out if she were not returned to work immediately.

Questions

1. Do the two remaining executive secretaries have appeal rights for review of their exclusion from the bargaining unit?
2. Were the activities of management within the framework of legal anti-union actions under existing labor laws?
3. Does the discharged secretary have appeal rights to the NLRB for unfair labor practices, even though she was not a member of the local union at the time she was fired?
4. Is picketing and striking by the local union in support of the discharged secretary legal?

Notification Preceding Collective Bargaining

Employees of a federal agency have a union to represent them in negotiations with the agency's management, and a new contract is negotiated every three years. One of the provisions states the union has the right to be present at any meeting between two or more employees and a representative of management when anything related to work (the working conditions, job performance standards, job assignments, proposed change of physical location of employees, times of break and lunch, etc.) is discussed. The union representative is to be notified forty-eight (48) hours in advance of such a meeting. The manner of the forty-eight hour notification is not specified in the contract.

Recently a meeting between the manager of a branch of the agency and the bargaining unit employees of the branch was held. The union steward was not notified and therefore was not present. The information passed to the employees was updated job-performance standards. These standards were created solely by management based upon past production levels that they considered outstanding, excellent, satisfactory, unsatisfactory, and cause for dismissal. The performance standards were for the various jobs within the branch and consisted of three areas in which the employee would be appraised: quantity, quality, and manner of performance.

Two weeks after the meeting, the union filed an Unfair Labor Practice with the Federal Labor Relations Authority, charging that:

1. The union did not receive proper and timely notice of the meeting between the bargaining unit employees and management.
2. The union had not participated in the formulation of the job performance standards and was not given the opportunity to review the standards before they were presented to the employees.

Questions

1. What do you think the limits of the union's authority should be in developing procedures to be applied by management in establishing performance appraisal systems?
2. Must the agency negotiate on a specific proposal for minimum performance standards?
3. What remedy would you impose against management for not notifying the union representative of the meeting?

Arbitration of Grievances Regarding Employee Discharge

Howard Knoblock belongs to National Truck Workers (NTW), Local 42, and works for an assembly plant in Cleveland as a repairman. He has worked there for eight years and has been a competent employee. He works hard and is known as "one of the best repairmen in Q Department" according to Q Department's supervisor.

Howard was transferred to R Department in November. Steve Silberg has been supervisor of R Department for six years. For 8 months Howard worked in R Department with no conflicts or problems. Then one day when he was working his 11:00 p.m. to 7:00 a.m. shift Steve approached him and asked, "Have you been drinking again?" Howard replied that he had not been drinking, nor did he ever drink on the job. Steve reprimanded him for doing sloppy work and warned that he should "never come in to work drunk again." The employees who were in the vicinity took notice of what was going on, and Steve told everybody to go back to work as he walked away, shaking his head.

A few days later, shortly after Howard arrived at work, Steve saw him drop a wrench. He immediately approached him and said, "Howard! I thought I told you a couple of days ago not to come to work when you've been drinking." Before Howard could reply, Steve said, "Look, buster, if you keep this up, I'm going to fire you." Other employees were looking on with interest as Steve was raising his voice. Howard's reaction was very cool and calm. He quietly explained that he had not been drinking and the dropping of the wrench was only a harmless accident. Steve returned to his office after warning Howard to be more careful in the future.

The following night, about an hour after Howard began his shift, he slipped on some oil and fell on the floor, cutting his knee and tearing his pants. Steve happened to see his fall and ran to him yelling, "Dammit, Howard, I warned you about coming here drunk. Don't lie to me this time, because I saw you going into the Silver Slipper Bar earlier this evening while I was driving to the post office." Steve was extremely angry and loud.

Some of Howard's co-workers had rushed over to aid him when he blurted to Steve, "You S.O.B.; I told you I don't come to work drunk. If you don't stop harassing me about it, I'm going to punch your lights out." As

Howard finished saying this, he started getting up off the floor. Howard's fellow employees thought he was getting up to hit Steve and attempted to restrain him. Steve's immediate reaction was to flinch and raise his fist. Howard, thinking Steve was going to strike *him* because of his threat, hit him and bloodied his nose. Howard immediately apologized, and Steve left the scene cussing and headed to the infirmary. Howard tended to his cut knee and returned to his work.

When Steve returned from the infirmary and found Howard working at his job as if nothing had happened, he approached him in a very professional fashion and told him he was fired. He did this by reciting a specific section of the contract agreement that deals with discharge in general as if he had just memorized it (i.e., management retains the right to discharge employees for dishonesty, fighting, intoxication, or other just causes). He told Howard he could come in the next day to get his wages, written notice of discharge, and personal belongings, but "to get the hell out of my sight" because he no longer worked at the plant. Howard said, "Okay, chump," as he dropped his tools and walked out.

The next day Howard met with his shop steward and filed a formal grievance. He then went in to get his personal belongings, received his written notice of discharge and wages, and left the plant with a smile on his face, whistling as he walked off the premises.

There was the usual conference and investigation of facts as provided for in the first step of the grievance procedure, but there was no agreement. Management's stand was strong - as was the union's. It was obvious after the third step of the grievance procedure that arbitration was inevitable. At this juncture, the facts accumulated through investigation by both sides had become somewhat complex.

Management's position was based on the following:

1. Management could prove that Howard had been in the Silver Slipper the evening of the incident and had been drinking while there. In fact, management could prove that he was a regular customer of the establishment.
2. Howard was known to be an excellent fighter and seemed to be proud of his reputation. It was known that Howard was fired from a previous job 8 years ago for fighting with a fellow employee.
3. Evidence was presented concerning Howard's drinking habits. He had been arrested two times during the past three years for being drunk in public.

4. Howard did receive written notice on the morning after the incident that, in accordance with the contract agreement, he was being discharged for fighting. Management argues that Steve, the supervisor, did not give written notice with an outline of the specific charges at the time he fired Howard because he thought it was obvious, and because he was in a great deal of pain with a broken nose.

The union's position was based on the following:

1. When Steve discharged Howard he only quoted the discharge clause *verbatim*, and never stated which specific reason he was being fired for. Furthermore, Howard did not receive written notice until the following day.
2. The union argued that the earlier reprimands of Howard were not warranted and were a direct attack on him because of some of Steve's personal problems involving drinking. The investigation revealed that Steve's wife has a serious drinking problem and only one week prior to Steve's first attack on Howard, she was involved in a serious car accident and charged with driving while intoxicated.
3. Howard only defended himself by hitting Steve because it appeared as if Steve were going to strike him first.
4. The union argued that the Silver Slipper is a restaurant where Howard frequently eats meals, and that he occasionally drinks beer with his meals. He has never been considered a rowdy drinker while there nor has he ever been involved in a fight in the bar.

Questions

1. In placing one's self in the position of an arbitrator, how much emphasis and/or weight can be placed on the extenuating circumstances surrounding the incidents in question?
2. Does the arbitrator have to make a decision based strictly on the simple facts - i.e.,
   a. Howard did, in fact, strike his supervisor;
   b. management did, in fact, fail to comply with the discharge procedures to give written notice setting forth the cause of discharge at the time Howard was instructed to leave the plant

   or...

should the arbitrator, to arrive at a "just" decision, include all the circumstantial issues?

3. What would your decision be if you were the arbitrator? Why?

Management Persuasion of Potential Union Members

A large textile corporation in the southeastern portion of the United States had an opening for the position of machine operator. The company had thirty machine operators already on their staff.

The company had in recent months been hearing rumors that the machine operators wanted to form a union because of what they considered inadequate pay for the job they performed. Mr. Hall, the President of the textile company, was informed of this rumor and quickly put out the word to his staff supervisors to try and squash this movement. He also stated to his Personnel Director, Mr. Jones, that the vacant position should be filled by an applicant with no prior record of union membership.

Mr. Jones had tried to recruit a candidate who would comply with Mr. Hall's request, but after several weeks, the only candidate to possess all other qualifications had prior union affiliation. Mr. Jones was very upset about this, since he had a candidate who was suitable in all other aspects. Mr. Jones went to Mr. Hall and discussed the situation. Mr. Hall flatly refused to even consider hiring an individual with prior union affiliation - even if it meant hiring one with less experience.

Mr. Jones continued to advertise for several more weeks without success. Mr. Swigart (the earlier candidate with prior union experience) noticed that the company was still in need of help and called Mr. Jones to ask why he had not been selected for the position. Mr. Swigart knew that he had all the qualifications and that because of the unique requirements not too many candidates would be suitable. Mr. Jones told Mr. Swigart over the phone that he wanted to talk to him about the possibility of hiring him for the job, but that they would have to clear up some matters first.

Mr. Swigart came in the next day, and Mr. Jones proceeded to say that he could have the job on the condition that he would not try to organize or bring in a union. Mr. Jones said that the company was anti-union and that they wanted no new employees with prior union background. Mr. Swigart readily agreed to the terms, since he had just moved into town and needed a job. Mr. Jones also stated that he would pay him a higher wage than any of his counterparts if he would refrain from any union activities.

Mr. Jones was very happy that Mr. Swigart readily agreed to his terms and thought that Mr. Hall would agree with what he had done. Since Mr.

Hall was out of town temporarily, Mr. Jones went ahead and hired Mr. Swigart at the higher pay rate.

Several months later, Mr. Hall happened to be going over the payroll and noticed Mr. Swigart's pay rate. He immediately called the Finance Department and asked what was going on. Mr. Hall was told that Mr. Jones had sanctioned the pay rate for Mr. Swigart. Mr. Hall immediately called in Mr. Jones and asked him why he had done this without prior approval. Mr. Jones outlined the circumstances surrounding the higher wage offer and said that his scheme was working well. Mr. Hall, still not very happy with the whole situation, called the Finance Department and told them that effective immediately Mr. Swigart would earn the same wage as the other machine operators.

When Mr. Swigart learned of this, he requested a meeting with Mr. Hall. Mr. Hall refused and instructed the foreman to start writing Mr. Swigart up for any and everything he could think of. As a result of this, Mr. Swigart resigned.

Questions

1. Has an unfair labor practice been committed? If so, what and by whom?
2. Should Mr. Swigart be reinstated?
3. Was the situation regarding Mr. Swigart's original pay rate legal?

Unfair Labor Practices

Tom Jackson has worked on the autoblock assembly line at the Cleveland, Ohio, plant of the American Metal Manufacturing Company for 13 years. During this time, he has been quite active in union activity, doing things like helping to organize workers, performing investigative work into health and safety standards and talking with other employees about problems they are having.

One investigation of health and safety standards by Jackson resulted in charges being brought against the American Metal Manufacturing Company for violation of the 1970 Occupational Safety and Health Act. Jackson testified before members of the agency regarding violations of the standards, some of which included improper ventilation, lighting, operation of equipment and excessive heat in the welding department. His testimony was largely responsible for the American Metal Manufacturing Company being assessed a stiff penalty and a warning of future fines if conditions did not improve.

Shortly after Jackson's testimony, he was told he was being promoted to the newly created position of assistant foreman of the day run. He was promoted even though there was a person in his department who had greater seniority than he did. His major responsibility was to take over for the foreman during his lunch period and on his days off and to help distribute work orders and keep track of employee mistakes. He had a few other small duties but had to confirm everything with the foreman and in all activities was under the foreman's control.

Now that Jackson had become an assistant foreman, he was put on a salary instead of getting an hourly wage and was also told that he would have to drop his union membership because, according to Taft-Hartley, supervisors and foremen cannot belong to a union.

This action on the part of management thoroughly enraged Jackson, as he felt that while the promotion was a step up in prestige, the job offer was simply a method management had used to get him out of the union. He felt that they had done this because of his recent testimony on safety matters and his continuous union activities over the years. Jackson went to the union and told them of his predicament and asked them to file an unfair labor practice charge with the National Labor Relations Board. The union agreed to file and represent Jackson.

The arguments each side presented before the NLRB were as follows:

Management:

1. The position of assistant foreman was created because of the need for someone to take over when the foreman was absent.
2. Tom Jackson was the person with the most seniority.
3. Since Jackson's job is now that of a foreman, according to Taft-Hartley, he must give up his membership in the union.

The union and Jackson countered these points by stating:

1. That while the job of assistant foreman may be needed, the duties being performed by Jackson do not contain any actual responsibility, because he needs to check out everything with his foreman. Thus he is not in *actuality* a foreman.
2. Jackson was promoted over a more senior employee for the purposes of getting him out of the union.
3. That the above constitutes an unfair labor practice under the Wagner Act because the company was discriminating to discourage membership in a labor organization.

The case went to the NLRB and is scheduled to be heard next week.

Questions

1. Is management discriminating because of Jackson's membership in a labor organization?
2. Are the responsibilities of the job sufficient to make Jackson a part of management?
3. If he is, in fact, part of management, must he relinquish his membership in the union under Taft-Hartley as management contends?

Transition and Turnover Problems Caused by Technological Advances

A large firm that manufactures stereophonic equipment and specializes in amplifiers has been a leading regional distributor for over 25 years. Until a few years ago it had been continually expanding due to ever increasing profits. In the past few years however, it has incurred a substantial reduction in sales and profits as a result of increased competition from foreign markets.

In an attempt to increase efficiency and sales, the main office called in consultants to advise on updating equipment. Based on their recommendations, new equipment was purchased and it was decided that several hundred employees would have to be laid off. The new machinery was to increase production and decrease staff by requiring a higher level of skills. Management felt if the new machinery had to remain idle during the training period for the present staff, it would cause further delays in production and that the process of training some employees and gradually reducing the staff would be too costly and too slow.

Since the older employees were unfamiliar with the new machinery, it was advised that an outsider be hired to oversee the training. A supervisor from a competitive company was offered an attractive salary, to which she agreed, and when she came she brought her own staff of operators. The new staff caused a further decrease in older employees and created conflicts between them and the new people. Many departments had a difficult time maintaining morale in light of the changes that were taking place.

After several months, the new staff and new machinery were working smoothly, but expenditures were still higher than the consultants had predicted. Suddenly, one day the main terminal broke down and production had to be halted until the parts arrived. If something were not done immediately, production would fall behind schedule, resulting in financial losses to the company. The only alternative was to return to the old machinery, even though it was slower and could probably not meet contract deadlines.

A problem developed because the new skilled employees were unfamiliar with the old machinery and there weren't enough of the older employees remaining to do the job. Pressed for time, the remaining older employees were asked to work nights and the following weekend.

Questions

1. Should management have dismantled the old system and dismissed the staff before the new machinery had all the bugs worked out and the new staff proved efficient?
2. How could the old system have been utilized to prevent production slow-down and company loss?
3. How could the impact of the machinery on the employees have been minimized?

Unfair Labor Practices During Union Organizing Attempts

John R. Snelt and Sons had been a non-union shoe factory since its inception in 1967. Lately, numerous supervisors had been reporting to their managers that talk of joining a union by the employees had been overheard. The owners were upset by this and a little puzzled as to why the employees would want a union. Mr. Snelt felt he had always paid competitive wages, provided good benefits and had been open to employee suggestions. He knew the business had changed dramatically since 1967 but didn't feel these changes warranted the need for a union.

Joe Snelt noted for his father that over the past five years they had hired a number of new employees and that the few employees left from the inception were now a minority. Perhaps these newer employees were the initiators of the union, Joe suggested.

Mr. Snelt decided that not only he and his managers, but also his first-line supervisors, should talk to the employees and see if they would be able to change their minds about needing a union. A few of the supervisors decided they would get to the heart of the problem and did so immediately. They proceeded to ask the employees under them what they thought of all this union talk and if they were going to join.

As the weeks went on, it seemed to Mr. Snelt that the union discussions were getting very serious. Supervisors were reporting that union literature was being passed out in the parking lot areas and that authorization cards were being distributed.

As the talk became more and more serious and a large number of the employees were signing authorization cards, the same group of supervisors decided to visit some of the homes of their friends who were employees to discuss the pros and cons of joining a union.

These employees reported to the other employees that management said many of them would be losing jobs if the union came in. However, these employees also claimed that the supervisors told them if the union didn't come in, management had made promises of raises and would try to promote a few more employees.

When the union organizers heard what was going on, they filed an unfair labor practice claim with the NLRB. They also argued that because of what had happened, the union should be recognized even without the election.

Mr. Snelt, of course, disagreed and demanded an election.

Questions

1. Does the union have grounds for their unfair labor practice charge? If so, what are they?
2. Is it possible to have a union represent this group (or any group) without an election?

Seniority vs. Ability in Layoff Determination

Lancor Tool and Maintenance Company has had a history of promotion from within based on longevity with the company. Employees were hired as apprentice workers and were promoted to better jobs as they learned skills and gained more experience.

The more established workers with the company were eager to get a job driving a company truck of their own and answering trouble calls to surrounding areas when these calls came into the Lancor Company. This traveling repair service was considered more desirable than staying on the premises of the Lancor Company and accepting and repairing equipment from off-the-street customers.

Recently, the company became concerned with the fact that the more senior workers could not repair the new, more sophisticated equipment as well as the younger, newer workers. Complaints were coming into Lancor concerning problems in the field. The older workers could not repair the equipment on the spot and were forced to bring it back to the in-house service department of Lancor so that the younger workers could complete the job.

The company finally negotiated an agreement with the union permitting it to use ability and skill tests in the selection of new repair crews. The older workers were no longer able to bid on the more desirable jobs. For the first time, Lancor was able to go outside the organization and hire young students just out of trade school. These students learned quickly and had the knowledge and understanding to work on the new equipment. After a while, the older repairmen who had come into their jobs prior to being screened were shifted to less desirable shop jobs.

The problem that now faces the Lancor Tool and Maintenance Company is one of declining business forcing a cutback in the size of the repair department. Since layoffs are based on seniority, nearly all of the relatively new and more able younger employees will be laid off if the present decline continues. Lancor fears the loss of their young, skilled workers will further erode their business and that, eventually, competitors will begin making inroads.

Question

1. What alternative courses of action are available to Lancor? What are the implementation problems and possible implications of each?

Favored Employees, Discrimination, and Unfair Labor Practices

About two weeks following the end of a strike of the registered nurses at St. Luke's Hospital, the hospital administrator sent a note of appreciation to the registered nurses who continued to work during the strike and to the extra RNs who were transferred from St. Mary's to help cover the shifts of the striking nurses. In the letter of appreciation, the RNs were praised for their hard work and long hours, and for "overcoming hardships and personal sacrifice in a definite gesture of dedication to duty." The letter indicated that nurses should be concerned with taking care of the sick rather than striking for higher wages.

For all the nurses who worked more than one shift during the strike, the chief nurse gave compensatory time or a day off. In addition, the LPNs were given time off with pay for their efforts in assisting in patient treatment during the strike, because without their services, the hospital would not have been able to meet patient needs, according to management.

The union filed an unfair labor practice charge with the National Labor Relations Board alleging that the hospital had infringed upon their right to strike and shown partial treatment in the working conditions afforded their peer employees. The union also alleged that they should have been consulted before other nurses were granted time off and the resultant change in work schedules was made.

Questions

1. Has management violated any part of the National Labor Relations Act?
2. Has management discriminated against the union members?
3. Can the NLRB force the hospital staff to grant days off with pay to all RNs, including the nurses on strike?

Just Cause for Separation

Mary Johnson had just graduated from the University of Florida with a Bachelor of Science in Business Administration. She moved to Miami immediately after graduation and looked for a job in retail management. She had worked as an Assistant Manager for a boutique in Gainesville for four years while she attended college and felt she was now qualified to be a manager.

Mary was hired as Manager of a fashionable boutique in Miami Beach. The boutique was part of a Florida-based chain and had a reputation for its high fashion merchandise and expensive accessories. Mary had the duties of a regular manager, as well as the responsibility for all hiring and firing of personnel. Although Mary had a degree in Business Administration, she had not majored in management and had taken only one basic human resource management course. Yet at the time she accepted the position as manager, she felt she would have no trouble handling the personnel responsibilities.

The chain of boutiques that Mary worked for was owned by a husband and wife who visited the stores approximately once a month. On their first visit since the hiring of Mary, they were quite pleased with the shape of the store. Sales figures were good and the store was making ever increasing profits under Mary's management.

A problem came up, however, when reviewing the new employees that Mary had hired. It seemed that two of the women that were hired did not fit the image of what the owners wanted for their sales personnel. Their merchandise was high fashion and expensive, and the salesgirls had to have "a special look." In other words, the two people in question were just not attractive enough. Mary was called into the back room and was told that she had to fire the two salespeople. Mary was upset over the situation, but had no choice in the matter. Either she fired the two young women or the owners would do it and replace Mary as well.

Mary made up some story to tell the salespeople about having to cut back the staff and informed them they would have to be the first ones let go. A month later the two girls found out from friends still working at the boutique the real reason they were fired. They considered filing suit against the boutique for wrongful dismissal.

Questions

1. Under what law, if any, could the two saleswomen have claimed discrimination?
2. Were the two young saleswomen entitled to Unemployment Compensation?
3. If Mary had refused to fire the employees, could she have legally been fired by the owners?
4. If Mary had been fired, could she have received Unemployment Compensation?

Distribution of Union Literature on Company Property

John Smith had been warned by his supervisor that if he were late one more time, he would be fired. The day after his last warning, John came to work at 7:45 - 45 minutes late. At 7:46, he was fired. He was told that his final pay would be ready around noontime.

As a rule, discharged employees were allowed to remain on the premises until receiving their final paycheck. After staying in the lunchroom for a half hour, Smith left the plant. Shortly afterward, he returned to the lunchroom with an NLRB pamphlet and some union literature.

During the morning coffee break, as the former employee was discussing the NLRB pamphlet with other employees, he was interrupted by a supervisor. The supervisor said that it was illegal to have the literature on company property. The supervisor threatened to have Smith arrested unless he left the plant and took the material with him.

Questions

1. Was Smith within his rights in handing out the NLRB pamphlet? In handing out union literature on company property?
2. What difference, if any, does the fact that Smith is no longer an employee make in the answers to Question 1?

Equal Work Or Sex Discrimination?

At Fort Confused (an Army installation in the Midwest) there was a requirement that a single guard be on duty at the post motor pool after normal duty hours. Because the guard was to be alone, the Post Commander decided that only males would be given this assignment. She also stipulated that the females who would normally be assigned to pull this guard duty would be assigned other additional duties, such as clean-up details.

Other than the fact that they would be alone, there were no requirements on this guard duty that could not be handled equally well by either a male or a female. There was no policy stating that females could not pull guard duty alone and, in fact, other installations did utilize females in such a capacity.

Although there were both males and females satisfied with this particular policy, there was also a contingent of males and females who felt it was discriminatory. There were personnel of both sexes who felt that the other was being favored. The Post Commander was informed by members of her command that one or both groups were about to file a discrimination case with the Post Equal Employment Opportunity Office.

Questions

1. Although the Post Commander might feel her policy is both morally right and equally fair to both sexes, is there still a legitimate case for discrimination by either side?
2. What rights, if any, do those personnel have who want to see the present policy maintained?
3. How would you handle this situation if you were the Post Commander?

Employee Discharges Preceding Union Representation Votes

A Midwestern department chain store called Plus Value was opening another unit in its chain. A reason for the location choice of the new store was that management knew the unions were not strong in that particular area. Some of Plus Value's stores were union and some were not, and the management strongly wanted the new store to be non-union.

Management undertook a massive recruitment campaign through advertising in the newspapers. After testing and interviewing all of the applicants, people were hired as sales clerks, cashiers, and loading dock clerks. As the company grew, the threat of a union organizing the workers was ever present. Upon opening, Plus Value hired about 40 people to handle the big crowds at the store's grand opening. About 30 of the 40 employees were originally hired as permanent help while the other ten were temporary.

About two weeks after the store had opened and the ten temporary employees were let go, union organizers came to the store and started to encourage the employees to sign authorization cards. Eventually, the union claimed it had at least the 30% necessary to call for a union election. The management, having only 30 employees, had a good idea who most of the pro-union employees were, and they also knew there were probably 12-15 employees who were against the union. Management knew it would be a close vote.

About a week before the election, a disciplinary incident occurred between the Assistant Manager of the store and one of the men on the loading dock. They had an agitated verbal exchange which climaxed in a shoving match. The cause of the fight was not clearly known, but the dock clerk was known to be very verbal about his pro-union views. As a result of this incident the employee was dismissed. In protest, two of his friends, who also were dock employees and were at the scene of the fight, quit their jobs. They said their friend's dismissal was not just, and he did not deserve to be fired. Management did not discourage the other two from quitting because they knew they were also pro-union.

Management was faced with 3 loading dock vacancies and 3 less pro-union employees. They realized the advantage they had gained in the union vote. Therefore, without hesitation, Plus Value hired three replacements from the pool of the ten temporary employees who were previously let go. These three happened to be anti-union.

Finally, when the vote for the union did come, the union only received 42% of the vote. The union was very upset about the outcome and claimed that Plus Value had staged the incident with the dock employee.

Questions

1. Does the union have a legal issue in questioning the firing of the pro-union employee?
2. Can the union bring charges against Plus Value for using unfair selection practices for hiring the three new anti-union employees?

Administration of Discharge Authority

Mr. West has been employed in the shipping department of the Zargo Company for 17 years. Through his years of employment with Zargo, Mr. West has become familiar with all the company rules, including the rule stating that employees are terminated when found guilty of crimes.

Mr. West committed a crime of moral turpitude which resulted in a jail sentence of two to three years in prison. His sentence was subsequently reduced, and he was placed on probation for three years while being ordered to obtain psychotherapy.

While under indictment, Mr. West was continued as an employee by Zargo but was discharged when he pleaded guilty to a morals charge in exchange for the modified sentence.

Zargo's company policy with respect to employees under indictment for crimes was that the employee was innocent until proven guilty, but if found guilty, the employee would be immediately discharged. This rule had been in effect at Zargo for years and had been administered uniformly. Zargo's position was that modification of the sentence handed down by the court did not change Mr. West's guilt.

After learning of his father's pending dismissal, Mr. West's son petitioned Zargo to grant his father a leave of absence rather than discharge him from the company, in consideration of the sentence modification. Zargo stated that its policy did not allow for leaves of absence.

Questions

1. Did Zargo unjustly discharge Mr. West?
2. What were some possible implications of Mr. West's discharge being overturned?
3. What were some possible alternative solutions to this problem?

Implicit Company Policies and Discharge

Alice, Betty and Carol are three of fifteen employees of a private-school cafeteria in a large eastern city. Alice is American-born and has worked at the cafeteria for five years. Betty and Carol were born in the West Indies and have been at the cafeteria one year.

Betty and Carol were observed taking leftover food home one afternoon. Taking leftover food home was not an unusual occurrence in this kitchen, but the pressure to hold down costs had caused management to decide to try to stop it. As a result, Betty and Carol were fired for stealing.

Betty sued for reinstatement claiming discrimination against her because she was foreign-born. She did not deny taking the leftover food but claimed that Alice had been observed doing the same thing and had not been fired. Management countered that while Alice may have been observed taking food home, it was before the decision to crack down, and thus no discrimination was intended. Betty and Carol were simply the first ones caught after the decision had been made.

Questions

1. If you were hired to arbitrate this case, what would your decision be?
2. Should Carol, who did not sue, be entitled to whatever relief, if any, Betty receives?
3. What can management do to avoid being sued again - without assenting to stealing?

Plant Closings Due To Union Demands

The ABC Electrical Company had been in business for more than 25 years. It was owned by two brothers and was located in the State of Maryland. The company was not unionized, and until last year union organizing activities had never occurred. The owners adamantly opposed unions and tried to be very fair with their employees in an attempt to keep unions out.

Last year, when some union organizing activity occurred, the owners brought all of their employees together and made it known that it would be up to each individual to decide if a union were desirable. During this assembly, the owners also announced increases in vacation and retirement programs for the employees. Within a week after this assembly, union-organizing activities had diminished. A year later they resumed.

The owners once again assembled their employees and informed them of their preference for a non-union environment. During this meeting, no changes in working conditions were discussed. Two months later a union was voted into the company.

As a result of the union being voted in, all employees were given two weeks' notice that the company was being shut down. Three months after the shutdown, the brothers opened up a new electrical company about 30 miles from their old location.

Questions

1. Did the company have the legal right to close and reopen the business in this manner?
2. Could the employees take legal action, under the premise that the company was trying to restrain employees from joining a union?
3. Did the employees have any legal rights regarding a position in the new company?
4. Was anything the brothers did during the first union organizing drive illegal? If so, what, and what legislation applied?

Union Influence on Construction Company Hiring Practices

Brown Bros. Construction Company operates in the suburban areas just south of a large, northern industrial city. The city proper has a 55% non-white population. The bulk of Brown Bros. construction work involves large housing subdivisions in predominantly white suburban communities.

The company has been in existence since 1988. In 1993, the electricians employed by Brown Bros. elected to be represented by Local #444 of the Brotherhood of Electrical Workers, which has its headquarters in the largest of the suburban communities that surround the city. Local #444 has remained the bargaining unit for electricians employed by Brown Bros. up to the present time.

There is another union local, Local #432 of the Brotherhood of Electrical Workers, that represents electrical workers who work within the city limits. Due to their different jurisdictions the racial composition of the two locals is quite different. The table below illustrates this point.

Analysis of Electricians Within A 50-Mile Radius of Brown Bros. Headquarters

	White		Non-white		Total
	No.	(%)	No.	(%)	No.
Local #432	267	(58)	193	(42)	460
Local #444	420	(92)	35	(8)	455
Non-union Electricians	165	(72)	65	(28)	230
Entire Labor Market	852	(74)	293	(26)	1145

The electricians employed by Brown Bros. are distributed as follows:

	White		Non-white		Total
	No.	(%)	No.	(%)	No.
Brown Bros.	15	(88)	2	(12)	17

The economic conditions are such that industries in the area employing electricians have fewer jobs open than there are unemployed electricians in the labor market.

The Local #444 contract with Brown Bros. calls for employment priority to be given to personnel furnished by the local's hiring hall. Among the members of Local #444, the unemployment rate has averaged 10% over the past 12-month period.

Brown Bros. recently won a federal contract to renovate a local defense munitions plant. The company president is apprehensive about Brown Bros.' compliance with Title VII of the 1964 Civil Rights Act as interpreted by the Office of Federal Contract Compliance.

Questions

1. To attain a more favorable racial balance, can Brown Bros. legally hire only non-white members of Local #444 as jobs in the company become available?
2. Can the union legally refer only non-white applicants to Brown Bros.?
3. What influences can be brought to bear on the Brotherhood of Electrical Workers to establish a more equitable distribution of non-white workers in the two locals?

Fired Before Quitting: The Implications for Unemployment Compensation

Chuck Nolson has been working with a merchandise liquidating company for 16 months. His job responsibilities included unloading tractor trailers full of merchandise, operating a fork lift, organizing the merchandise in the warehouse, loading the company's trucks with various merchandise, driving the trucks to the different outlet stores, and assisting with their unloading. In other words, Chuck did everything from sweeping up the warehouse to cleaning up after the warehouse cat. Because merchandise was bought on a sporadic basis, his working hours were also sporadic. His wages were five cents an hour above minimum wage.

Chuck disliked his job, but more than that, strongly disliked his boss, the warehouse supervisor. He felt the supervisor took advantage of his easy-going nature and constantly assigned him the unpleasant tasks.

He had already enrolled for the upcoming fall semester at a local college and planned on quitting his job two weeks prior to the beginning of classes in order to take a vacation. Because of his animosity toward his supervisor, he was not going to inform him of his departure until the end of his final working day. Unfortunately, a few days prior to this, it slipped out in conversation with some fellow workers and made its way back to the supervisor.

The supervisor became irate, realizing in two days he would be under-staffed. When he asked Chuck why he did not notify him, Chuck shrugged it off and replied "I forgot." The supervisor, not one to take things lightly, fired Chuck on the spot. Chuck felt he was entitled to collect unemployment compensation.

Questions

1. According to the law, is Chuck entitled to unemployment compensation?
2. If he is entitled to unemployment compensation, will it continue while Chuck is in college and not seeking employment?
3. Was Chuck's behavior sufficient grounds for dismissal?

Selection of Union Members for Supervisory Positions: A Conflict of Interest?

Wagner Auto parts is in the business of producing and selling quality automobile parts for American-made cars. It started as a family business over 50 years ago and is still run by the son of the original owner. Its central management and research headquarters is located in St. Louis and its two manufacturing plants are located in Detroit and Newark.

All of the laborers within the plants are unionized. One of the unwritten rules between management and the union concerns seniority. It was well understood that promotions within the plants would be based on seniority. When it came time for a new foreman to be hired, the production worker who had the best combination of merit and seniority was traditionally promoted to fill the vacancy.

This method proved to be less and less effective. The foreman invariably remained a member of the union, most often becoming one of the officers. Despite his new status and position within the management of the company, it usually seemed that his major priority was to work for the goals of the union and the workers rather than those of the company as a whole.

Two weeks ago, a foreman position in the Newark plant became available. The union members within the plant immediately began to speculate about who among them would be chosen. The union had their candidate pretty well picked out when management announced their plans to hire someone from outside the plant. By the time the new foreman showed up for work the next day, members of the union had already held a meeting and decided to strike. They demanded that a clause be written into their contract guaranteeing that all foremen would be chosen from within their membership. Management attempts to compromise with the union failed and three days later, the workers in the Detroit plant went on a sympathy strike.

Questions

1. Did the union members have a right to demand that the foreman be chosen from within their membership?
2. Did management have the right to choose the person whom they felt would best fill the job, regardless of whether or not he was a union member?
3. What are some of the possible implications of the strike?
4. Discuss possible alternatives and solutions to this problem.
5. Discuss what steps you would suggest be taken to guard against such a problem arising in the future.

Resistance to Safety Management

Mr. White has recently been appointed Safety Director of Atlas Steel, Inc. Atlas has approximately 1,000 unionized production and maintenance employees at its plant in Detroit, Michigan.

As the Safety Director, Mr. White is very concerned over the high accident rate the company has been experiencing for the past several years. To help solve the problem, a better program of machine guarding and plant maintenance has been initiated. While this program did reduce the severity of accidents, it did not reduce the number significantly.

Mr. White decided to analyze all of the work injuries that had occurred over the past year. He found that in a majority of instances most of the injuries were due to (1) failure to follow safety rules, (2) incorrect use of machines and hand tools, and (3) sloppy cleaning of work areas. Furthermore, Mr. White looked into some literature concerning industrial safety and found some research studies that proved employee attitudes, emotions and knowledge greatly influenced accident rates on the job.

Mr. White concluded that a plant-wide employee education program needed to be initiated. To educate employees in safety, Mr. White decided to have each foreman hold a safety meeting with their employees once a month. He found that the foremen vehemently objected to the added burden, claiming the extra time needed for the meeting would slow down production.

Questions

1. How should Mr. White handle the foremen who refuse to conduct the safety meetings?
2. What, if any, involvement should Mr. White seek from the union?
3. What is the employer's legal responsibility under OSHA if the employees and foremen refuse to attend the meeting?

Abuses of Compensatory Time

The Sperry Univac Corporation sells, rents and services electronic data processing equipment and employs a large staff of service people to keep its customers' equipment in order. The 30 service people who work out of the St. Paul district office (which covers most of the Midwest) all live in the St. Paul area and are often required to travel to customers in distant locations. They usually travel by air.

A given trouble call may take several hours or even days of work. When an assignment is completed, the workers fly back to St. Paul and often arrive home late in the evening or even after midnight. Under these circumstances, management has always allowed the service people to report to the office late the next day.

Recently, there have been signs that the workers have begun to abuse this privilege. A few people have developed the habit of taking the entire morning off after every out-of-town trip even if they arrive back at their home by 5:00 p.m. the previous evening.

Management has considered requiring all service people to report for work at 9:00 a.m., regardless of what time they arrived the night before. They realize that in some cases this would impose an obvious hardship, and it might encourage the employees to spread their work out so that instead of finishing their job in the afternoon and returning home late, they would work through the next morning, returning home in the afternoon.

Above all, management is anxious not to adversely affect the employees' high morale and interest in their work. These service people are paid a salary, receive liberal fringe benefits, and are treated almost like members of management.

Question

1. What action, if any, would you recommend?

Forming A Union

Mary is a nurse at County Hospital. Although she loves her work and is considered one of the best nurses at County, Mary is dissatisfied with working conditions, pay and benefits. After talking with other nurses, she has come to the conclusion that a union would be the answer to the nurses' grievances with County Hospital.

One of the most important issues facing the nurses concerns the staffing situation. More nurses are needed to handle the workload, but the hospital administration says the budget will not allow the hiring of additional personnel.

Another item of contention is the differential pay scale for nurses on the day, evening and night shifts. Evenings and nights get ten percent more than day, but the nurses want a further differential between the evening and night shift, since the night shift is the hardest of the three. The nurses would also like an across-the-board pay raise.

Another concern is lack of any benefits for the part-time nurses. They get no life insurance, medical, dental, nor credit union benefits, even though these part-timers often work as much as the full-timers due to the staffing problems.

To get a nurses' union started, Mary and a few friends had flyers printed up calling for an organizational meeting. However, these flyers were intercepted by the hospital administration, and Mary was verbally reprimanded by her Head Nurse.

Mary found that on her next monthly schedule she was shifted from days to evenings, two weeks prior to normal shift rotation, and that she did not get her requested days off. Suspecting harassment as a result of her union activities, Mary confronted her Head Nurse and was told that if she refrained from union organizing activities she would find her schedule a bit more to her liking. She was also told that if she continued trying to organize the nurses she might find herself out of work.

Question

1. What, if anything, has the hospital administration done that is illegal?

About The Author

Dr. Kenneth A. Kovach is a Full Professor in the School of Business at George Mason University where he has been voted Outstanding Faculty Member and received the Distinguished Faculty Award. He specializes in Human Resource Management/Labor Relations research and has published eight books, over sixty articles, and over two hundred cases in these areas.

Dr. Kovach is also a consultant to numerous local and national firms, including the U.S. Department of Defense, American Red Cross, and the American Council on Education. He is on retainer with numerous employer and labor organizations in the areas of contract negotiation, mediation, arbitration, diversity and sensitivity training, employee motivation, etc.

www.ingramcontent.com/pod-product-compliance
Ingram Content Group UK Ltd.
Pitfield, Milton Keynes, MK11 3LW, UK
UKHW020122290926
15471UKWH00003B/232

9 780761 80581